WELFARE, CHOICE AND DEVELOPMENT

WELFARE, CHOICE AND DEVELOPMENT

Essays in Honour of Professor Amartya Sen

Edited by:
Biswanath Ray

KANISHKA PUBLISHERS, DISTRIBUTORS
NEW DELHI-110 002

KANISHKA PUBLISHERS, DISTRIBUTORS
4697/5-21A, Ansari Road, Daryaganj,
New Delhi-110 002
Phones : 2327 0497, 2328 8285
Fax : 011-2328 8285
E-mail : kanishka_publishing@yahoo.co.in

First Published 2001
Edition 2008

ISBN 978-81-7391-384-6

PRINTED IN INDIA

Published by Madan Sachdeva for Kanishka Publishers, Distributors, 4697/5-21A, Ansari Road, Daryaganj, New Delhi-110 002. Typeset by Sunshine Graphics, Delhi, and Printed at Nice Printing Press, Delhi.

To
Rama
Subhendu

Contents

List of Contributors

Professor Samir Guha Roy, Former Head of the Population Studies Unit and Professor-in-Charge of the Social Sciences Division, Indian Statistical Institute, Calcutta, (WB).

Dr. Debabrata Dutta, Senior Lecturer in Economics, Asutosh College, Calcutta, (WB).

Dr. Debasish Sarkar, Assistant Professor, Department of Economics, Hooghly Mohsin College, Hooghly, (WB).

Professor Satya R. Chakravarty, Economic Research Unit, Indian Statistical Institute, Calcutta, (WB).

Dr. Krishna Mazumdar, Associate Professor, Economic Research Unit, Indian Statistical Institute, Calcutta, (WB).

Dr. Debaprasad Bandopadhyay, Lecturer, Linguistic Research Unit, Indian Statistical Institute, Calcutta, (WB).

Anindya Bhukta, Lecturer in Economics, Netaji Mahavidyalaya, Arambagh, Hooghly, (WB).

Abhijit Kumar Pal, Research Scholar, Serampur Girl's College, Hooghly, (WB).

Dr. Bhola Nath Ghosh, Lecturer, Sociological Research Unit, Indian Statistical Institute, Calcutta, (WB).

Kunal Bandopadhyay, 18, R. N. Chatterjee Lane, Ichapur, North 24 Parganas, (WB).

Dr. Sumita Bajpai, Reader in Zoology, Raja Peary Mohan College, Uttarpara, Hooghly, (WB).

Dr. Surendra Nath Banerjee, Lecturer, Psychology Research Unit, Indian Statistical Institute, Calcutta, (WB).

Pranati Dutta, Associate Scientist, Population Studies Unit, Indian Statistical Institute, Calcutta, (WB).

Biswanath Ray, Associate Scientists, Economic Research Unit, Indian Statistical Institute, Calcutta, (WB).

Foreword

It is an arduous task to edit a book on the theme of economic welfare, choice and development and more so when the volume is published in Honour of Professor Amartya Sen: a pioneer in Welfare Economics and Development. Dr. Biswanath Ray with his docile nature and devotion successfully completed this ambitious endeavour through his co-authors. This book performs the much-needed role of tracing the changes that has taken place in India for human welfare and development. The reader will be given a road map for a few major issues relating to human welfare and development. Selection of topics and the authors show the ingenuity of the editor and no doubt his vast experience in editing several books on different socio-economic themes enriched this endeavour with more zest.

Three chapters are devoted to reappraise the economic thinking of Professor Sen: one deals with social choice, measurement of inequality, on relationship between inequality and welfare, and so on; the other one discusses the concept of development as visualised by Sen; and the third one deals with the views of a critique on welfare economics from the perspective of post-modern theories. Human well-being is measured in a chapter by constructing an achievement index as a function of social well-beings. Human development is not possible with high prevalence of diseases in the population. Two chapters are devoted on the aspects of health and health care:

(i) one deals with the epidemiologic transition in India and the disparity of curative health care between urban and rural areas, and
(ii) other chapter proposes an efficient health care system based on some micro-level observations.

Elimination of gender inequalities in schooling and market place is necessary for development and a few chapters demonstrate the status of gender inequality in educational system. Status of transfer of technology through Panchayati Raj and leadership for rural development are discussed by covering two chapters through case studies. Current status of primary education and massive illiterate population may be the factor for non-development and one chapter deals with such aspect.

Response of development may be reflected through demographic transition and the last but one chapter deals with such factors. Last chapter provides a biographical sketch of Prof. Sen and his achievements.

The area of welfare, choice and development is wide; however, the editor is successful in depicting a few major issues. Contributors of this book have also taken enough pain to pinpoint several lapses, drawbacks and policy questions through their research. Thus contributors have succeeded in transferring their messages.

Readers ignorant about economics and development may apprise themselves with thinking of Prof. Amartya Sen and some issues regarding welfare and development.

Researchers in social sciences, managers in Non-Governmental Organisations and policy as well as programme planners especially in the area of welfare and development may have this volume as a reference material.

I must congratulate all contributors for their informative articles and Dr. Ray for his sincerity in editing these ambitious endeavours in honour of Prof. Sen and his thinkings.

Rest, I leave for the readers.

Prasanta K. Majumdar
Professor
Population Studies Unit
Indian Statistical Institute
Calcutta

Preface

"Welfare, Choice and Development: Essays in Honour of Prof. Amartya Sen" reviews the prevalent social, economic and demographic features in India. Such diverse issues as overview of epidemiologic transition, health care services, theory of collective choice and welfare, measuring human well-being of the countries: achievements and development indices, post-modern response of welfare economics, Sen's sense of development, gender inequality in the education system, leadership and development, transfer of technology through Panchayati Raj, inequality, problems of primary education and economic development, demographic indicators of economic development, the concluding chapter contains a comprehensive account of Professor Amartya Sen's career and his manifold academic and other activities.

It is imperative that in spite of recommendations made by several committees and commissions constituted since independence, for reforms of gender disparities, the essential character of our education has remained more or less unchanged even after fifty years of independence. Impact of tribal planning and tribal transformation has been evaluated in this venture. No doubt, it will be a valuable reference book for planners, economists, professors, teachers, researchers and students.

This book has been possible obviously through the generosity of the contributors. I express my deep sense of gratitude to them all. I must mention my appreciation of the editorial and technical help received from Dr. Prasanta Majumdar, Professor of the Indian Statistical Institute who has written the Foreword.

I am grateful to Professors Atish Dasgupta, Samir Guha Roy, Arijit Chowdhury, Kumarananda Chattopadhyay and Suraj Bandopadhyay for their encouragement for this venture. None of them is, however responsible for the views of other contributors and the errors and mistakes of omissions and commissions in this volume, which hopefully are not galore or glaring. I have a long list of well-wishers who inspired me in preparing this book. To save space, I omit their names, I, however, take solace from Keat's words, "Heard melodies are sweet, those unheard are sweeter." I am thankful to Kanishka Publishers, Distributors, New Delhi for their interest and co-operation in publishing this book.

I do not claim that I could cover all the aspects of the Indian economy within the limited space, but I firmly believe that this book will be very useful to all concerned.

Biswanath Ray

Introduction

Chapter One studies the phenomenon of epidemiologic transition in India. In the recent period in India, there has been considerable progress in the quantity and possibly also the quality of health service that have helped epidemiologic transition in a selective way. The country was quick enough to adopt most recent advances in medical innovations for effective management of many diseases. An important contribution of the application of medical technologies has been the reduction in case fatality rates. The use of new life-saving drugs and antibiotics has reduced the probability of death from such diseases such as pulmonary tuberculosis, cholera or acute diarrhoea and such other diseases taking a great toll of life earlier. Rural areas contain the majority of the population in the country and need much greater access to health care than that which currently exist; however, health service provision is concentrated in urban areas and remains relatively inaccessible to the population in rural areas. Despite India's moving towards increased privatisation, the public sector continues to play an important role in the field of health, particularly for the care of acute episodes and among the poorest. However, in recent years, private health care has expanded rapidly in both rural and urban areas. Nearly 80 per cent of the registered doctors of the country work in the private corporate sector. The private corporate sector dominates the health care system through large and specialized hospitals in big cities.

Chapter Two studies the health care services in India. The maxim that health is wealth is no exaggeration. Good health is a benefit, and perhaps the most precious benefit of an individual of its own. Good health is an essential part of well-being and without sufficient improvement in health care, human development is impossible. Apart from the intrinsic benefit of health, it has a number of other significant benefits. These economic benefits are more for poor people who are typically most handicapped due to ill health. In view of these benefits of health, the study of issues relating to health in particular, the economic dimensions receiving the attention of policy-makers, scientists and researchers. This particular paper addresses the basic question of why health matters, and distinguishes between two aspects of health care namely primary and secondary health care. The role of Government and the market in development of these health care services have been considered. The focus is placed on the limitation of the role of market in primary health care in particular and the necessity of developing an efficient health care system with Government, Non-Government Organisations and market participation. In the second part of the article we depict the pros and cons of health care facilities in India and current status through some micro level data. On the basis of observation of this study, some broad suggestions are, prescribed to improve the health scenario of the country.

Chapter Three presents a summary of Professor A.K. Sen's works on choice of technique, nonstrategic social choice, majority voting, measurement of inequality and poverty, and living standard. It particularly summarises Sen's suggestions on interpersonal comparisons of utility under alternative measurability assumptions for existence of social welfare function. In other words, these suggestions become helpful to get rid of disappointing conclusion of Arrow's impossibility theorem. A discussion on relationship between inequality and welfare has also been made.

Chapter Four deals with human well-being of a country as a social well-being function and measures the level of human well-being of a country in terms of achievement indices. The change in human well-being over a period of time has been estimated by the improvement indices. This study takes into account 92 countries representing all levels of income and all the geographical regions and estimates achievement indices for two points of time 1960 and 1994 and formulates the relevant improvement indices also. In this connection, the study throws light to a number of findings.

Chapter Five is a critique of Welfare Economics (WE) from the perspective of post-modern theories. This paper reads WE-discourse by deploying Foucault's anti-discourse on modern (im-)morality. The critique mainly circles around the dubious duality of present day mainstream WE, which at a time is propagating war as well as welfare which leads to "death industry" as suggested by the author. It is also alleged that WE ignores the ecological entitlement and thus enhances the State-controlled manipulation of docile human body. The paper, thus, describes the panoptical characteristics of State and statistics.

Chapter Six concentrates on Sen's sense of development. Amartya Sen received the Nobel Prize in Economics in 1998 for his contribution to welfare economics. But his contribution to development economics is no less important. In fact, the concept of development has been given a new direction through his thinkings. Professor Sen adds a human flavour to the concept of development. Development economics breathed his first in the post-war period. Initially it was believed that an increase in per-capita real GNP is a good indicator of development. Development economists then believed in the 'trickle down theory.' But soon after it was felt that the theory does not work. The emphasis then included also on distributive equality. Later on Professor Sen discarded all these development criteria. According to Professor Sen, development in material terms is meaningless so long as it does not guarantee increase in human-welfare. An increase in real GNP, no doubt, indicates increases in the level of development of the country. But this increase does not always reflect in the betterment of human-welfare. Sen speaks of development in terms of capability. Development means capability-enhancement. He also talks about entitlement. Capability and entitlement are closely interrelated. If one is not entitled to do or have something, certainly he wouldn't be capable of doing or having something. In earlier writings on development economics Sen argued that betterment of living standard makes people entitled to have or do something. Recently he tries to measure development in terms of various types of freedom.

Chapter Seven concentrates on gender inequality in the education system. The National Policy on Education 1986 and its Programme of Action, 1992 led special emphasis on the constitutional directives for removal of disparities and equalise educational opportunity by attending to the specific needs of women, who have been denied equality so far. The removal of Women's illiteracy and obstacles inhibiting their access to and retention in the educational system, according to this policy, should receive overriding priority through provision of special support services, setting of time targets of ten years and effective monitoring by their programme of action. But it is a teasing reality that in spite of all the plans, programmes and provisions of special support services for removal of factors which result in discrimination against women at all levels of education, the actions which need to be taken to promote women's education can hardly be improved upon during the last 14 years, and the number of female illiterates in the country at present reach 195.64 million which is 70 million more than that of males, even though the female population is less than male population by 32 million. So, it is a pity that in spite of recommendations made by several committees, commissions that constituted since independence for reforms of gender disparities, the essential character of our education has remained more or less unchanged even after more than fifty years of independence. Thus we have to proceed to the twenty-first century with a huge number of illiterate women population.

Chapter Eight intends to interface rural leadership with development. It shows that rural leaders mostly come from high and middle caste Hindus, male, and from middle age-group. Most of them are from middle income categories having more than one source of livelihood besides small farming. Their educational level is upto secondary. Most leaders give highest priority to economic issue like income generation and creation of means of production whereas other issues especially environmental issues still occupy low priority. Leadership qualities would not quite flourish among the rural leaders due to their lack of access to objective information. Political parties are often not consistent with the ideologies they preach and there is therefore a great difference between the leader's precepts and their practices.

Chapter Nine discusses the problem of transfer of technology through Panchayati Raj System. Through the PR system has been running since last 21 years and the State Government with its good intention to make the system effective to decentralize, power and planning for upgradation of rural mass living on agricultural, yet the farmers in parts of States are bereft of the fruits of the system. Indeed, the PR as a self-governing unit, as has been envisaged, can become active in implementing benefits of technological changes, if some of the constraints of its functioning can be rectified. This has been the realisation from a case study of a Gram Panchayat in Nadia District, West Bengal.

Chapter Ten re-examined the gender inequality in education. 'SWAMATA VIGYAN UTSAV' is a specialised programme of Paschim Banga Vigyan Mancha concerning the aspect of literacy, self-reliance and equality of the women. It opted some open questionnaire sessions in some orientation camps on the 'Samata Mela' of the Women for intervention of science activities. These interventions unfold the situation that economically deprived, illiterate and malnourished ladies practice various degrees of superstitions, so also the educated, well established ladies. Experiences could hardly distinguish the origin of modern superstitions among illiterate and literate ladies. It has been experienced that the sense of equality is partially a gender-biased product. 1998 being marked by UNICEF as International Year for Safe-motherhood, programmes were organised including the aspects of Self-motherhood. It is a painful experience that familial and social situations avert a girl child to create gender biasness. It was planned to intervene with their concepts of social ethics related with obstetric and maternal life of women. Degrees of superstitions of urban and rural slums show variations with specific characteristics. Urban ladies have acquired modern superstitions in their limited life-cycle, which can be well marked as the effect of consumerism.

Chapter Eleven discusses the problems of primary education and economic development in India. Nobel Laureate Professor Amartya Sen opined, in his famous articles 'Education and Economic Growth' and also in different speeches in India, that primary education of our country has been neglected in comparison with the higher education. Successive Government policies, also, vastly overestimate the requirement of university educated manpower and vastly underestimates the necessary speed of the expansion of primary education to fulfil the stated objectives. The continued failure since independence to fulfil the constitutional directive of providing education to all children upto the age of 14 years is an unrelated reality. In spite of considerable progress in the spread of educational institutions, 50 per cent of world's illiterate population still lives in India. Though the number of primary schools increased from 2.10 lakhs in 1950-51 to 6.10 lakhs in 1997-98, about 20 per cent of the rural population are still deprived of any primary school in their habitation. Though the gross enrolment ratio in primary classes during 1997-98 is 89.7 per cent, the drop-out rate during the same period is 39.58 per cent in primary and 54.14 per cent in upper primary classes. Moreover there are 4.5 crores of children *i.e.*, about one fourth of the schoolgoing age group are as child labour and are deprived of education. The issues of social justice with respect to educationally backward sections and gender bias rooted in the Patriarchal Indian Societies are some of the other significant factors that thwarted the Universalisation of Elementary Education in the country. Without elementary education, economic development of any country is not possible so, time has come to plan appropriate planning for the universalisation of elementary education to improve the situation and if we still hesitate, we shall prove to the world that we richly deserve the trouble in which we find ourselves today.

Chapter Twelve deals with infant mortality rates, expectation of life at birth, crude birth rate, age specific death rate, neonatal and postnatal mortality rate. Economic development is a long-term process of fundamental structural change so that a low-income country is transformed into high-income country by proper utilisation of natural resources. In a much wider sense it incorporates aspects of social development including egalitarian distribution, removal of poverty, demographic aspects relating to fertility and mortality decline, improvement in education, health status and environmental aspects etc. Demographic transition may act as a determining factor of economic development. The process of development can be explained in terms of demographic transition. We would like to concentrate mainly on some fertility and mortality indicators of economic development. Gradual decline of child woman ratio, crude birth rate, general fertility rate, general marital fertility rate, total fertility rate, gross reproduction rate, age specific fertility rate and slight rise in the mean age at effective marriage pinpoint that India is in the process of demographic transition. Similarly, gradual decline of infant mortality rate, crude death rate, age specific death rate, prenatal and postnatal mortality rate is an indicator of process of mortality transition in India. Expectation of life at birth has shown an increasing trend. Couple protection rate has also increased over a long period of time. Mortality transition is an index of economic development. Though India experience declining trend in fertility and mortality over past years, mortality and fertility rates are still higher compared to other developing countries *e.g.*, China, Sri Lanka, India's total fertility rate (TFR) 3.5 in 1993 suggests that India still needs a long way to reach below replacement level fertility. However keeping in view the present level of achievement, it is expected that net reproduction rate, NRR-1, would be achieved in the period of 2011-16 AD. India has made considerable progress in the reduction of mortality from high to low and even though the inverse relationship between mortality decline and economic development holds true but the link between the two has weakened. Mortality decline may be attributed mainly to public health and disease control measures imported through the international organisations. However further mortality decline is only possible through economic development emphasizing health programmes for rural masses.

The concluding chapter reflects a comprehensive account of Professor Amartya Sen's career and his manifold academic and other activities.

EDITOR

CHAPTER 1

Epidemiologic Transition in India

S. Guha Roy

BACKGROUND AND DEFINITION

Epidemiologic Transition

The term 'epidemiologic transition' is just two and a half decades old. Originating from Omran (1971) it has served as a major breakthrough in the understanding of long-term changes in the leading causes of death in populations. It is generally referred to as a period rather than as a process of change.

Thus the epidemiologic transition has a starting point, when infectious diseases were predominant, and an end when chronic and degenerative diseases dominated the causes of death. It is, however, important to consider the transition as a dynamic process, whereby the health and disease patterns of a society evolve according to demographic, socio-economic, technological, political, cultural, and biological changes (Frenk, *et al.*, 1991).

The study of health in populations comprises two major objects: on the one hand, the health conditions of the population; on the other hand, the response to those conditions. According to this simplifying dichotomy, the health transition may be divided into two main components. The first is the epidemiologic transition strictly speaking, which is defined as the long-term process of change in the health conditions of a society, including changes in the patterns of disease, disability, and death. The second component, which may be called health care transition refers to the changes in the patterns of the organised social response to health conditions in terms of public health measures and the availability and access to basic health services.

Epidemiologic transition acts through three major mechanisms, these have traditionally involved; a fall in fertility levels, which transforms the age structure, variations in risk factors, which affect the disease patterns and improvements in health care technology and infrastructure, which modify case-fatality rates (Mosley, Jamison and Henderson, 1990). Whilst such an analytical framework for examining occurrence of epidemiologic transition (ET) may be useful, it is difficult to apply in countries like India where the relevant information on the different factors involved and by region remains poorly documented. This is mainly due to the fact that India lacks a sound data base of national and State level statistics that can record the health status of its ever growing population. Official recording of disease occurrence is far less deficient than health reporting. Generally, the routine sources of morbidity data such as reporting of certain acute diseases to health officials, registration of certain diseases, medical statistics, hospital reports and other sources are incomplete.

Some Sources of Routine Data

As in many other developed and developing countries hospital records are considered foremost on the list of sources of epidemiologic information. But reports from hospitals in India appear to be the least informative of all sources. As a matter of fact, the country lacks a complete disease census of its population for estimation of prevalence or incidence.

Registrar General of India (RGI)

The Registrar General of India (RGI) has, however, initiated a scheme on medical certification of causes of death based on the returns from the district headquarters and teaching hospitals. The Sample Registration Scheme (SRS) collects data on type of medical attention at death. But such information on morbidity and mortality are mostly not published by age break-ups so that the older segment of the population cannot be studied separately. This applies also to other age categories. Besides the RGI, SRS, Central Bureau of Health Intelligence (CBHI) and several local surveys, the National Sample Surveys (NSS) and National Council of Applied Economic Research (NCAER) have provided some evidence of trends in morbidity and mortality in India. The following sections summarise the available evidence.

NATIONAL AND REGIONAL STUDIES ON HEALTH STATUS AND UTILISATION OF SERVICES AT OLDER AGES

National Sample Survey Organisation (NSSO) (1956, 1973-74, 1986-87)

In addition to earlier surveys in 1956-57 and 1973-74, the NSSO has collected data on a nation-wide basis on morbidity and the utilisation of medical services on the one hand and nature and dimensions of socio-economic problems of the elderly on the other in its 42nd round (July 1986-June 1987). This survey covered 50,000 households spread over a sample of 8,312 villages and 4,546 urban blocks.

Indian Council for Medical Research (ICMR) Study of the Rural Aged (1984-1986)

This study sponsored by the Indian Council for Medical Research, is among the most widely quoted on the aged in India. Its findings were published in 1991. The study was conducted among a sample of 1910 older people attending specialist geriatric clinics in a district of South India. The main aim was to collect socio-demographic information. General health status information was collected in an incidental manner. However an in-depth study was undertaken among a sub sample of the population in order to highlight psychiatric disorders.

This showed that almost half the sample were suffering from some form of depressive illness. One of the most significant aspects of this study was to highlight the need for improved methodological tools to differentiate cultural artefacts from actual pathology and the need for training among research workers in this field.

National Council for Applied Economic Research (NCAER) (1992a, 1992b, 1994, 1995)

The NCAER first conducted a health survey during May-July 1990 followed by a survey, entitled "Differentials and determinants of morbidity in India," during May-June 1993. It covered 18,693 households across the country in 718 villages and 1,509 urban blocks. A total of 1,03,245 persons reported sickness (if any) during a 30-day reference period for major states by rural and urban residences. Despite its methodological leanings towards market research, the NCAER surveys (especially that of 1995) have captured for the first time a national picture of the prevalence of morbidity by disease type and by the nature and cost of health care sought by gender, socio-economic group and age categories. The information by disease type illuminates for the first time, a national profile of the health transition.

Kerala Sastra Sahitya Parishad (KSSP) (1987)

Another useful survey on "Health and development in rural Kerala" was conducted in 1987 in Kerala, the southernmost state of India. It covered a population of some 10,000 households in districts throughout the state to provide baseline data on health status of the population. The study highlights enormous cultural variations in reported morbidity between this state, other states in India and in the country as a whole. It also suggests that the health and demographic transitions are well established in the state which is characterised by low levels of fertility and mortality. Earlier to this study the Centre for Development Studies at Trivandrum (Panikar and Soman, 1984) carried out a smaller scale study based on hospital data.

The Indian Council for Social Science Research (ICSSR)) and Centre for Research into Ageing, Tirupati Venkateswara University.

Study on the Physical and Mental Health Status of Widows in a District of Southern India (Tirupati) 1989-1991.

This study involved some three thousand rural and urban widows and an assessment of their functional and mental health status, by comparison to non-widows. The main conclusion of this rare study among widowed women was to show a positive correlation between economic insecurity, depression and poor mental health functioning. Such health conditions were found to be worse among widows and older widows in particular than non-widows and younger widows, due to the greater physical and economic vulnerability of the former. As a result, older widows had particular problems of adjustment compared with younger widows. Among all groups of widows those living in rural areas suffered from the greatest isolation.

Limitations of Multi-Source Data

It is well established that cause-of-death statistics in most countries are problematic. For example, the presence of more than one pathologic condition has made it difficult to classify deaths by cause. On the recommendations of various international bodies, some countries began issuing death certificates bearing multiple causes. This change had a profound effect on the statistics of some diseases (MacMahon, *et al.* 1960). Moreover, most of the studies referred to above, collected data through conventional enquiries by non-medical field investigators. As a result, they were subject to inaccurate diagnoses, lack of precise causal information, and ethnologic differences which were not validated or accounted for in the methodology. In addition types of diseases in India are culturally and socially sensitive. Respondents are suspected not to report very often sicknesses such as tuberculosis, leprosy, leucoderma, STDs, psychiatric and gynaecological disorders, (NCAER, 1995).

The absence of standardisation in coding illness, as developed by the WHO has limited the scope for measuring shifts in morbidity levels. Though the broad features of the epidemiologic transition are fairly evident even from the untidy mess of morbidity statistics. It is only when one wants to measure quantitatively the prevalence and incidence rates that the limitations of the data stand squarely in the way of such estimation.

Specific Issues Related to Old Age

In addition to these limitations, firm data is often lacking on the incidence and prevalence of disease particular to old age, epidemiologic determinants and characteristics of disease episodes in terms of repetition, duration and seasonal manifestations, frequency of hospitalisation, and so on. Morbidity data in a given time-perspective are yet to be built up methodically in studying relationship between health and the different bio-social characteristics of the aged population in India.

Implications for Health Planning

The paucity of information on morbidity is a detriment to health care in India. Planning is undertaken without sufficient information and decisions are often based upon outdated and inaccurate data. Added to this is the regional variation in fertility and mortality levels which manifests itself in the health transition. Given the inadequacy of resources especially in public sector provision coupled with the health burdens of uneven development the lack of a strategy can only undermine the health and well-being of all sections of the population, but especially so of the most vulnerable among the old and the young.

One Indian Example in More Depth—West Bengal

The true age structure of a population at the current data is a result of the past trends of some demographic events, such as fertility, mortality and migration. Since the volume of migration is not significant in the context of total size of the Indian population, the role of this factor in determining age structure may at best be ignored. It is true that a decline in mortality increases the probability of survival to old age, but its effect is not yet as strong as that of even moderate fertility decline.

The crude birth rate in India was about 42 per 1,000 population in 1941-51, which declined to about 30 per 1,000 in 1990. It is estimated that crude birth rate may attain a rate of 25 or so and crude death rate less than 9 at the end of the twentieth century. These phenomena will corresponding effect on the shape of population pyramid, which will change from a wide base, narrow top to steep barrel-shaped form.

The Example of West Bengal

The onset of a fertility decline took place in West Bengal, the state on which we focused, after 1971. The state meets the three United Nations' criteria (UN, 1990) considered as a late initiator of demographic transition. The criteria, which are satisfied by the population are:

(*a*) Total fertility rate (TFR) was above 5 in or around 1950-55;
(*b*) TFR was below 5 in 1985-90; and
(*c*) TFR fell by more than 1.5 children from 1950-55 to 1985-90.

Table 1.1
Estimated Age Specific Death Rate by Sex (1993)

	India			*West Bengal*		
Age Group	*Person*	*Male*	*Female*	*Person*	*Male*	*Female*
50-54	11.2	13.2	9.0	10.1	11.0	9.2
55-59	17.6	20.6	14.4	16.9	20.2	13.3
60-64	27.5	30.7	24.2	24.6	26.8	22.4
65-69	40.3	46.2	34.6	40.5	43.3	37.7
70+	87.6	94.5	81.1	79.4	81.9	77.2

Source: Registrar General, India 1995. Sample Registration System: Fertility and Mortality Indications, New Delhi.

As a result of fertility transition, the age structure will tend to an incipient ageing of the population. Between 1961 and 1991, the proportion of "under age 15" category declined by 4 per cent and that of the aged population (60 and over) increased by 2 per cent.

Table 1.2
Reported and Projected Trend (in per cent) of Selected Segments of Population of West Bengal (1961-2001)

Segment of Population	*1961*	*1971*	*1981*	*1991*	*2001*
Children (under 15)	41	43	39	37	33
Youth Population (15-24)	19	17	21	19	20
Aged Population (60 and over)	5	5	6	7	7

Source: Guha Roy (1993).

In epidemiological terms, the implication of this process of change in age structure is an increase of persons exposed to non-communicable diseases (NCD). As a result even with constant age specific incidence rates, the absolute number of patients and deaths from such diseases increases. However in India there is no firm data for the empirical evidence of a shift in morbidity patterns and especially so in a given time perspective.

An all India study by the National Council of Applied Economic Research (NCAER, 1995) however suggests that in urban areas representing relatively affluent society, of six states of India, non-communicable disease (NCD) is more predominant than communicable diseases (CD). These states are Andhra Pradesh, Himachal Pradesh, Kerala, Orissa, Tamil Nadu and West Bengal. Even in rural areas of these three states, namely Andhra Pradesh, Kanataka and Kerala, the proportion of persons suffering from NCD is more than that of CD (Ebrahim 1993, Kalache and Sen 1996 forthcoming).

There are two arguments which consider a gradual epidemiological transition in the Indian population. The first is the overall control of infectious diseases over the past few decades. The second, is the identification of non-infectious and chronic diseases among adults and within the older segments of the population. As mentioned above, the volume of the elderly group has also been increasing as a result of changes in the demographic age structure.

There is sufficient evidence from the NCAER study of 1993 to suggest that while children under age 15 have been suffering from a high incidence of infectious diseases, the older age groups, (60 and over) are subject to very high (about 50 per cent) incidence of non-infectious diseases. This is confirmed by several emerging studies (Dugal and Amin 1989, Sundar 1995, Kumar (eds.) 1995). What is more alarming is the fact that mortality data after the age of 60 years, classifies most deaths as those from 'senility' in most official classification which is highly misleading.

A study undertaken by the authors (Sen and Guha Roy) also verifies a long-standing hypothesis that the onset of disease and disability occurs at an earlier age in countries such as India and that the boundary between chronological and functional ageing is quite distinct and cannot be confused (Kalache 1991, Sen 1994).

Table 1.3
Percentage Distribution of Persons by Age Group and Broad Type of Illness: India, 1993

Age Group	*Infections*	*Non-infections*	*Fever/Others*
Less than 5	52	5	43
5 - 14	42	11	47
15 - 34	32	27	41
35 - 59	29	38	33
60 and over	22	50	28

Source: Sheriff (1995).

The second mechanism involved with the epidemiologic transition is the change in the risk factors. Risk is defined (Last, 1983) as a certain probability of suffering a loss of health, thus resulting in illness or death. Such risk arises from a change in the factors (Frenk *et al.*, 1991) associated with development and include socio-economic, demographic, biological and environmental dimensions.

Age

As we know that age of the individual is a major determinant influencing risk of morbidity. Referring to the NCAER study (Sundar 1995), it can be observed that there is initially a declining and then an increasing trend of morbidity with age. Late childhood (5-14) and young adult (15-34) categories have the lowest risks and those above 60 years the highest when compared with the reference category of under 5 years. This was also the conclusion of a study on patterns of morbidity and the nature of health care utilised in Maharashtra western India in 1989 (Dugal and Amin, FRCH 1989) which suggests that a health transition is very much underway in the Indian subcontinent yet receives limited research and documentation to the detriment of the adult and elderly population.

Gender

In the context of age structure changes, mentioned earlier, the observed J-shaped association (true for both sexes) between age and morbidity is significant for India. Moreover, high risk associated with females of age range 15-39 has important implications for reproductive health. This also intensifies the need to examine the long-term health effects of reproductive morbidity in addition to malnourishment coupled with socio-cultural discrimination in early life, in relation to female survival into later life. An assessment of the prevalence of morbidity among adults or elderly people by age specific ratios remains largely untouched.

Mortality Decline

The decline in mortality among elderly people in India is evidenced even from the not-too-recent series of information presented. Elimination of famines and epidemics and control of infectious and parasitic diseases, seem to have caused some real decline in mortality. Although the ageing of the aged necessarily resulted in a higher rate of death, the decline in mortality had still occurred in the old-old segment. Contrasting the sex pattern of mortality in childhood and adult ages, the female mortality was lower almost uniformly than males in the old age range.

The estimates of Indian life tables (Malaker and Guha Roy, 1990) suggested a modest gain in longevity by the elderly in the course of this century. It cannot be claimed, however, that the prolongation of life was all free from chronic illness and disabilities. Models of dynamic disability, free life expectancy have been developed to incorporate risk factors, recovery and rehabilitation into the analysis of expectation of life (Rogers, *et al.*, 1989; Manton and Stallard, 1991). These methods require detailed data that are not available for this country. As data collection improves in India, however, these methods should prove useful in establishing levels and variability in the decline of physical functioning.

Disability

Background

There is urgent need to understand the extent of function and levels of activity among older people over and what is considered to be 'productive activity.' Reductions in the activities of daily living and participation in community activities not only increases exponentially with age but are also associated with changes in organ function (Ebrahim 1995). However it is very rare for national data to record levels of functional ability or levels of disability, despite the fact the available evidence shows the doubling of levels of disability by five year age bands after the age of 70 years in countries as far apart as China and Spain (UN *Demographic Yearbook* 1993). More significant is the fact that the onset of disability in countries such as India is likely to occur at an earlier age due to social, economic and environmental disadvantages.

Statistical monitoring of daily and functional activities of older persons and the environment and the socio-economic barriers confronted by them is intrinsically tied to the study of disability. Many countries across the world attempt to collect disability statistics through their censuses. But a major problem in the collection of statistics is the proper definition and classification of disability which is culturally and socially varied. (UN, *Ibid.*)

WHO Classification

In 1981 the World Health Organisation (WHO) classified disability through the standardisation of human function at 3 main levels:

(i) At the level of the organ (Impairment)
(ii) At the level of the person (Disability)
(iii) At the level of social circumstances brought about by interaction of disabled persons with society or community (Handicap)

Following much discussion the ICIDH was prepared by the WHO, and a number of major revisions have also taken place. In

India the procedure followed for the classification of disability is described below. It must be stressed however that much of this has focused upon disability among children and younger adults rather than upon the elderly. Hence this important field remains an underdeveloped one.

The major sources of statistics on disability in India are the following:

1. Office of the Registrar General of India: Census of India 1981: The Physically Handicapped — Report and Tables.
2. National Sample Survey Organisation: Report on Survey of Disabled Persons, Thirty-sixth Round, 1981.
3. Indian Council of Medical Research: Collaborative Study on Prevalence and Aetiology of Hearing Impairment, 1983.
4. Ministry of Social Welfare.

Different types of disability have been defined (see "Child in India: A Statistical Profile," Ministry of Welfare, New Delhi, 1985) as:

Visual disability: Either have no perception of light in both eyes or have perception of light, but could not currently count fingers of a hand (with or without glasses) at a distance of 3 metres in good day light.

Hearing disability: Unable to hear normal sound with one or both the ears without the help of hearing aids.

Speech disability: Having voice and ability to cry and cough, but cannot speak.

Locomotor disability: Unable to move because of

(i) paralysis of limb or body,
(ii) deformity of limb,
(iii) amputation,
(iv) dysfunction of joints of limb, and
(v) other deformity in the body *viz.* in spine, in neck, hunchbacks, dwarfs, etc.

Ageing and Disability

Increasing age is associated with a higher incidence of disability. The impairment of vision is one of the most common non-lethal health conditions among the elderly in this country. Females appear to suffer more than males in visual disability, as a result of more nutritional deficiency in general and vitamin A deficiency in particular. This has been the result of neglect of women, and their poor access to nutrition and health care services. Loss of hearing and deafness were the other common health problems of the aged. Old persons also suffered from speech disability, but the incidence rate revealed by studies was low at 282-285 persons per 1,00,000 population. Among the aged persons, more or less 2.5 per cent of the population were unable to move from place to place due to paralysis or deformity of limb or body. Gender differences were also found in hearing, speech and locomotor disabilities, but unlike visual impairment, males were more afflicted. Prevalence of disability in rural areas was greater than that of towns and cities for all types of physical disorders.

Visual disability was the most prevalent condition among the aged at the national level, it is in order to discuss it for some small population groups. Ophthalmological investigations were carried out in 1981 among indigenous high altitude populations in Darjeeling district of West Bengal, India (Forsius *et al.*, 1985). The results of this survey suggests that whilst cataractous eyes were hardly found before the age of 60 years, but appeared to increase quite considerably (about 15 per cent) thereafter. Arcus senilis in old age appeared to be less severe in these populations possibly because of lesser senile changes in the cornea. Myopia-endemicity found in many populations did not seem to occur in the population studied, but the cause of increasing myopia prevalence with increasing age might be related to high prevalence of cataract among the aged persons. Age-specific disability and the earlier onset of disability is highlighted at Table 1.4.

Health Outcomes

Despite the high risk associated with the elderly, it may not be the most appropriate segment of population to target health interventions. In a study based on epidemiologic evidence, (Elo and Preston, 1992) hold that infection contacted in childhood may manifest itself much later. In other words, later life condition is often a carryover of ill health in childhood. The sub-population of elderly at the current date had originated from various birth cohorts, which experiences in course of life different health care services and mortality levels and patterns.

Table 1.4
Per 1,000 Distribution of Physically Disabled Persons Ages 60 Years and Above by Age at Onset of Disability, 1991, All India

Age at onset	*Rural*				*Urban*			
	Visual	*Hearing*	*Speech*	*Loco-motor*	*Visual*	*Hearing*	*Speech*	*Loco-motor*
0-4	8	9	42	29	12	7	35	21
5-9	8	6	23	19	15	13	39	16
10-14	9	12	24	17	7	10	9	15
15-19	2	9	—	17	3	11	—	9
20-24	3	11	10	10	6	9	23	12
25-29	3	10	—	8	5	14	—	8
30-34	4	12	12	22	5	13	7	13
35-44	18	41	25	59	18	55	27	41
45-59	255	280	262	278	236	215	287	280
60+	689	609	594	541	690	651	572	586
Total (inc. NR)	1,000	1,000	1,000	1,000	1,000	1,000	1,000	1,000

Source: NSS, Government of India, 1994. A Report on Disabled Persons, 1991.

Socio-Economic and Environmental Variables and Risk of Morbidity

The disease mixes and other conditions do vary across the heterogeneous group of survivors of these cohorts. Besides the shift in age structure, the socio-economic changes in the form of moderate expansion of education in this country have a profound impact on the transition from communicable to non-communicable diseases. The National Council for Applied Economic Research (NCAER) study presents some important relationships between education and morbidity prevalence, through a legit analysis. However, it should be noted that higher educational attainment may improve reporting of diseases, which in turn may give a false impression of higher incidence of morbidity. This highlighted by studies from Kerala and West Bengal (Kanan *et al.* 1991, Sen & Roy 1996).

Indian censuses provide evidence of impressive improvements in educational levels and a moderate increase of female participation in the labour force, especially in the rural areas. An important implication of such changes is the improvement in nutrition, housing, water supply, and sanitation, which reduce health risks (McKeown, 1976; Evans, Hall and Warford, 1981). Such an advantage seems to be restricted mainly to urban areas and some pockets of more developed regions within the country. With the introduction of basic urban infrastructure and adoption of health action plans, the incidence of infectious diseases (*e.g.* cholera, malaria, chickenpox, acute gastro-enteritis, etc.) has been declining, as is suggested by Table 1.5.

Table 1.5
Percentage Distribution of Deaths by Major Cause Groups: India-Rural (1989-1993)

Major Cause Groups	*1989*	*1990*	*1991*	*1992*	*1993*
Senility	23.8	24.4	23.8	23.5	22.9
Coughs (disorders of the respiratory system)	20.2	18.9	18.9	19.6	19.2
Causes peculiar to infancy	9.8	9.8	10.2	9.6	11.0
Diseases of circulatory system	10.9	11.1	11.1	10.8	10.6
Other clear symptoms	8.2	8.5	8.3	8.4	8.9
Accident and injuries	7.4	8.5	8.5	8.7	8.4
Digestive disorders	6.6	6.2	6.4	6.2	6.8
Fevers	7.4	7.3	7.3	7.7	6.7
Disorders of the central nervous system	4.8	4.2	4.4	4.5	4.2
Child birth and pregnancy	0.9	1.0	1.1	1.0	1.3
All causes	100.0	100.0	100.0	100.0	100.0

Source: Registrar General, India, 1995. Survey of Causes of Death (Rural): India Annual Report 1993, Series 3, No. 26, New Delhi.

As is well-known, the pattern of deaths by causes reflects the health status of a population. But rural India lacks adequate medical facilities to build up such statistics based on medically certified cause of death. This gap in the data has been partially bridged by the Registrar General's "Survey of Causes of Death (Rural)" in sample villages of selected Primary Health Centres through "Lay Diagnosis Reporting (Post-death verbal autopsy)" method of investigation employing trained paramedical staff. In 1993 the survey was conducted in 1,407 sample villages of 23 States and 2 Union Territories.

The major cause groups are shown below along with the individual diseases falling under them:

Fevers: Typhoid, influenza, malaria, not classifiable.

Digestive disorders: Acute abdomen, gastro-enteritis, dysentery, peptic ulcer, food poisoning, cholera, not classifiable.

Coughs: Asthma and bronchitis, T.B. of lungs, pneumonia, whooping coughs, not classifiable.

Disorders of central nervous systems: Paralysis, convulsions, meningitis, not classifiable.

Diseases of circulatory system: Heart attack, anaemia, other heart diseases.

Other clear symptoms: Cancer, jaundice, diabetes, cirrhosis and chronic liver diseases, mental diseases, uraemia, tetanus, measles, poliomyelitis, hyperplasia of prostate, leprosy, obstructed hernia, chickenpox, other medically certified diseases.

Reporting of Morbidity

There is evidence also from the NCAER study that reporting of morbidity incidence is less reliable in larger households (6 and more members) than in smaller households. It is also suggested that the reporting of sickness is underestimated among the poor. Any conclusion on this occurrence of epidemiologic transition in the population, should therefore exclude the latter group.

Combined and Uneven Development

Whether urban and rural poor, this section of the population lacks access to minimum levels of schooling, have high fertility and short birth intervals, a low age at marriage, low survival of children and poor acceptance of contraceptive methods (CI Indian demographic statistics from censuses and sample registration system). Thus with limited access to the process of modernisation and the fruits of development, they are exposed to high risk of infectious diseases. In view of this uneven development across the population segments, the transition from infectious and acute to chronic and degenerative diseases, due to reduced exposure to risk is at best selective.

Improvements in Medical Technology and Health Care

In the recent period in India, there has been considerable progress in the quantity and possibly also the quality of health services that have helped epidemiologic transition in a selective way. The country was quick enough to adopt most recent advances in medical innovations for effective management of many diseases. An important contribution of the application of medical technologies has been the reduction in case-fatality rates. The use of new life-saving drugs and antibiotics has reduced the probability of death from such diseases such as pulmonary tuberculosis, cholera or acute diarrhoea and such other diseases taking a great toll of life earlier.

A decrease in these cause specific deaths has its impact on the overall mortality and longevity is illustrated by Tables 1.6 and 1.7.

Rural Populations and Private Sector Health Provision

One consideration that complicates health service provision in India is the largely rural character of society. Rural areas, contain the majority of the population in the country and need much greater access to health care than that which currently exists (UN 1991, Sen 1994); however health service provision is concentrated in urban areas and remains relatively inaccessible to the elderly population in rural areas. Despite India's moving towards increased privatisation, the public sector continues to play an important role in the field of health particularly for the care of acute episodes and among the poorest.

Table 1.6
Death Rates Based on a 3 Year Moving Average for India

	Death Rate Per 1,000	
Period	*Rural*	*Urban*
1970-1972	17.6	10.1
1975-1977	16.6	9.7
1980-1982	13.5	7.7
1985-1987	12.4	7.6
1990-1992	8.3	

Source: Sample Registration Bulletin (1992).

Table 1.7
Life Expectancy [e(x)] at Birth and at Age 60 by Sex, India

	Males		*Females*	
Period	*e (0)*	*e (60)*	*e (0)*	*e (60)*
1970-1975	50.513.4	49.0	14.3	
1976-1980	52.5	14.1	52.1	15.9
1981-1985	55.4	14.6	55.7	16.4
1991-2001	61.2	18.3	61.8	20.0

Source: Sample Registration based life Tables and Malakar and Guha Roy (1990).

In recent years private health care has expanded widely in both rural and urban areas. Nearly 80 per cent of the country's registered doctors work in the private corporate sector (Sundar, 1995). Increasingly the private corporate sector dominates the health care system through large and specialised hospitals in big cities. In the present context of an expanding private corporate sector coupled with demographic ageing and rising levels of chronicity in the population, the future for elderly people does not augur well. The next part of the study will explore the economic burden of rising levels of morbidity among adult and elderly people in one particular region of the country.

References

Official Sources

Census of India (1961), Volume I, part 11 C(i), India, Socio Cultural Tables.

Census of India (1971), Series I, part 1 C(ii), Social and Cultural Tables, 1976.

Census of India (1981), Series I, part IVA, Socio-cultural Table, 1988.

Chakrovorty, C. and Singh A.K., *Household Structure in India*, Occasional Paper No. 1 of 1991, *Census of India*, 1991.

The International Labour Office (1992), *The ILO and The Elderly*, International Labour Office, Geneva.

Ministry of Home Affairs, Vital Statistics Division (1991), *Survey of Causes of Death (Rural)*, New Delhi, 1991.

Office of the Registrar General, (1995), *Survey of Causes of Death (Rural)*, Ministry of Home Affairs, New Delhi, Series 3, No. 26, New Delhi, 1995.

Ramachandran, C.R. and Shah, B., (1994) (eds.), *Public Health Implications of Ageing in India*, Indian Council of Medical Research Division of Non-communicable Disease, New Delhi, India.

Sharma, S.P. and Xenos, P., *Ageing in India*, (1992) Demographic Background and Analysis Based on Census Materials, Office of the Registrar General Census Commissioner India, Ministry of Home Affairs, Government of India, Occasional Paper No. 2 of 1992.

United Nations (1979), *The Ageing in Slums and Squatter Settlements*, UN, New York.

United Nations (1988), *World Population Prospects*, UN, New York, 1989.

United Nations (1990), *Population Newsletter* No. 50, New York.

United Nations (1991), *The World Ageing Situation*, UN, New York, 1991.

United Nations (1993), *Demographic Yearbook*, Economic and Social Information and Policy Analysis Statistical Division, UN, New York.

US Department of Commerce, *Economics and Statistics Administration Bureau of the Census (1992) Population and Health Transitions International Population Reports.*

Other Sources

Anker, R., Khan, M.E., and Gupta R.B. (1988), *Women's Participation in the Labour Force: A Methods Test in India for Improving its Measurement*, International Labour Office, Geneva.

Bennet, S., and Tangcharoensathein, V. (1994) , *A Shrinking State? Politics, Economics and Private Health Care in Thailand in Public Administration and Development*, Vol. 14, 1-17 (1994).

Berman, P., and Khan, M. (eds.) (1993), *Introduction: Paying for India's Health Care*, Sage Publications, New Delhi, India, pp. 21-31.

Bhatt, R., *The Private Health Care Sector in India* in Berman and Khan (eds.) (1993), *Paying for India's Health Care*, Sage Publications, New Delhi, India, pp. 161-97.

Bose, A. (1991), *Population of India 1991 Results and Methodology.*

Biswas, S.K.(1987), *Ageing in Contemporary India, Indian Anthropological Society*, Calcutta, India.

Biswas, S.K. (1987), *Ageing in Contemporary India, Indian Anthropological Society*, Occasional Papers, Calcutta, India.

Biswas, S.K. (1991), *Role of Elderly Persons as Family Decision-Makers: Rural Urban Situation in Quality Ageing*, edited by Indira Jaiprakash, Association of Gerontology (India), Varanasi, 1991, pp. 98-101.

Bose, A.B., and Gangrade, (1988), *The Ageing in India: Problems and Potentialities*, Abhinav Publications, New Delhi, India.

Buvinic, M., and Rao Gupta, G., (1992), 'Targeting Poor Women-Headed Households and Women Maintained Families in Developing Countries: Views on a Policy Dilemma,' Washington DC: International Centre for Research on Women (ICRW).

Caldwell, J.C. (1990), *Introductory Thought on Health Transition* in J.C. Caldwell *et al.* (eds.), *What We Know About the Health Transition*, Canberra: Australian National University.

Caldwell, J.C. (1994), 'New Challenges for Demography,' *Journal of the Australian Population Association*, Vol. 11, No. 2, pp. 9-19.

Cleland, J. (1990), The Idea of the Health Transition in J.C. Caldwell *et al.* (eds.), *What We Know About the Health Transition*, Canberra: Australian National University.

Chanana, H.B., and Talwar P.P. (1987), *Ageing in India: Its Socio-economic and Health Implications, Asia Pacific Population Journal*, Vol. 2 (3), pp. 23-28.

Das Gupta M., Krishnan T.N., and Chen L., *Health and Transitions in India: Public Policies and Action*, Corbett.

Dreze J., and Sen A., (1991), *Public Action for Social Security* in Ahmad, E. Dreze, J. Hills, and Sen, A., *Social Security in Developing Countries*, University Press Limited, Dhaka.

Duggal, R., and Amin, S. (1989), *Cost of Health Care: a Household Survey in an Indian District, The Foundation for Research in Community Health* (FRCH), Bombay, India.

Ebrahim, S. (1994), *Methodological Issues in Mortality, Morbidity and Disability*, in Ramachandran and Shah (eds.), *Public Health Implications of Ageing in India*, pp. 61-67.

Ebrahim, S. (1995), Public Health Implications of Ageing; *Journal of the Royal College of Physicians*, London, Vol. 29, No. 3.

Elo, I.T., and Preston, S.H. (1992), *Effects of Early Life Conditions on Adult Mortality: A Review, Population Index*, Vol. 58, No. 2.

Evans, J. R., Hall, K.L., and Warford, J. (1981), *Shattuck Lecture—Health Care in the Developing World: Problems of Scarcity and Choice, New England Journal of Medicine.*

Frenk, J., Bobadilla, J.L., Stern, C., Frejka, T., and Lozano, R. (1991), *Elements for a Theory of the Health Transition, Health Transition Review*, Vol. I, No. 1.

Gowariker, G. (1991) (eds.), *Population Science and Development*, Asish Publications, New Delhi, India.

Guha Roy, S. (1994), *Morbidity Related Epidemiological Determinants in the Indian Aged—An Overview* in Ramachandran C.R., and Shah B. (eds.), *Public Health Implications of Ageing in India*, ICMR, Delhi.

Guha Roy, S. (1984), *Population Estimates for India, Demography India*, 13 (1&2).

Guha Roy, S. (1985), *Demography of Ageing: Indian Experience, Journal of Indian Anthropological Society*, Vol. 20, pp. 58-83.

Guha Roy, S. (1993), *Demography of West Bengal*, in B. Roy (ed.) *West Bengal Today*, Publications, New Delhi, India.

Gulati, L. (1991), *'The Female Dimension of Population Ageing in Kerala State in India,' Proceedings of Expert Group Meeting on Integration of Ageing and Elderly Women into Development*, Vienna, October, 1991.

Indrayan, A., *Towards Developing a Health Atlas of India: An Exercise in Cartograph in Health and Population Perspectives and Issues*, Vol. 11, No. 4, October-December, 1988, *Journal of National Institute of Health and Family Welfare*, New Delhi.

Kalache, A. (1991), *Ageing in Developing Countries* in Pathy W.J. (eds.), *The Principles and Practice of Geriatric Medicine*, John Wiley and Sons, Surrey UK Ltd.

Kalache, K., and Sen K. (1996 forthcoming), *Ageing in Developing Countries—Case Studies of Brazil and India* in Pathy W.J. (eds.), *Principles and Practice of Geriatric Medicine*, John Wiley and Sons, third edition.

Kannan, K.P., Thankappan K.R., Kutty V.R., Aravindan, K.P. (1991), *Health and Development in Rural Kerala: A Study of Linkages between Socio-Economic Status and Health Status*, Integrated Rural Technology Centre of Kerala Sastra Sahitya Parishad (KSSP), Kerala, India.

Kinsella, K., and Taeuber, C. (1992), *An Ageing World 11, US Department of Commerce Bureau of the Census.*

Kjellstrom, T., and Rosenstock, R. (1990), *The Role of Environmental and Occupational Hazards in the Adult Health Transition, World Health Statistics Quarterly*, No. 43, pp. 188-95.

Kumar, V. (1991), *Family Life and Socio-Economic Problems of the Aged*, Ashish Publishing House, New Delhi, India.

Kumar, S. Vijaya, (1995) (eds.), *Challenges Before the Elderly — An Indian Scenario*, MD Publications Private Limited, New Delhi, India.

Lakshmana, T. (1989), *Implications of Demographic Change in Indian Population by 2001* in Pati and Jena (eds.), *Aged in India*,1989.

Last, J. (1983), *Dictionary of Epidemiology*, Oxford Medical Publications, New York.

Lemer, M. (1973), *Modernisation and Health: A Model of the Health Transition*, paper presented at the annual meeting of the American Public Health Association, San Francisco, November.

MacMahon, B., Paugh, T.F., and Ipsen, J. (1960), *Epidemiologic Methods*, J.A. Churchill Ltd., London.

Mahadevan, K., Audinarayana, Jayasree, R., and Ramalingam S.P. (1993), *Demographic Implications of the Elderly in India* in *Journal of Social Research* special issue of *Anthropology of Ageing*, Vol. 31, Nos. 1 and 2, pp. 14-23.

Mahajan, K., and Joshi S. (1991), (eds.), *Studies in Medical Anthropology*, Ashish Publications, New Delhi.

Malakar, C.R., and Guha Roy S., (1990), *Reconstruction of Indian Life Tables for 1901-81 and Projections for 1981-2001, Sankhya*, Vol. 52, Series B, Part 3.

Martin, L.G. (1990), *Status of South Asia's Growing Elderly Population, Journal of Cross Cultural Gerontology*, Vol. 5.

McKeown, (1976), *The Modern Rise of Population*, Edward Arnold, London.

Mosley, W.H., Jamison, D.T., and Henderson, D.A. (1990), *The Health Sector in Developing Countries: Prospects for the 1990's and Beyond, Annual Review of Public Health*, Vol. 11, pp. 335-58.

Mohanty, S.P. (1989), *Demographic and Socio-Cultural Aspects of Ageing in India — Some Emerging Issues* in Pati and Jena (eds.), *Aged in India*, Asia Publishing House.

Murray, C.J.L., and Lopez, A.D. (eds.) (1994), *Global Assessments in the Health Sector*, World Health Organisation, Geneva.

Muthayya, B.C. (1995), *The Rural Elderly: A Study of their Existing Conditions and Problems* in Kumar (eds.), *Challenges Before the Elderly, An Indian Scenario*, Asia Publishing House.

Omran, A.R. (1971), *The Epidemiologic Transition: ATheory of the Epidemiology of Population Change* in *Milbank Memorial Fund Quarterly*, Vol. 49, pp. 509-38.

Omran, A.R. (1982), *Epidemiologic Transition Theory* in J. Rose (ed.), *International Encyclopaedia of Population*, Free Press, New York.

Pati, R.N., and Jena, B. (1989) (eds.), *Aged in India (Socio-Demographic Dimension)*, Ashish Publishing House, New Delhi, India.

Panikar, R.G., and Soman, C.R. (1984), *Health Status of Kerala: Paradox of*

Economic Backwardness and Health Development, Centre for Development Studies, Trivandrum, Kerala, India.

Phillips, M., Feachem, R.A., Murray, C.J.L., Over, M., Kjellstrom, T. (1993), *Adult Health: A Legitimate Concern for Developing Countries, American Journal of Public Health*, Vol. 83, No. 11, November 1993, pp. 1527-30.

Ramamurti, P.V., and Jamuna D. (1987), *Psychological Research on the Aged in India* in Biswas (eds.), *Ageing in Contemporary India*, Indian Anthropological Society.

Ramamurti, P.V., *The Status, Psychological Adjustment and Mental Health of Middle Aged and Older Widows*, (report) Indian Council for Social Science Research and Centre for Research on Ageing, S.V. University Tirupati,1989-1991 unpublished report.

Reddy, P. Jayarami, (1989), Inter-generational Support — A Reality or Myth in Pati and Jena (eds.), *Aged in India (Socio-Demographic Dimensions)*, Asia Publishing House, New Delhi, India.

Sarkar, B.N., *Demography of Aged People* (1989), in Pati and Jena (eds.), *Aged in India*, 1989.

Sen, K. (1994), *Women and Ageing* in Ramachandran and Shah (eds.), *Public Health Implications of Ageing in India*, ICMR, New Delhi, India.

Sen, K. (1994), *Ageing — Debates on Demographic Transition and Social Policy*, Zed Press, London and New Jersey.

Sen, K. (1996), Old Age Security and Pensions in India: A Critique of the Current Paradigm in Lloyd, Sherlock and Johnson, P. (1996), *Ageing and Social Policy — Global Comparisons*, Suntory and Toyota International Centres for Economics and Related Disciplines, *Occasional Papers*, The London School of Hygiene and Tropical Medicine.

Shariff, A. (1995), *Health Transition in India, National Association of Applied Economic Research* (NCAER), New Delhi, India.

Sundar, R. (1995), *Household Survey of Health Care Utilisation and Expenditure, National Council for Applied Research (NCAER)*, New Delhi, India.

Tracy, M.B. (1991), *Social Policies for the Elderly in the Third World*, Westport, Greenwood Press.

Tulasi Dhar, V.B. (1992), *States Financing of Health Care in India Some Recent Trends*, National Institute of Public Finance and Policy, New Delhi, March 1992.

Tout, K.(1989), *Ageing in Developing Countries*, Oxford University Press, Oxford, UK.

Vatuk, S. (1991), Gerontology in India: The State of the Art, *Journal of Cross Cultural Gerontology*, 6: 259-71.

Yesudian, C.A.K. (1990a), *A Study of Health Services Utilisation and Expenditure, Bombay: Department of Health Service Studies*, Tata Institute of Social Sciences, Bombay, India.

CHAPTER 2

Issues of Health Care Services: Some Reflections

Debabrata Datta & Debasish Sarkar

"It is perhaps a mistake to see the development of education, health care and other basic achievements only or primarily as expansion of 'Human resources' — the accumulation of 'human capital' — as if people were just the means of production and not its ultimate end. The bettering of human life does not have to be justified by showing that a person with a better life is also a better producer" (Sen and Dreze: Economic Development and Social Opportunity).

Health is Wealth!

As the above line suggests the issue of health should be viewed from two aspects — *health is wealth* and also *health creates wealth.* The maxim that health is wealth highlights the increasing importance of health. Health is valuable on its own. It is perhaps the supreme element of economic development. We cherish for developed world but we cherish no less for healthy world.

According to Sen, education and health can be seen to be valuable to the freedom of a person in at least five distinct ways.

1. Intrinsic importance—Education and health are valuable achievements in themselves.
2. Instrumental personal roles—A person's education and health help him to do many things.
3. Instrumental social roles—Education and health encourage demand for social needs.
4. Instrumental process roles—The education and health broadens the horizon of the people and generate benefits.

5. Empowerment and distributive roles—with better health and education, disadvantaged groups can better resist oppression and inequality.

When we look at the above-mentioned benefits of health we also find out that these gains are more for poor people who are typically most handicapped by ill health and who stand to gain the maximum from the development of health care facilities.

The primary gain of good health arises from gains in workers' productivity. Healthier worker earns more because they are more productive and can get better paying jobs. In Cote d'Ivory daily wage rate are estimated to be 19 per cent lower, on an average, among men who lose a day of work per month because of illness than among healthier men. The worker in the less developed country often gets daily wage on the basis of no work no pay. If he misses the work due to illness, his income is reduced.

There are evidences of substantial gain in health improvement among the children. When the children are healthy and do not suffer from nutritional deficiency there is marked improvement in their ability to learn. In a study of Brazil, it is found out that inadequately nourished children score 20 per cent less than the average score in the class. Ill nutrition often creates bad eyesight, damaging educational progress.

There is a very close interlinkage between poverty and poor health. A vicious circle is operating here. Poverty causes poor health and poor health causes poverty. The improvement in health care can be an important step in reducing the level of poverty.

When we consider a problem of health care in the context of less developed country, it is found out that poverty and low income causes major difficulties in the lives of the common man. So a good health care is highly needed and this has the following components.

(a) Nutritious diet.
(b) Hygienic condition of living.
(c) Safe drinking water.
(d) Information about good health care.
(e) Existence of good health care facilities.
(f) Existence of hospitals and medical treatment facilities.
(g) Financial ability to incur the medical expenses.

Health, A Public Good

It is evident that among these requirements, most of them remain unfulfilled in the less developed countries. The poor people do not get nutritious food or hygienic condition of living. Illiteracy also makes them uninformed about the basic health care. This implies that if the task of health care improvement facilities is left to the individuals themselves, the situation is difficult to improve. There is necessity of social and Government intervention in the matter of health facilities so that the overall health care system can improve. Some of the aspects of health improvement as noted earlier fall within the category of public good. Safe drinking water should be provided by the society. This has increasing returns to scale for which optimal allocation needs Government intervention. Similarly the information about health care is another public good with significant positive externality. This should therefore be the area of Government intervention.

From the above point of view we should make a distinction between primary health care and secondary health care. Primary health care implies the development of socio-economic conditions, which leads to general improvement of health. Primary health care is more social in nature than personal. There is externality in the benefits of primary health care. This primary health care also requires lumpy investments, which can be provided only by the society. Certain programmes of vaccination or inoculation can be conducted only at the social or Government level. So the primary health care is basically a public good.

Compared to it, the secondary health care is more personalized in nature. This is the medical treatment, which an individual undertakes in the event of any illness. In this case the individual himself derives the benefits and so is required to pay for the benefits. The market can provide secondary health care for the people who can afford them. There is need for Government provision only on distributional consideration. The poor people, who cannot afford to pay for their own medical treatment, should be helped by the Government. So there is need for subsidising secondary health care only for the poor and so it is in the area of distributional objectives of Government.

Our distinction of the health care facilities between primary and secondary health care makes the position clear with regard to policy proposals. A primary health care needs active Government intervention. However, since primary health care requires the involvement of both medical and non-medical personnel, a large area of this primary health care may not be that expensive. Secondary health care however is basically dependent on the medical professionals, modern and sophisticated medical equipment and therefore the cost of secondary health care per person may be very high. However the major part of secondary health care does not involve externality and therefore it can be left to the market forces.

We can consider in detail the role of Government in the area of primary health care. The primary health care is mostly a public good. The key characteristic of this public good *i.e.*, public health is that one individual can consume it and benefit from it without reducing the benefit for the other. An information regarding the benefit of the use of oral rehydration salt or the benefit of the use of iodised salt is basically a pure public good with non-excludability and non-rivalry.

The necessity of Government also arises on account of externality. If an infectious disease is cured, spread of this disease is prevented. The persons who are not attacked by the disease will never be required to pay anything for this benefit of escape from infection. So obviously the total payment will not match the total benefit. There is necessity of Government intervention in internalising this externality.

Health Economics: Some Stylised Facts

Health is multidimensional. With the exception of the dichotomy between life and death, there is no completely objective ordering across individuals or populations with respect to health. Health can be defined on the basis of life expectancy, mortality rate, work capacity etc.

Economists feel that the individuals make trade off between health and other goods and therefore a question of allocation is also involved here. This requires a valuation of health. The two leading approaches in this regard are *(a)* willingness to pay and *(b)* discounted future earning. The first approach is preferred on theoretical ground (Schelling, 1968, Mishan, 1971, Jones and Lee, 1974) but it is difficult to estimate empirically.

There is a strong positive correlation between income and health in the low-income level but this result becomes weaker in the high level. So LDCs can improve health situation by increasing their income and particularly with improved distribution of health.

Health has two dimensions; one as an intermediate commodity that affects production, and the other as a final commodity which directly affects utility. The externalities associated with health are often quite significant but some of them are difficult to measure and evaluate. For example when one person suffering from an infectious disease gets cured early, others are benefited but it is not easy to measure the extent of this benefit.

The percentage of expenditure on health may vary from country to country but while comparing them the prices of the services is to be taken into account. For example, the health services are much costlier in USA than in India and this factor has to be taken into account. The role of the Government is also important here. The Government in all countries plays a role as provider of medical care, subsidiser, regulator etc.

The issue of health is closely related with insurance, as there is risk and uncertainty here. Arrow (1963) and Phelps (1973) make seminal contribution in this area. The two problems that arise with regard to insurance are

(a) moral hazard and
(b) asymmetry of information.

Moral hazard leads to overspending on medical care. (Pauly, 1968) Similarly asymmetric information also create excess medical spending. Contingent or compulsory insurance can be a solution to this problem.

Despite the difficulty of measuring output, many estimates of short and long run have been made. (Lave and Lave, 1970) In the short run marginal cost is below average cost in most hospitals but the long run average cost falls up to 200 beds and thereafter it is constant with a possible rise after 500 beds. This can help in determining the optimum size of a hospital.

Disparate World Health

The world health scenario is characterised by inequality as is expected, given the skewed nature of income distribution of the world economy. The life expectancy, mortality rate, both adult and infant points out a grim situation of the health profile of the Less Developed Countries. The position of course is worst in Sub-Saharan Africa but the position in the South-East Asia is no less uncomfortable. We can look at the Tables 2.1, 2.2 and 2.3 to get a clear idea of the disparity. This also shows that there is enough scope for improvement in the health care system in the LDCs.

With this end in view, in 1978 the World Health Organisation and UNICEF convened the world conference in order to endorse the Alma-Ata declaration of advancing towards "Health for All" by the year 2000. The declaration called for a potentially revolutionary approach. Primary health care was conceived as a comprehensive strategy that would not only include an equitable approach to health services but also address underlying social and political aspects of health. It called for accountability of health industry to the common people and for social guarantees to make sure that the basic needs particularly the food needs of all people are met. Unfortunately these high expectations of Alma-Ata have not been met. Today it is painfully evident that the goal of health for all is receding more distant and the poor is deprived of the basic health needs as earlier.

Three factors that can be identified as responsible for sabotaging the revolutionary essence of primary health care are:

1. The introduction of the idea of selective health cares since late 70's.
2. Structural adjustment programme and introduction of user financed health services.
3. The take over of Third World health cares policy-making by the World Bank in 90's.

UNICEF had been a strong advocate of comprehensive primary health care as declared at Alma-Ata. But gradually it started introducing selective primary health care through its "Child Survival Revolution"(CSR). UNICEF prioritised four interventions programmes as GOBI (G — Growth monitoring, O — Oral rehydration therapy, B — Breast feeding, I — Immunization). UNICEF later broaden this package to GOBIFFA (Food sufficiency, Female education and Family planning). But only two areas get some attention, namely ORT and immunization. But here also one

Table 2.1
Health Infrastructure and Services

Demographic region and economy	Doctors per 1000 population 1985-90	Nurses to doctor ratio 1982-90	Hospital beds per 1000 population 1985-90	Percentage of children immunised, age less than 1 year third dose of DPT 1990-91	Total health expenditure Official Exchange rate Dollars		Health Expenditure as a percentage of GDP		
					Millions 1990	Per capita 1990	Total 1990	Public sector 1990	Private sector 1990
Sub-Saharan Afica	0. 12W	5.1W	1.4W	52W	12080t	24W	4.5W	2.5W	2.0W
India	0.41	1.1	0.7W	83	17740	21	6.0	1.3	4.7
China	1.37	0.5	2.6	95	12969	11	3.5	2.1	1.4
Other Asia & Islands	0.31W	3.0W	1.8W	81W	41752t	61W	4.5W	1.8W	2.7W
Latin America & the Caribbean	1.25W	0.5W	2.7W	71W	46660t	105W	4.0W	2.4W	1.6W
Middle Eastern Crescent	1.04W	1.5W	2.9W	75W	38961t	77W	4.1W	2.4W	1.7W
Formerly Socialist Economies of Europe (FSE)	4.07W	2.2W	11.4W	77W	49143t	142W	3.6W	2.5W	1.0W
Established Market Economies (EME)	2.52W	2.1W	8.3W	80W	1483196t	1860W	9.2W	5.6W	3.5W
FSE &EME	3.09W	2.1W	9.3W	79W	1532340t	1340W	8.7W	5.4W	3.4W
Demographically Developing Group	0.78W	0.9W	2.0W	80W	170115t	41W	4.7W	2.3W	2.5W
World	1.37W	1.4W	3.6W	80W	1702455t	323W	8.0W	4.9W	3.2W

Source: World Development Report 1993.

Table 2.2
Population Structure and Dynamics

Demographic region and Economy	*Population and Fertility*					*General Mortality*			*Age-specific Mortality Rates*					
	Population 1990 (millions)	*Under 15 years old, 1990 (per cent)*	*60 Years and over, 1990 (per cent)*	*Total fertility rate, 1990*	*Total live births per year, 1990 (hundreds of thousands)*	*Life expectancy at birth*		*Median age at death, 1990*	*Perinatal mortality rate, 1990*	*Child mortality rate*			*Adult mortality rate, 1990 (ages 15-59)*	
						1960	*1990*			*1960*	*1975*	*1990*	*Male*	*Female*
Sub-Saharan Africa	510	46	5	6.4	251.8	43	52	5	68	251	212	175	381	322
India	850	37	7	4.0	258.1	47	58	37	64	235	195	127	272	229
China	1134	27	9	2.5	251.3	43	69	64	25	210	85	43	201	150
Other Asia and Islands	683	37	6	3.3	188.7	50	62	42	49	182	135	97	243	177
Latin America and the Caribbean	444	36	7	3.3	124.6	54	70	55	33	161	104	60	228	163
Middle-Eastern Crescent	503	41	6	5.0	195.8	44	61	24	46	242	174	111	228	174
Formerly Socialist Economies	346	23	17	2.2	52.9	66	72	72	19	68	36	22	281	112
Established Market Economies	798	19	18	1.7	104.0	70	76	75	9	36	21	11	147	73
World	5267	32	9	3.4	1427.1	53	65	55	40	195	135	96	234	169

Source: World Development Report, 1993.

Table 2.3
Annual Drug Expenditure Per Capita, Selected Countries, 1990

Countries	*Expenditure (in US $)*
Japan	412
Germany	222
USA	191
Mexico	28
Brazil	16
Philippines	11
China	7
Pakistan	7
India	3
Bangladesh	2

Source: World Development Report, 1993.

problem that appears is the role of the market that has made the ORS quite costly and has promoted market immunization in doubtful areas like hepatitis B.

A big set back to primary health care occurs when under structural adjustment programme most of the Government have tried to reduce expenditure and without being able to reduce the spending for the better off section of the society has reduced the expenditure of the health services for the poor.

The World Bank prioritises health intervention by calculating their relative cost-effectiveness. This is measured by the number of disability adjusted life years (DALY) set through each intervention. Each disease is classified according to how many years of productive life, the individual loses because of the disease. Refer to Table 2.4 in this connection. The Bank has studied and prioritised 47 different public health and clinical intervention, expressing their benefits in DALY achieved. For example Leukaemia treatment provides only 10 DALYs for 10,000 dollars while vitamin A supplementation achieves 1 DALY for dollar 1.

The problem with the World Bank approach is that it glosses over the fact that the dependence of private sector solely for health care may be quite dangerous. The US health system dominated by

Table 2.4
Estimated Global Burden of Disease from the Selected Environment Threats, 1990, and Potential World-wide Reductions Through Environmental Interventions

Type of environment and principal related diseases	*Burden from these diseases (millions of (DALYs/year)*	*Reduction achievable through feasible interventions (%)*	*Burden averted by feasible interventions (millions of DALYs/year)*	*Burden Averted per 1000 population (DALYs/year)*
Occupational	318	—	36	7.1
Cancers	79	5	4	0.8
Neuropsychiatric	93	5	2	0.9
Chronic respiratory	47	5	2	0.5
Musculoskeletal	18	50	9	1.8
Unintentional injury	81	20	16	3.1
Urban air	170	—	8	1.7
Respiratory infections	123	5	6	1.2
Chronic respiratory	47	5	2	0.5
Road transport (Motor vehicle injuries)	32	20	6	1.2
All the above	473	—	50	10.0

Source: World Development Report, 1993.

a strong private sector is an example. The health care there is so expensive that some US health indicators among the low-income people in US cities are worse than those of even Third World countries.

It is observed that even in developed countries particularly in Europe and USA the money made available for health services by the Government appears to be inadequate in the face of growing demand contributed mostly by development of new high cost medical Technology. The dominant approach presently followed to this problem is to attempt to deploy services more efficiently and effectively so as to achieve a greater return for a given output. Emphasis is given to place direct cost to the consumer and enable the private sector to develop.

Although Government looking after the health needs of people may be welcomed, in view of the present scenario of paucity of fund for health care, the approach should be to make clear distinction between the primary and secondary health care. Unless the Government resources are withdrawn from secondary health care and deployed for the primary health care, it is very difficult to improve the general health standard of the people of the less developed country. The people who can finance his own secondary health care should provide it, so that the state fund can be used for general benefit of the society. For example, in India the primary and public health programme get less than one-third of the total allocated resources when around 71 per cent is spent on secondary programme. This situation is to be reversed for effective improvement in national health.

What Ails India's Health?

The health care situation in India always merits serious attention in view of vast population size of the country. In the world, every sixth individual is an Indian and therefore unless health care facilities improves in this part of the world, the world health situation can never be satisfactory. Here lies the importance of the slogan "Health for All," coined in 1982 in the National Health Policy.

Fifty years, after independence, have witnessed definite improvement in the health indicators. Life expectancy has doubled and the death rate has declined to a single digit level. Table 2.5 reflects the situation at the time of independence and in the nineties.

Table 2.5
Basic Indicators of Human Development

Year	*Life expectancy at birth (years)*	*Literacy rate (%)*	*Birth rate*	*Death rate*	*Infant mortality rate*
			(Per Thousand)		
1951	32.1	18.3	39.4	27.4	146
1971	45.6	34.5	36.9	14.9	129
1991	59.4	52.2	29.5	9.8	80
1997	62.4 (1996)	62.0	27.2	8.9	71

Source: Indian Economy Survey, 1999-2000.

The picture becomes clearer if we focus our attention to the expansion of health services over the plan period. The number of hospitals has increased around six times and the number of medical colleges has also achieved similar expansion. Table 2.6 shows the trend of expansion pattern of health care services in India during the plan period.

The most notable feature witnessed in the above table is a phenomenal rise in the number of primary health centres (PHC). This is because of the policy of health improvement as per the report of the Bhore Committee (Health Survey and Development Committee, GOI, 1946). This Committee had some important suggestions as under:

(a) That no individual should lack access to medical care because of inability to pay for it.
(b) That medical relief and preventive health care should be urgently provided to the rural people.
(c) That special emphasis should be placed on preventive methods.

The Bhore Committee laid down norms for rural health infrastructure and the construction of primary health centres

Table 2.6
Expansion of Health Services

(in numbers)

Item	*1951*	*1961*	*1971*	*1981*	*1992*	*1996*	*1997*
Medical Colleges **	28 *	60	98	111	146	165	165
Hospitals**	2694	3094	3862	6804	13692	15097#	NA
Dispensaries**	6515	9406	12180	16751	27403	28225#	NA
Community Health Centres@	0	0	0	217	2186	2572	2628
Primary Health Centres@	725	2565	5112	5740	20701	21917	22446
Sub-Centres@	NA	NA	28489	51405	131370	134931	136379
Hospital Beds (All Types)**	117178	230000	348655	569495	834650	870161#	NA
Doctors**	61840	83756	151129	268712	395851	375291(P)	484401P
Dentists**	3290	3582	5512	8648	11300	23953 #	NA
Nurses**	16550	35584	80620	154280	385410	565696	NA

NA : Not available
* : Pertains to 1950
** : As on December 31
@ : As on March 31
# : As on 31.12.95
P : Provisional

Source: Ministry of Health and Family Welfare.

began in the early fifties in accordance with the Bhore Committee's recommendations. The pattern adopted was to have one PHC for every block. The National Planning Commission also advised at that time a rapid increase in the number of medical personnel.

Another watershed in the development of the Government policy towards health is the announcement of National Health Policy in 1982. It accepts the policy of providing health for all by the year 2000 A.D. The overall goal of the policy is the "universal provision of comprehensive primary health care services" which is "relevant", "affordable by the people" and "participatory" of community and voluntary organization. It aims to provide an integrated package of services to tackle the entire range of poor health conditions. It wants to focus on

(*a*) modification of existing system of medical education and Paramedical training
(*b*) reorganization of health services infrastructure and
(*c*) integration of health issues with overall socio-economic development.

The Eighth Plan however restated the goal as "Health for Underprivileged by 2000" instead of "Health for All by 2000." The Ninth Plan noted the inter-state disparity in health care and highlighted the need for improvement of referral linkages and operationalisation of Health Management Information System.

Given the above policy framework, what ails the India's health economy? Of course one major problem is the poverty of a large section of the society and similarly the inability of the Government of a low-income country to mobilise enough resources for improvement of the health care system of the nation. If we look at the picture of the developed countries it is observed that a major part of health expenditure of these countries is borne by the Government. Refer to Table 2.7 in this connection. This is a hard reality that our Government cannot spend as much as one developed country can, and therefore, we have to make it doubly sure that whatever we spend is optimally spent and benefit the man who needs it most. Rather than Pareto criterion, a Rawlsian criterion can be more useful in this regard.

Table 2.7
Expenditure on Health

(Rs. in Million)

	1950-51	*1975-76*	*1991-92*
Revenue Expenditure on Health	218.50	6111.66	52010.60
Total Revenue Expenditure	8136.10	174933.00	1670133.00
Per cent of Health Expenditure	2.69	3.49	3.11

Source: Finance and Revenue Account, CAG.

It could be nobody's case to argue that the Government did not increase the spending on health. The per capita expenditure on health has gone up by 100 times over the period 1950-51 to 1990-91. In real terms this signifies an increase of more than four times.

Table 2.7 shows the trend of increase in health expenditure during the plan period. But yet the conditions of health care facilities appear to be deplorable in most of the Government hospitals. The rural health care system assiduously built up during the fifties has been crumbling on account of non-availability of doctors, paucity of funds for purchase of medicines, poor work culture of the hospital staff and misuse of fund for non-health care purposes. The Ninth Plan document observes that the existing primary health care institutions are functioning sub-optimally for

(a) inappropriate location
(b) lack of professional staff
(c) lack of funds for drugs and
(d) lack of first referral units.

When we look at the global health expenditure pattern and compare it with the health expenditure of India, we find that while for 15 per cent of world population, the established developed economies spend US $1483 billion in the year 1990, India for 16 per cent of world population spend only US $18 billion (Table 2.1). Much more notable is that the share of public sector spending in the total expenditure is lowest in India, being only 22 per cent of total expenditure. This is however not at all surprising, if we consider the level of income that we have. But the pity is that even this small expenditure is not properly directed to optimise the benefit and provide the help to the person who need it most.

The problem arises because from the very onset of our planning process, the Government only verbally emphasised the preventive care. In 1982, in its document on national health policy, the Government of India admitted that health services in India were more curative than preventive. In 1990-91, the Government spent 60 per cent on curative care and only 26 per cent on preventive services. This pattern of expenditure has played havoc with the communicable disease eradication programme like malaria eradication, leprosy control etc.

There has been rapid private sector expansion and corporatisation in health care in India since the mid 70's. Another trend is the neglect of rural areas. Today out of 1.1 million registered medical practitioners, 60 per cent are located in cities although 70 per cent of our population lives in villages. Among allopathic practitioners 75 per cent are practising in cities. The purchasing power for health care is higher in urban areas and this attracts doctors mostly to the urban areas. The scheme of reimbursement of medical expenses for the organised sector gives a boost to this tendency of concentration of doctors in urban areas. Refer to Tables 2.8 and 2.9 to get an idea of rural-urban divide in health facilities.

Table 2.8
Mortality Rates, All-India, 1978 (SRS) Showing Differences Between Rural and Urban Areas, Males and Females, and 5-years Age Groups

Age-group	*Rural Persons*	*Urban Persons*	*Combined*		
			Males	*Females*	*Persons*
0-4	53.2	26.3	44.7	52.1	48.3
5-9	4.8	1.5	3.7	4.7	4.2
10-14	2.2	1.0	2.0	2.0	2.0
15-19	2.8	1.6	2.1	3.0	2.5
20-24	3.6	2.5	2.7	4.1	3.4
25-29	4	2.6	3.4	4.1	3.7
30-34	4.2	2.7	3.8	3.9	3.9
35-39	5.2	3.9	5.2	4.7	4.9
40-44	7.6	4.9	7.4	6.7	7.1
45-49	9.6	9.4	11.4	7.6	9.5
50-54	15.6	14.7	17.5	13.0	15.4
55-59	24.1	21.1	26.9	19.9	23.6
60-64	38.3	34.2	42.7	32.4	37.5
65-69	53.8	42.3	56.5	47.1	51.7
70+	108.4	106.2	110.2	106.0	108.8
All ages	15.3	9.4	13.8	14.5	14.2

Source: Office of the Registrar General, (1983b).

If we look at the expenditure pattern in India, we see that the health expenditure as a percentage of total expenditure has declined during the period 1981-82 and 1994-95. We get the similar trend when we look at the state expenditure as well. The situation regarding medical care expenditure which are the responsibilities of State Government is moving from bad to worse.

Table 2.9
Rural Urban Disparities in Health Care Spending and Facilities 1990-91

States	*Urban health services@* *Rs. per capita* 1	*Rural health services* *Rs. per capita* 2	*Urban/Rural disparities (times) in spending* 3=1/2 *(in round fig.)*
Punjab	124	38	3
Kerala	171	16	11
Tamil Nadu	109	14	7
West Bengal	142	13	11
Maharashtra	76	19	4
Gujarat	84	15	6
Andhra Pradesh	92	9	10
Madhya Pradesh	68	12	6

@ — Includes Medical Education and ESI scheme.
Sources: Demands for Grants of the respective States Health Information of India, CBHI.

What is actually needed in the area of health care system, provided by Government, is an out and out professional approach. In a micro level study it has been found out that in West Bengal and India only 20 per cent of the total patients go to Out-Patients Departments of hospitals. The findings in this regard is presented in the Table 2.10. In many Government hospitals there is elaborate arrangement, big halls and qualified doctors for the outdoor treatment but still a major part of the patients, many of whom are poor, prefer to visit the private practitioners for domiciliary treatment.

The location factor is an important reason for this preference of private practitioners. Another reason is the round about process where only after two three visits one patient may be referred to the specialists. The bigness of the hospitals, the formalities and the lack of proper information and guidance system also deter people particularly the illiterate to visit the hospitals.

The problems can be effectively tackled if Out Patients Departments are decentralised and run from different centres in the area, served by a hospital. It may add upto the cost but there

Table 2.10
Percentage of Patients of Outdoor Treatment in India and West Bengal

Place of Treatment	*West Bengal*		*All India*	
	Village	*Town*	*Village*	*Town*
Govt. Hospital	12.48	19.52	17.67	22.60
PHC	6.08	0.58	4.94	1.19
Pvt. Hospital	0.93	1.95	15.13	16.18
Pvt. Physician	74.74	69.60	53.01	51.83
Others	5.77	8.35	9.25	8.20
Total	100.00	100.00	100.00	100.00

Source: National Sample Survey, 1986-87.

should not be any hesitation to realise this additional cost from the beneficiaries who in any case is ready to spend some money for treatment. The paying bed system is working for a long period and there is no reservation in the society about that. The political parties often make unnecessary fuss over pricing of Government services and in the present circumstances, there is little public support to these agitations.

More serious problem, however, is the transaction cost of this pricing. If too many formalities are set in this regard, the result may be self-defeating. This part, therefore, has to be made as simple as possible. The entire task may be left to the staff involved, which should collect revenue, bear cost and pay a certain amount to the Government.

The shortage of doctors similarly is an outcome of our misguided policy regarding the pricing of education. After the independence, the fund was not so limited, the burden of debt did not become so unbearable and Government could double the number of medical college over a span of ten years. But thereafter the resource crunch emerged and the establishment of new medical colleges came almost to a halt during the seventies. Only in the eighties when Government allowed private medical colleges, the rate of establishment of new medical colleges picked up. But state like West Bengal that blocked the entry of private colleges on account of ideological blinkers did not manage to set up a single Government medical college over a period of long thirty years. This caused havoc with the health care system of West Bengal where the shortage of doctors left many parts of the rural areas at the mercy of quacks, minted at the alternative medicine system that mushroomed all over the state in the eighties and nineties, as per the rule of the market.

The issue of the pricing and privatisation of the medical education can be resolved very easily by standard textbook result. The medical education confers private benefits to the students and also there is strong positive externality in this education. It is therefore a merit good, which should be subsidised. But that does not mean that the private beneficiary *i.e.* the student should not be properly charged. Unless the private benefit part is priced, it is quite natural that there will be insufficiency of fund.

The argument that is extended to support the practice of low-fee medical education also does not stand the test of textbook result. It is a standard rule in Economics that the income of a person should not be judged by his current income; rather it should be judged by lifetime income. By that rule, no student in medical college can be regarded as low-income and can deserve Government support in study. What he of course needs is a good lending system which can finance his present expenditure and which he can easily pay back once he starts earning. In our country, it is necessary to remind the high-educated persons how much they owe to their alma mater for their present earning.

Similarly, there is no reason to find fault with the system of capitation fees. Again there is a standard result in the analysis of discriminating monopoly that there are some markets where no production takes place under uniform pricing. But if higher price is charged to the high demand persons the market can function and society can gain. If a few medical colleges can be established with capitation fees, the benefits will go to many other students and the society will also be benefited. It is not necessary in this regard to compromise with the standard of medical education and the examination can be as tough as necessary. One valid objection is that this will give admission opportunity to the rich students but this is rule of the game that the rich get all the good things in the market and medical education can be one of them.

The increase in the number of qualified doctors can solve the problem of sending medicos to the rural areas. Here again there is a wishful thinking that doctors can be sent to villages through bonds and diktats. This betrays poor understanding of the law of demand and supply. All the problems of high fees, non-availability of doctors can be tackled only by increasing the supply of doctors. The society is aging and it will gradually need more and more doctors and unless we make ourselves alive to this situation and understand the role of market in this case, a grim situation waits for us. The need of the hour is therefore increasing the facility of medical education at a rapid rate.

The paucity of funds is no doubt a major barrier in improving the health care situation in India. The growing population makes the problem much more complicated and serious too. It is not very easy to mobilise more funds for medical services when the Centre as well as all the State Governments suffer from severe resource crunch. So attention must be given to the raising of more resources wherever possible. Charging of some fees for the services by the Government is never a bad idea but there should be free benefits for the destitute. The issue involved, therefore is one of proper targeting. This is never a simple task. One method can be income certificates but often these certificates are casually issued and the purpose is defeated. It is a good idea if the Government identifies the poor with utmost seriousness and issues Below Poverty Line (BPL) card that should be used for various Government benefits like cheap food, doles, social employment etc. If the names of the BPL beneficiaries are openly displayed with prominence, the problem of presence of Non-BPL persons in the list may be less by what is known as stigma factor. Another way is to provide the benefit in those areas where the incidence of poverty is maximum, like the tribal areas. It has been estimated that even if a very small amount is collected from the beneficiaries, the quality of services can much improve. This will also entitle the paying beneficiaries to voice their protest in case of poor or non-existent services.

The problem of insufficiency of fund however should be addressed more from the expenditure side rather than from the revenue side. The hospitals have been made overstaffed with large contingent of General Duty Attendants and sweepers many of them are recalcitrant and undisciplined. A study of a medical college reveals that there is post of carpenters and tailors although there is no job for them. Abolition of such unnecessary posts and handing over the cleansing job to agencies can reduce the cost substantially in the long run.

One major requirement is to set our priority right. Dreze and Sen have noted massive displacement of health care activities by family planning programmes. While family planning programmes are definitely important, it should never be at the cost of general health care particularly when the general health care can help a lot in progress towards family planning. Much more serious is too much importance attached to AIDS when in terms of virulence and casualty, diseases like malaria or gastroenteritis are more dreaded in our country. In the Ninth Plan Perspective, while diseases like cholera and diarrhoea do not find a place, AIDS occupies a central place as a cent per cent centrally aided programme. It is a pity that our problems are often viewed through the looking glass of West and hype about AIDS is an example of that.

Certain innovative scheme can be useful in improving the health care system in our country. Instead of establishing hospitals, building staff quarters and making a large overhead expenditure, mobile health unit may be planned. Programme like doctor comes to the door can be introduced under which a mobile unit equipped with necessary medical accessories can go to village at a fixed hour. Similarly, village people can be trained about the basic health care by literacy campaign bodies. The success of immunization programme like Pulse Polio Programme should be emulated in other areas like safe drinking water, sanitation etc.

Health, A World Agenda

The gigantic task of "Health for All" cannot be left to the Governments of the LDCs alone. It is a World responsibility. Within the Less Developed Country it needs all-round participation. The community involvement, the improvement of female literacy and the awaking of environmental consciousness can go a long way in moving towards a healthy world. The primary health care should be the focal point in this fight and the policy orientation to that direction not just at the country level but also at the global institutional level is the need of the day. The writing of

Sen has worked here, as the conscience of the world and his twin focus on health and education will be the guideline in all future policy framing.

References

1. Chatterjee, Meera (1998), *Implementing Health Policy*, Manohar Publishers.
2. ICSSR and ICMR (1981), *Health for All*, Indian Institute of Education.
3. *Indian Economic Survey*, Various Issues.
4. John Eatwell, Murray Milgate and Peter Newman ed. (1988), *The New Palgrave Dictionary of Economics*, The Macmillan Press Limited.
5. Nayar, R.K., 'Health in the Ninth Plan,' *Economic and Political Weekly*, Vol. 34, No. 8, 1999.
6. Datta Roy, S. (1994), *Paschimbangabashi*, Bagchi, K.P. & Co.
7. Sen and Dreze (1999), *The Amartya Sen and Jean Dreze Omnibus*, Oxford University Press.
8. *World Development Report*, Various Issues.
9. Datta, D. (1999), 'An Overview of the Economics of Health Care, *Samajtattva*, Vol. 5, June-December 1999.
10. Bhattacharya, S. (1996), 'Socio-Biological Perspectives in Resurgence of Malaria,' *Samajtattva*, Vol. 2.

CHAPTER 3

On Professor A.K. Sen's Contributions to the Theory of Collective Choice and Welfare

Satya R. Chakravarty

Professor Amartya K. Sen has been awarded the 1998 Nobel Prize in Economic Sciences for his contributions to Welfare Economics. Professor Sen's contributions have been substantive to all the areas he has touched upon, some of them are highly technical. But from the very beginning his major concern was the welfare of people, especially the poor.

Professor Sen raised basic questions about welfare theories and how market prices can be taken as reflections of welfare indicators. He chose a path of research which is different from market failures, co-ordination problem and asymmetric information. He was looking for methods of aggregating the values individuals in a society attach to different alternatives into values for the society as a whole. In the early 1950s, problems associated with social choice motivated Professor Kenneth J. Arrow to examine the possibility of aggregating individual preferences into a social preference. A social preference relation or a social welfare ordering (SWO) generates a complete and consistent ranking of all economic situations (social states). Completeness means that every social state can be compared and ranked to another. Consistency means reflexivity and transitivity of the relation. If a continuity assumption is made, the SWO can be represented by a social welfare function. If t_1, t_2 and t_3 are social states, where t_1 is regarded as socially better than t_2 and t_2 is better than t_3, then continuity requires any curve connecting t_1 and t_3 to cross the social indifference curve containing t_2, there are no sudden jumps from being better than t_1 to being worse than t_1. Arrow's fundamental result is that there does not exist any social preference that fulfils five axioms, each of which seems to be quite reasonable. This result is popularly known as the Arrow impossibility theorem. This strong negative result casts doubts on all claims that there can be a 'will of the people,' a 'social contract,' a 'public good,' a 'social benefit,' a 'people's voice,' and so on. That is, it casts doubts on all notions that explicitly or implicitly attribute preferences to society. Evidently, any theorem that casts so much doubts will generate a lot of responses. Investigation proceeded along the line how could individual preferences be aggregated and different social states evaluated in a satisfactory manner.

Now, social states cannot be ordered if we do not make some prior value judgements. Value judgements, which are generally regarded as statements of ethics, cannot be found to be true or false on the basis of factual evidence. A natural value judgement in the context of rankings of alternative social states is to require that rankings depend only on personal utility levels, so that two arbitrary social states are ranked entirely on the basis of personal utilities in the respective states. This value judgement, which demands that a social welfare ordering should ignore all nonutility features, has been referred to as welfarism by Sen. He also developed sufficient conditions for welfarism. These conditions are universality on unrestricted domain (URD), independence of irrelevant alternatives (IIA) and Pareto indifference (PAI). According to URD, any logically possible n-vector of individual utility functions is admissible in determining the social ranking, where n is the population size. That is, the same SWO must be employed to aggregate individual utilities irrespective of the forms of utility functions. IIA demands that the social ranking of any two social states s and t will be the same whenever the utility levels attached to s and t by the individuals involved are the same. This also means that if people's feelings change about some set of alternatives, but do not change about the pair s and t, then a collective choice rule must preserve the social ordering of s and t. Finally, PAI means that if all individuals are indifferent between two social states, then the SWO must rank them equally.

Another value judgement imposes certain informational requirements on the choice of a social preference rule. Specifically, information about each person's preference over social states and about how a given level of utility for any individual compares with that of another individual are required. These requirements are called *measurability* and *comparability* requirements respectively. Sen initiated the idea how assumptions about measurability and comparability of individual utility functions can affect the possibility of determining a consistent rule for social decision. Formally, a measurability assumption regarding a particular utility function will determine the set of transformations that can be applied to the utility function without altering the usable information. A strict type of measurability assumption is ratio scale measurability. According to ratio scale measurability, if a set of numbers u represents utilities of different objects, then $v = bu$, where $b > 0$ is a scalar, can also be used. An example here can be the measurement of height of a person. It does not matter whether we measure the height in feet or in metres, since the former can always be converted into the latter through a positive scalar transformation. A somewhat looser assumption is cardinal-scale measurability. Cardinal scale measurement says that any affine transformation of the utility numbers u such as $v = a + bu$, where a and $b > 0$ are scalars, conveys the same information as u. For instance, we can say that Centigrade and Fahrenheit scale temperatures are cardinally equivalent, since $C = -160/9 + 5F/9$, where C (F) indicates temperature in the Centigrade (Fahrenheit) scale. The least restrictive measurability assumption is that utility is measurable only with an ordinal scale. Formally, this permits the utility function of an individual to be rescaled taking any increasing transformation of it. If the only admissible scale transformation is the identity transformation, then the individual's utility function is fully measurable or measurable with absolute scale. Clearly, this is the most restrictive notion of measurability. As stated earlier, a comparability assumption means the extent to which the utility information available for an individual can be meaningfully compared across individuals. For instance, when I say 'I would like to be person A rather than being person B in a situation,' I am indulging in an interpersonal comparison. As Sen showed, all assumptions about measurability and comparability can be formalized by considering the set of transformations that can be applied to a utility profile without changing the SWO. Technically this is known as information invariance requirement. We can consider some examples. Let $f = (f_1, f_2, \ldots, f_n)$ be a vector of transformations, with one co-ordinate for each individual's utility function. Suppose that $u = (u_1, u_2 ..... u_n)$ is a utility profile associated with some social state s. In Arrow's framework we have ordinally measurable, noncomparable utilities.

Ordinally measurable, noncomparable utilities (OM-NC):

f_i is an increasing function for all i.

Ordinally measurable, fully comparable utilities (OM-FC):

$f_i = f$ for all i, where f is an increasing function.

Cardinally measurable, noncomparable utilities (CM-NC):

$f_i(r) = a_i + b_i r,$

where $b_i > 0$, *for all* i.

For any two social states s and t, in this case, we can compare utility gains and loses $[U_i(s) - U_i(t)]$ intrapersonally, but not interpersonally.

Cardinally measurable, unit-comparable utilities (CM-UC):

$f_i(r) = a_i + br$ for all i.

This permits comparison of utility differences interpersonally, but comparison of utility levels is not allowed.

Cardinally measurable, fully comparable utilities (CM-UC):

$f_i(r) = a + br.$

We may compare here both utility levels and utility differences.

In order to discuss Sen's suggestions rigorously, it may be worthwhile to state the Arrow theorem formally.

Theorem: Assume welfarism axioms. Then a SWO satisfies information invariance with respect to ordinally measurable, noncomparable utilities and the weak Pareto principle if and only if it is a dictatorship, where the weak Pareto principle declares a gain by everyone to be a social improvement and a dictatorship demands that there is someone whose preferences always dictate the SWO.

Thus, Arrow's theorem says that social orderings must coincide with the preferences of some individual regardless of preferences of others.

Sen showed that if in Arrow's theorem we assume that the SWO satisfies information invariance with respect to CM-NC utilities instead OM-NC utilities, then the theorem remains valid. However, a nondictatorial rule emerges if we include a comparability assumption in the framework. The following theorem of Professors Claude d'Aspremont and Louis Gevers exemplifies this.

Theorem: In the presence of welfarism axioms, a SWO satisfies information invariance with respect to cardinally measurable unit-comparable utilities, the weak Pareto principle and anonymity if and only if it is the utilitarian rule; the alternatives are ranked by sum of utilities across individuals.

According to anonymity if u' is a vector of utilities associated with the social state s and u'' is a permutation of the elements of u', then the social ranking of u' and u'' with respect to other utility vectors must be the same. Thus, anonymity shows the irrelevance of the names of the individuals. Two important observations can be made from this characterisation of the utilitarianism. First, the characterisation is a concrete demonstration of Sen's idea that if a social choice rule is to be designed for comparing alternative social states, then the framework must be broadened to include international comparisons of utility. Second, the characterisation requires only partial comparability of utilities. Thus, in a society of two persons, if one of them gains from a proposed move and the other loses, then the utilitarian rule requires that the loss can be compared to the gain. Later research in collective choice theory relies to a large extent on Sen's taxonomy of information about measurability and comparability of individual utilities.

For cross population comparisons of income distributions or to look at intertemporal changes in income distribution within a particular country, an index of inequality is required. Such indices are related to social welfare functions representing the welfare of the society. Along with Professors Partha Dasgupta and David Starrett, Sen substantially generalised a result of Professors Anthony B. Atkinson and Serge C. Kolm to show how Lorenz curves can be employed to compare welfare levels of alternative income distributions of a given total. The Lorenz curve of an income distribution indicates the share of total income received by the bottom t proportion ($0 \leq t \leq 1$) of the population. It is assumed that the social welfare function W, defined on income distributions, is individualistic. That is,

$$W(x) = F[u(x_1),..., u(x_n)] \quad (1)$$

where $x = (x_1, ... x_n)$ is the income distribution and u is the common utility function of individuals.

To discuss the Dasgupta-Sen-Starrett result let us consider two income distributions x and y of a given total over a fixed population size n. Suppose that x Lorenz dominates y, that is, the Lorenz curve of x is nowhere below that of y and at some places (at least) it lies strictly inside the latter. Then the Dasgupta-Sen-Starrett theorem can be stated as follows:

Theorem: Let x and y, where $\sum_{i=1}^{n} x_i = \sum_{i=1}^{n} y_i$, be two arbitrary income distributions. Then the following statements are equivalent:

(a) x Lorenz dominates y.
(b) $W(x) > W(y)$ for all equity oriented social welfare functions W, where by equity orientation we mean that a rank preserving transfer of income from a person to anyone who has a lower income increases welfare.

To illustrate this result, let $x = (4, 5, 7)$ and $y = (3, 6, 7)$. Here Lorenz domination of x over y implies that $W(x) > W(y)$ for all equity oriented social welfare functions W and conversely. What is interesting about this result is the use of a graphical technique to rank two income distributions in terms of society's preference by a large class of welfare functions. However, the ordering generated is a quasi-ordering: it is transitive, but not complete. If two Lorenz curves cross, then we can get two different equity oriented social welfare functions that will rank the income distributions in different directions. In the Dasgupta-Sen-Starrett theorem efficiency considerations are absent. Therefore, attempts have been made by researchers to generalize this result when both equity and efficiency vary.

One interesting example of equity oriented social welfare functions is the Gini social welfare function

$$W_G(x) = \frac{1}{n^2}\sum_{i=1}^{n}[2(n-i)+1]x_i \tag{2}$$

It is assumed that x_i's are nondecreasingly ordered, that is, $x_1 \leq x_2 \leq .... \leq x_n$. Sen also developed an economically attractive axiomatic characterization of the welfare function W_G. It may be noted that the welfare function W_G can be rewritten as

$$W_G\ (x) = \bar{x}\ (1 - G), \tag{3}$$

where $\bar{x}$ is the mean income and G is the well-known Gini coefficient. Thus, W_G is an increasing function of an efficiency index (x) and an equity index ((1 – G). The inequality index G is a particular member of the Atkinson-Kolm-Sen ethical inequality index

$$I\ (x) = 1 - \frac{xe}{\bar{x}}, \tag{4}$$

where x_e is the equally distributed equivalent income associated with x. More precisely, x_e is that level of income which, if given to each individual, will make the existing income distribution x ethically indifferent. Thus, x_e is implicitly defined by

$$W\ (x_e, x_e, ..., x_e) = W(x), \tag{5}$$

where the social welfare function W is continuous, increasing in individual incomes and equity oriented. I is bounded between zero and one, where the lower bound is achieved whenever incomes are equal. I determines the fraction of aggregate income that could be saved if society distributed incomes equally without any loss of welfare. Thus, if $I = 0.4$, it can be said that if incomes were equally distributed, then we should need only 60 per cent of the present national income to achieve the same level of welfare. Evidently, if the social welfare function in (4) is of the type W_G in (2), then I

becomes the Gini coefficient. Other existing measures of inequality (*e.g.*, the coefficient of variation and the entropy index suggested by Henri Theil) can also be interpreted in the Atkinson-Kolm-Sen framework.

In one of his outstanding articles, Sen viewed poverty measurement problem as involving two exercises:

(i) the identification of the poor in the total population and
(ii) the aggregation of the characteristics of the poor into a device that will quantify the extent of poverty.

The identification problem requires the specification of a poverty line that represents the level of income necessary to maintain a subsistence standard of living. A person, is said to be poor if his/her income falls below the poverty line. This is called the income method of identifying the poor. Before Sen published his article on poverty measurement in 1976, the aggregation problem was being handled using crude indices such as the head-count ratio H (the proportion of population below the poverty line) and the income-gap ratio R (the gap between the poverty line and average income of the poor, expressed as a proportion of the poverty line).

Sen suggested three axioms for an index of poverty — the focus axiom, the monotonicity axiom and the transfer axiom. The focus axiom requires the poverty index to be independent of nonpoor incomes. The monotonicity axiom requires that a poverty index should increase if there is a reduction in the income of a poor. The transfer axiom, on the other hand, demands sensitivity of the poverty index to the redistribution of income involving the poor, a postulate which is verified by neither the head-count ratio nor the income-gap ratio. The head-count ratio violates the monotonicity axiom also. To see this, let us consider a 5-person society with the income distribution $x = (2, 3, 4, 10, 18)$ and the poverty line $z = 8$. For this example, the head-count ratio H equals 3/5 and the income-gap ratio R equals 5/8. Now, if we generate the distribution $y = (1, 3, 4, 10, 18)$ from x by reducing the income of the worst off person from 2 to 1, then H remains unchanged but R increases to 2/3. Next, the distribution $q = (1.5, 3, 4.5, 10, 18)$ is obtained from x by transferring 0.5 units of income from the poorest person to the richest poor person and in this case both H and R remain unaltered.

Sen therefore axiomatically derived a more sophisticated index of poverty. For a large number of poor persons, the Sen index is given by

$$S(y, z) = H[R + (1 - R)G_p], \tag{6}$$

where y is the income distribution, z is the poverty line and G_p is the Gini coefficient of inequality taken over the vector of poor incomes. In S the weight attached to income gap of person i from the poverty line is i's rank order in the poor incomes. If we take a relativist view of poverty, then a poor person's feeling of deprivation may be taken as the number of others in his group who have more income. In this sense this weighting scheme can be motivated by a notion of relative deprivation. The measure S satisfies the three axioms set forth by Sen. His work has led to a large body of literature dealing with the aggregation problems associated with the measurement of poverty. Particularly, attempts have been made to introduce additional axioms for a measure of poverty and to suggest alternatives and variations of the Sen index.

In later works, Sen argued that well-being of a population and hence its poverty, which is a manifestation of insufficient well-being, are essentially multi-attributed phenomena, income is just one of these many attributes. In contrast to the income method, a direct method of identification of the poor checks if a person has minimally acceptable levels of different quality-of-life attributes, such as, food, housing, health, provision of public goods and so on. In the words of Sen 'In an obvious sense the direct method is superior to the income method, since the former is not based on particular assumptions of consumption behaviour which may or may not be accurate'. If direct information on different attributes are not available, then one can adopt the income method, 'so that the income method is at most a second best.' Multidimensionality of well-being is evident if we look at the problem from the view-point of Sen's 'capability-functioning' approach, where functionings deal with what a person can ultimately do and capabilities indicate the freedom that a person enjoys in terms of functionings. In this approach functionings are closely approximated by different quality-of-life attributes. According to this view poverty is a problem of functioning failure. Following Sen, most of the recent attempts to the measurement of inequality and poverty have taken this route.

Building on ideas put forward by Sen, UNDP suggested the human development index (*HDI*), which can be regarded as an index of well-being in terms of functioning achievements. It aggregates the functioning levels of the three attributes life expectancy, per capita real GDP and educational attainment rate. More precisely, *HDI* of a country is given by

$$HDI = \frac{1}{3}\sum_{i}\frac{A_i - m_i}{M_i - m_i}$$

Here A_i is the actual attainment level of attribute i, m_i and M_i indicate its minimum and maximum attainment levels respectively, where i = life expectancy, educational attainment rate and per capita real GDP. UNDP has put forward suggestions for calculating the minimum and maximum values of the attributes. Thus, *HDI* is a measure of the extent to which a country has performed in providing basic ingredients of life to its citizens. Alternatives and variations of the *HDI* have been suggested by various researchers.

Sen also analysed famines with his theoretical approach to welfare measurement. He argues that famines can occur even when the supply of food is not significantly lower. In his view lack of opportunities and capabilities are responsible for poverty and famines. In other words, hunger is essentially a problem of functioning failures. For instance, one of the functioning failures which gave rise to Bangladesh famine in 1974 is lack of work opportunities for agricultural workers (hence inability to purchase food), since one of the crops could not be harvested during that year because of flood. For understanding famines a thorough analysis of different factors that influence well-being of a population is necessary.

Another important aspect which he investigated in details is gender inequality. He established that in countries like India, unequal distribution of food entitlement among the male and female members of a family may cause malnutrition of the female members which in turn affects their health and longevity. Existence of high inequality in educational attainment rate between males and females demonstrates another dimension of gender bias.

In my opinion the best tribute that our country can pay to Nobel Laureate Professor Amartya K. Sen is by speeding up the social sector programmes on education, health and improvement in living conditions of women.

CHAPTER 4

Measuring Human Well-being of the Countries: Achievement and Improvement Indices

Krishna Mazumdar

Introduction

Human well-being has been defined by Professor Sen (1985, 1987) in terms of 'functioning' and 'capability.' Functioning denotes 'achievement of different attributes' such as education, health, nutrition etc. and capability indicates 'ability to achieve' these attributes. In a pioneering paper Kakwani (1993) has introduced a class of 'achievement indices' to represent the actual 'levels' of standard of living and a class of 'improvement indices' to represent the improvement in the standard of living of a country over a period.

This chapter attempts to provide an overview of the changing pattern of human well-being of the countries over the period 1960 to 1994. In this context the overall achievement indices representing overall human well-being for the sample countries have been estimated for five points of time: 1960, 1970, 1980, 1990 and 1994. The improvement indices for the periods 1960-94, 1960-70, 1970-80, 1980- 90 and 1990-94 have been derived. A comparison of the relative position of a country is attempted on the basis of the overall achievement index and other composite indices used to measure human well-being, *e.g.* Weighted index formed with the same indicators (Wtd8), Physical Quality of Life Index (PQLI) introduced by Morris (1979), Human Development Index (HDI) introduced by United Nations Development Programme (UNDP) in 1990. Also comparison of relative position of a country has been attempted for Per Capita Real Gross Domestic Product (PCRGDP).

Choice of Indicators

In welfare analysis the basic notion that welfare (*human well-being*) should be measured on the basis of as large a number of attributes as is relevant and feasible, has enjoyed widespread support. (For example, see Slottje, 1991; Hirschberg, Maasoumi and Slottje, 1991; Sen, 1985, 1987; Maasoumi, 1986; Atkinson and Bourguignon, 1982; and Kolm, 1977). At the same time the selection of appropriate indicators to represent human *well-being* or *social indicators of development* requires attention to comprehensiveness and comparability. The basic requirements of a particular society may not tally with the basic requirements of another society. Therefore, one should be careful when choosing indicators for any cross-country analysis. However, a wider breadth of agreement is possible if indicators of social life which are directly related to the provision of long-life, health and education are used.

In this study choice of indicators is governed by two apparently conflicting principles: wide coverage of various aspects of human development, and parsimony regarding the number of indicators. The indicators chosen are:

Life expectancy at birth (LIFE), Infant survival rate as per 1,000 of live births (INFS), Adult literacy rate as percentage

Broad Group	*Variable*	*Variable Name Used in the Study*
1. Population	Urban population (% of total)	UPOP
2. Demographic characteristics	Life expectancy (years)	LIFE
3. Health and nutrition	Calorie supply per capita (% of requirement)	CALO
	Infant survival rate (per 1,000 of live births)	INFS
	Physician per 1,000 of population	PHYS
4. Education	Adult literacy rate (% of total population over age 15 yrs)	ADLI
	Teacher-pupil ratio primary level	TPRP
5. Consumption	Passenger car per 1,000 of population	PCAR

of total population over age 15 years (ADLI), Calorie supply per capita as percentage of requirement (CALO), Physician per 1,000 of population (PHYS), Urban population as percentage of total population (UPOP), Teacher-pupil ratio in primary schooling (TPRP), Passenger car per 1,000 of population (PCAR).

These indicators are considered to be representative of the list of indicators within the broad group. Some of these indicators are also listed as representative variables in Hicks-Streeten (1979) study.

Broad Group	*Variable*
Health	LIFE
Education	ADLI
Food	CALO
Water supply and sanitation	INFS

Next few paragraphs present rationales behind choice of each indicator.

LIFE. Life expectancy at birth is the number of years a random newborn baby can expect to live, on the assumption that current age-specific mortality rates will persist. It is mathematical expectation of a person's longevity as seen from the vantage point of his date of birth if age-specific mortality rates are not expected to alter. LIFE directly reflects the levels of health, nutrition and income and thus indirectly links employment and shelter. A low figure usually shows there is a sizeable percentage of the population facing poor living conditions and there is a lack of proper health facilities in the country.

INFS. Infant mortality rate is the number of babies those die before reaching their first birthday out of every 1,000 of live born babies during a year. Infant survival rate is obtained by 1,000 minus infant mortality rate. Plainly, this is not unrelated to LIFE, but it focuses on something quite different: nutrition and hygiene at the earliest stage of life. This indicator also reflects the degree of existence of contagious disease in a country, as infants are more susceptible to these diseases. It is also closely related to the health of the mother and to the duration of lactation. It is also related to the educational attainment of the mother because literate women are more likely to know how to protect their infants' lives. Moreover, literate women possess higher status in the family than the illiterate women, which helps to advance interests of the infants in the family. The infant survival rate, reflects nutrition and sanitary conditions of the country. This indicator shows very rapid response to many health policies. It is obvious that where the infant mortality rate is very high there are many people living in conditions under which basic health needs are not met.

ADLI. Adult literacy rate is percentage of literate population above age 15. This is a direct measure of achievement of one basic right of the human beings, minimum education. This indicator is also well correlated with many other indices of quality of life such as measures of employment, income or health and therefore, adult literacy can be considered the most excellent overall quality of life indicator.

According to Professor Das Gupta (1992) LIFE, INFS and ADLI along with income are key indicators of general well-being. This study considers LIFE, INFS and ADLI as the *core indicators* of human well-being. Five other background indicators have been incorporated in this study in order to have better idea about the inter-country inter-temporal pattern of human well-being.

CALO. Calorie intake per capita as percentage of requirement is an indicator of level of nutrition of a country. Of the various social indicators that can be used to describe the conditions of life, the standard of nutrition is the most fundamental. Food is the most basic need for survival and in many cases the definition of poverty is based on nutritional level of the households. Also the problem of malnutrition is closely associated with the problem of low productivity and ultimately low national income. And the countries where the available calorie per person fall short of the required calorie per head, almost certainly there exists a significant problem of malnutrition. The problem of malnutrition is closely associated with the problem of low productivity and ultimately low national income.

UPOP. The indicator used to represent urbanization of a country is, percentage of total population residing in the urban areas. Although increasing urbanization is widely accepted as a natural phenomenon, the justification of inclusion of this indicator is that it carries profound implications for both the immediate well-being of citizens and the prospects of a nation for future welfare gains. In reality, more is the percentage of total population residing in the urban areas, more is the people (at least some of) with urban facilities such as better sanitation, medical and educational facilities, better communications, access to safe water etc. There is a close association between urbanization and industrialization. Moreover, "urbanization promotes values favourable to participation, entrepreneurship, and industrial growth; in particular, cities typically tend to innovate and accept change, since in the relatively impersonal and fragmented setting of urban life the all embracing bonds of traditional community systems are difficult to maintain."

PHYS. The health situation of a population depends mainly upon the health services available. The old industrialized countries have experienced slow but steady progress in regard to health services. In the newly independent poor countries, it is an enormous task to build up health services approaching the levels now existing in the rich countries. Education and various kinds of paramedical personnel on a large scale are required. It is expected that there are many more patients to share the service of one physician or nursing person in the poor countries than in the rich ones. Physician per thousand of population, therefore, provides a general picture of the quantity of health care available in a country.

TPRP. Teacher-pupil ratio in the primary level of education gives an indication of quality of educational care available in the primary level of education. The higher the number of pupil per teacher the lower is the quantity and quality of personal care available for each pupil.

PCAR. The passenger car per thousand of population reflects the level of communication and transportation in the country. In fact, better the transportation system in a country more widespread is the medical and educational facilities and more mobile is the population.

PCRGDP. The standard measure of *economic growth* is per capita gross domestic product (PCGDP). No doubt it is an acceptable indicator for measuring a specific country's economic performance, but its utility in cross country study is not beyond question. The major problem associated with the choice of PCGDP as an indicator for comparing the level of economic development of a number of countries is the conversion of each country's PCGDP to a common currency. The most widely used method is to convert the PCGDP of each country to US dollars using exchange rates between the country's currency and the US dollar. This method implicitly assumes that the purchasing power parity of US $1 is equivalent in all the countries being compared. This assumption may not be correct. For the purpose of comparison the indicator used to measure economic growth should be adjusted for purchasing power parity. Therefore the indicator chosen in this study to measure economic well-being of the countries is the Per Capita Real Gross Domestic Product (PCRGDP) which is adjusted for purchasing power parity.

Data

The data for 1960, 1970, 1980, 1990 and 1994 on all the indicators representing human well-being considered in this study have been obtained from different issues of *World Tables, World Development Reports* published by the World Bank and *Human Development Reports* published by the UNDP. Figures not available for these five years have been imputed in some cases by figures from around these years. The data for per capita calorie intake as percentage of requirement for 1990 and 1994 are not available. These figure are approximated using the ratio between percentage of requirement and actual supply for the year 1980.

A few indicators incorporated in this study are required to be transformed to make all the indicators move in the same direction. Data obtained from the official sources mentioned are infant mortality rate, population per physician, pupil-teacher ratio. These variables are negatively related with the level of development while other variables have positive correlations with the level of development. These variables are transformed as follows:

(*a*) Infant survival rate (INFS) = 1,000 - Infant mortality rate
(*b*) Physician per 1,000 of population = 1,000/population per physician.
(*c*) Teacher-pupil ratio = 1/pupil-teacher ratio.

The data for per capita real gross domestic product (PCRGDP) have been taken from Summers and Heston (1984, 1988, 1991).

Sample

The principle followed in choosing the sample countries is wide representation of countries from various income levels and various geographical regions. At the same time the study attempts to obtain uniform sample for five years under study and to have all the variables for all samples. Consequently, the sample consists of 92 countries. Broadly these countries may be divided into three income groups: high, middle and low following the World Bank classification of countries for 1990 per capita gross domestic product. A list of the sample countries is provided below:

High income group: Australia, Austria, Belgium, Canada, Denmark, Finland, France, Federal Republic of Germany, Hong Kong, Iceland, Italy, Japan, Netherlands, New Zealand, Norway, Singapore, Spain, Sweden, United Kingdom, United States of America (20).[1]

Middle income group: Algeria, Argentina, Barbados, Bolivia, Brazil, Cameroon, Chile, Colombia, Congo, Costa Rica, Cyprus, Dominican Republic, Ecuador, El Salvador, Greece, Guatemala, Guyana, Iran, Iraq, Ireland, Israel, Jordan, Korea Republic, Malaysia, Mauritius, Mexico, Morocco, Panama, Papua New Guinea, Paraguay, Peru, Philippines, Portugal, Surinam, Syrian Arab Republic, Thailand, Trinidad and Tobago, Turkey, Uruguay, Venezuela (40).[1]

---

[1] Figures in the parenthesis are the number of observations in the respective income group.

Low income group: Bangladesh, Benin, Burundi, Central African Republic, Egypt, Ethiopia, Gambia, Ghana, Guinea, Haiti, Honduras, India, Kenya, Liberia, Madagascar, Malawi, Mozambique, Myanmar, Nicaragua, Niger, Nigeria, Pakistan, Rwanda, Sierra Leone, Sri Lanka, Sudan, Tanzania, Togo, Upper Volta, Zaire, Zambia, Zimbabwe (32).[1]

Time Frame

Our choice of the points of time are restricted by the availability of data. Unfortunately, suitable data is not available for most of the countries and indicators prior to 1960. Year 1994 is the latest available year for which data for all the variables and sample countries could be gathered. Most of the analysis have been carried out for five points of time, *i.e.* 1960, 1970, 1980, 1990 and 1994.

Construction of Achievement Indices and Improvement Indices

The achievement function is derived as an univariate function of the indicators representing well-being of the nation and the aggregate achievement index for a particular country for a particular point of time is the simple arithmetic mean of the achievement indices of the constituent indicators. In fact, the weighting pattern has greater significance in formulation of any index. Flexible weighting is better in this respect, as in reality some countries may prefer LIFE to ADLI, some others may have choice for ADLI over LIFE. But in practice, flexible weighting is likely to be complicated. If constant weights are to be used, then the obvious candidate is equal weighting since it is difficult to rationalize a greater valuation being placed on achievement in one particular indicator. In order to form the achievement indices the maximum and the minimum values of the particular indicator have been taken from the data set at particular point of time. In some other similar studies arbitrary values have been chosen for the maximum and minimum. For such choice the justification

[1] Figures in the parenthesis are the number of observations in the respective income group.

offered is that if one chooses maximum and minimum values from the sample set, the improvement in the highest and the lowest performing country would affect performance of all other countries in the sample. In reality, however, choice of an arbitrary value depends on the value judgement of the particular researcher and obviously this choice varies from person to person. Whereas, choice of value of the maximum and minimum for a definite data set would be impartial. Moreover, biological and physical maximum and minimum varies with region, climate, time and other conditions of life. Therefore, this study uses actual maximum and minimum values for each indicator as are obtained from the values of the sample countries. The assumption behind is that the maximum and the minimum obtained for a particular point of time is the possible maximum and possible minimum value for the respective indicator at that point of time for the given set of countries. The achievement index thus obtained leads to give an impression of the relative position of a country at a particular point of time in respect of a particular indicator of well-being.

The overall achievement index provides the overall standard of living of the country. This is estimated as a composite index formed with the achievement indices derived from the indicators of well-being. The overall improvement indices for a period of time is derived as the difference between the overall achievement indices of two points of time.

The estimation procedure precisely is as follows:

The achievement index for a particular indicator of well-being for a country at a point of time is:

$$A_{ij} = \frac{X_{ij} - X_{imin}}{X_{imax} - X_{imin}}$$

where X_{ij} = value of the *i*th indicator for *j*th country.
X_{imin} = minimum value of the *i*th indicator.
X_{imax} = maximum value of the *i*th indicator.

The overall achievement index for the *j*th country at any point of time is obtained as:

$$A_j = \frac{1}{n}\sum_{i=1}^{n} A_{ij}$$

where, n = Number of constituent indicators.

The improvement index over a period $(t_2 - t_1)$ for the ith indicator is derived as:

$$I_{ij}(t_2 - t_1) = A_{ij}(t_2) - A_{ij}(t_1)$$

The overall improvement index of well-being is obtained as

$$I_j(t_2 - t_1) = A_j(t_2) - A_j(t_1).$$

Observations

The general observations regarding the achievement and improvement indices of 92 countries have been summarised in the following paragraphs. Table 4.1 presents overall achievement indices and overall improvement indices for the sample countries over the period 1960 to 1994. It has been observed from the table that there is wide variation in the achievement levels among the sample countries considered. It is an useful exercise to look at the best and the worst performers of the set. Looking at the achievement indices (first five columns of the table) it has been observed that the lists of the highest performers and the lowest performers are not the same for five years under study but they are strikingly similar. Among the ten highest ranked countries for five years (1960, 1970, 1980, 1990, 1994) five countries are same: Australia, Canada, Denmark, Iceland and USA. It has also been found that among the ten toppers of 1994, Belgium, France and Italy were outside the orbit of first ten in 1960 while among the ten performers of 1960 Israel, New Zealand and Sweden failed to retain their position among the first ten in the latter years. The table shows that among the ten lowest ranked countries for the five years six common names occurred are: Benin, Guinea, Malawi, Sierra Leone, and Upper Volta (Burkina Faso). It is of interest to have a picture of the countries belonging to different ranges of achievement. If the countries are grouped on the basis of their overall achievement indices, it has been observed that for all the five points of time considered in the study a tri-polar picture is

Table 4.1
Overall Achievement and Improvement Indices: 1960-94

Country	Achievement Indices					Improvement Indices				
	1960	1970	1980	1990	1994	1960-94	1960-70	1970-80	1980-90	1990-94
1	2	3	4	5	6	7	8	9	10	11
ALGERIA	27.48	28.19	33.25	38.33	45.78	18.30	-7.68	5.06	5.08	7.43
ARGENTINA	61.81	70.35	68.31	64.51	63.58	1.77	1.96	-2.04	-3.80	-1.07
AUSTRALIA	73.36	77.05	80.63	78.36	76.66	3.30	-0.06	3.58	-2.27	-1.70
AUSTRIA	67.34	72.73	76.20	73.39	72.90	5.56	0.02	3.47	-2.81	-0.43
BANGLADESH	15.07	19.91	20.06	17.94	21.38	6.31	-1.36	0.15	-2.12	3.43
BARBADOS	43.42	56.77	58.70	59.66	58.41	14.98	3.22	1.93	0.96	-1.40
BELGIUM	57.19	76.19	79.90	81.64	82.36	25.17	13.51	3.71	1.74	0.79
BENIN	9.46	18.12	21.64	21.87	24.34	14.88	4.08	3.52	0.23	2.37
BOLIVIA	15.64	30.30	35.40	31.03	38.38	22.74	6.88	5.10	-4.37	7.38
BRAZIL	35.36	46.34	49.67	49.94	50.44	15.08	2.61	3.33	0.27	0.50
BURUNDI	17.34	20.08	20.47	20.83	15.69	-1.65	-2.04	0.39	0.36	-5.12
CAF REP	14.58	20.28	22.08	28.39	23.55	8.97	1.53	1.80	6.31	-4.82
CAMEROON	16.09	21.59	28.30	29.95	22.90	6.82	0.24	6.71	1.65	-7.11
CANADA	72.71	77.14	77.39	77.35	76.08	3.37	4.43	0.25	0.04	-1.31
CHILE	43.17	51.87	55.25	56.95	55.58	12.41	8.70	3.38	1.70	-1.37
COLOMBIA	35.48	47.23	49.07	50.87	52.21	16.73	3.42	1.84	1.80	1.20
CONGO	19.11	32.17	34.01	28.63	28.96	9.85	5.39	1.84	-5.38	0.30
COSTA RICA	34.53	51.99	54.65	54.52	50.35	15.82	7.64	2.66	-0.13	-4.10
CYPRUS	43.84	58.66	60.49	60.82	68.71	24.87	2.55	1.83	0.33	7.87

DENMARK	68.01	84.43	84.38	76.88	76.27	8.26	12.22	-0.05	-7.50	-0.56
DOM REP	28.66	40.92	42.91	45.25	46.99	18.33	4.11	1.99	2.34	1.60
ECUADOR	28.68	39.39	42.81	44.83	47.51	18.83	0.91	3.42	2.02	2.68
EGYPT	29.00	35.95	40.01	37.56	40.63	11.63	0.74	4.06	-2.45	3.04
ELSALVADOR	26.49	38.10	39.48	40.54	41.43	14.94	1.70	1.38	1.06	0.83
ETHIOPIA	14.66	18.25	16.94	17.92	14.21	-0.45	-4.18	-1.31	0.98	-3.70
FINLAND	56.42	67.43	73.15	71.75	69.04	12.62	4.80	5.72	-1.40	-2.65
FRANCE	66.56	75.33	76.05	75.66	76.42	9.85	4.41	0.72	-0.39	0.80
FRG	67.34	76.17	79.62	80.04	79.07	11.73	4.67	3.45	0.42	-0.98
GAMBIA	16.86	16.86	15.95	15.57	17.06	0.20	-2.17	-0.91	-0.38	1.38
GHANA	22.59	29.99	31.32	30.30	29.47	6.88	0.94	1.33	-1.02	-0.79
GREECE	49.56	62.67	68.33	66.97	66.94	17.38	2.81	5.66	-1.36	-0.18
GUATEMALA	28.72	36.69	36.71	37.21	36.31	7.59	0.96	0.02	0.50	-0.90
GUINEA	12.34	16.84	16.86	11.61	13.23	0.89	0.41	0.02	-5.25	1.51
GUYANA	37.71	47.79	48.75	41.27	41.78	4.07	0.41	0.96	-7.48	0.56
HAITI	14.76	23.96	26.06	24.78	25.94	11.19	1.20	2.10	-1.28	1.24
HONDURAS	24.99	35.19	35.94	37.01	39.95	14.96	2.96	0.75	1.07	2.86
HONG KONG	49.58	61.19	63.05	62.35	60.90	11.32	1.24	1.86	-0.70	-1.49
ICELAND	67.64	76.12	79.55	82.93	83.12	15.48	1.29	3.43	3.38	0.17
INDIA	19.07	26.45	26.10	27.26	30.23	11.16	0.38	-0.35	1.16	2.98
IRAN	21.52	33.56	35.89	39.07	42.05	20.53	3.51	2.33	3.18	2.99
IRAQ	25.32	37.98	44.69	48.04	40.02	14.70	6.11	6.71	3.35	-7.92
IRELAND	58.84	66.22	67.05	65.33	63.79	4.95	0.20	0.83	-1.72	-1.56
ISRAEL	65.66	75.90	74.69	70.53	69.67	4.01	2.17	-1.21	-4.16	-0.82
ITALY	62.44	75.24	80.96	80.14	80.40	17.96	5.22	5.72	-0.82	0.33
JAPAN	53.15	68.00	69.62	68.94	67.51	14.37	4.73	1.62	-0.68	-1.45
JORDAN	26.36	40.11	44.19	49.11	52.70	26.34	6.05	4.08	4.92	3.67
KENYA	18.25	27.89	30.08	29.97	31.78	13.54	3.44	2.19	-0.11	1.70
KOREA REP	31.50	47.61	51.97	60.60	61.99	30.48	6.25	4.36	8.63	1.36

(Contd.)

Country	Achievement Indices					Improvement Indices				
	1960	1970	1980	1990	1994	1960-94	1960-70	1970-80	1980-90	1990-94
1	2	3	4	5	6	7	8	9	10	11
LIBERIA	20.81	24.97	28.00	22.57	19.53	-1.28	-0.56	3.04	-5.44	-3.17
MADAGASCAR	20.86	28.40	30.26	24.55	21.11	0.25	3.42	1.86	-5.71	-3.34
MALAWI	13.26	18.52	17.03	15.13	13.59	0.33	-0.45	-1.49	-1.90	-1.52
MALAYSIA	35.09	42.73	44.45	49.76	52.78	17.69	-0.09	1.72	5.31	3.01
MAURITIUS	36.29	47.29	50.50	49.44	49.58	13.29	1.58	3.21	-1.06	-0.02
MEXICO	40.74	49.23	52.74	55.91	55.69	14.95	1.84	3.51	3.17	-0.38
MOROCCO	20.30	30.06	32.16	35.42	36.83	16.53	2.62	2.10	3.26	1.46
MOZAMBIQUE	12.48	19.60	19.19	14.53	11.47	-1.01	2.23	-0.41	-4.66	-3.03
MYANMAR	18.92	32.70	37.15	38.31	35.33	16.42	6.17	4.45	1.16	-2.97
NETHERLANDS	64.17	71.88	74.49	75.14	73.74	9.57	1.12	2.61	0.65	-1.33
NEW ZEALAND	73.71	78.03	77.09	75.29	74.79	1.08	0.43	-0.94	-1.80	-0.52
NICARAGUA	32.29	41.22	43.61	47.07	40.78	8.49	4.09	2.39	3.46	-6.28
NIGER	12.65	17.68	16.81	13.26	12.53	-0.12	0.37	-0.87	-3.55	-0.68
NIGERIA	14.00	22.07	24.21	22.18	24.73	10.73	2.27	2.14	-2.03	2.57
NORWAY	58.80	69.98	78.78	83.36	79.94	21.15	3.60	8.80	4.58	-3.36
PAKISTAN	18.34	25.34	26.09	24.63	26.74	8.40	-0.93	0.75	-1.46	2.20
PANAMA	40.00	53.26	55.69	54.27	51.35	11.34	3.13	2.43	-1.42	-3.06
PAPUA NG	15.69	24.91	26.05	27.18	30.34	14.65	1.95	1.14	1.13	3.26
PARAGUAY	41.38	48.60	50.38	49.54	48.99	7.61	-0.74	1.78	44.16	-44.52
PERU	34.05	43.85	45.43	44.88	45.98	11.92	4.18	1.58	-0.55	1.06
PHILIPPINES	31.96	43.10	43.32	42.98	43.96	12.00	1.93	0.22	-0.34	0.87
PORTUGAL	40.11	52.39	60.31	61.30	61.60	21.49	3.11	7.92	0.99	0.34

RWANDA	14.47	21.26	21.62	16.08	15.23	0.76	-0.09	0.36	-5.54	-0.83
SIERRA LEONE	10.27	17.45	16.83	13.54	10.23	-0.04	0.44	-0.62	-3.29	-3.41
SINGAPORE	49.08	62.91	63.77	61.56	60.93	11.85	3.39	0.86	-2.21	-0.62
SPAIN	51.95	64.43	73.43	73.72	73.29	21.34	2.98	9.00	0.29	-0.43
SRI LANKA	34.70	48.20	44.51	45.33	42.21	7.51	2.53	-3.69	0.82	-3.15
SUDAN	13.59	21.06	25.41	31.42	22.79	9.20	1.11	4.35	6.01	-8.55
SURINAM	41.92	51.59	54.01	50.48	53.44	11.52	0.07	2.42	-3.53	2.96
SWEDEN	74.86	77.93	79.41	74.68	75.96	1.09	-1.83	1.48	-4.73	1.35
SYRIAN AR	25.69	37.64	45.09	44.11	44.57	18.88	4.43	7.45	-0.98	0.49
TANZANIA	13.59	28.22	30.07	31.88	24.37	10.78	7.15	1.85	1.81	-7.48
THAILAND	28.91	39.88	41.92	42.94	42.91	14.01	1.58	2.04	1.02	0.03
TOGO	14.22	22.25	22.84	24.36	24.95	10.73	1.47	0.59	1.52	0.60
TRIN & TOB	44.46	51.01	52.65	61.28	57.76	13.30	-1.62	1.64	8.63	-3.55
TURKEY	26.73	37.60	41.69	44.36	47.39	20.67	5.17	4.09	2.67	3.00
UK	71.41	75.42	74.45	73.20	71.09	-0.32	0.16	-0.97	-1.25	-2.06
UPVOLTA	7.01	12.18	12.12	13.59	16.89	9.88	-0.76	-0.06	1.47	3.32
URUGUAY	56.62	62.53	65.68	62.40	61.44	4.82	-2.01	3.15	-3.28	-0.99
USA	80.45	82.55	81.54	77.34	76.09	-4.36	2.12	-1.01	-4.20	-1.26
VENEZUELA	45.51	54.88	58.91	58.39	63.19	17.68	4.00	4.03	-0.52	4.64
ZAIRE	21.03	12.17	30.56	25.34	25.56	4.53	-14.92	18.39	-5.22	0.27
ZAMBIA	19.13	29.00	30.37	33.78	27.08	7.94	3.58	1.37	3.41	-6.70
ZIMBABWE	29.18	34.24	34.23	38.75	34.77	5.59	-1.03	-0.01	4.52	-3.98

obtained where most of the countries of North America, Western Europe and Australia are found to have high human development, most of the countries from Central and South America and East Asia have obtained middle level of human development and the rest are characterised by the low human development. For example, Australia, Canada, New Zealand, Sweden, UK and USA have achievement indices above 70.00, while Bangladesh, Benin, Burundi, Central African Republic, Congo, Ethiopia, Gambia, Haiti, India, Malawi, Mozambique, Niger, Nigeria, Pakistan, Papua New Guinea, Rwanda, Sierra Leone, Sudan, Tanzania, Togo and Upper Volta have achievement indices below 30.00 and Argentina, Barbados, Cyprus, Greece, Finland, Ireland, Hong Kong, Japan, Panama, Surinam, Trinidad and Tobago, Uruguay and Venezuela have value of the overall achievement indices between 50.00 to 69.99. It has been observed that most of the countries having achievement indices below 30.00 belong to Africa. Only Bangladesh, India and Pakistan are from (South) Asia, Haiti from Latin America and Papua New Guinea from the Australia-New Zealand zone. In this context it is worthy to note that the improvement indices of these countries are not significant.

It is very surprising to found that the region which had the rich heritage of Indus Valley Civilisation is lagging behind the other regions of the world in respect of human development! In reality, the annual additions to the South Asian population exceed the total population of fifty of the smaller UN member countries. This population could have become the real wealth of these nations, if sufficient investment had been made in human development. But South Asia spends very little on the education and health of its people — less than five per cent of its combined GNP. And that is why rapidly multiplying populations have become a major liability rather than an asset. In case of Haiti and Papua New Guinea, it may be noted that these countries are suffering from continuous political and economic turmoil.

It has further been observed from the table that the overall improvement indices for the period 1960-94 is very high (above 15.00) for some of the countries, *viz.*, Korea Republic, Belgium and Jordan. Among them Korea Republic has improved very significantly (30.48) over the period. The table also throws light to the fact that 8 countries have shown retardation over the same period. Except UK and USA all are from Africa and belong to the low income group in the World Bank classification. These countries are Burundi, Ethiopia, Liberia, Mozambique, Niger and Sierra Leone. Most of these countries are suffering from economic and political turmoil. The table portrays that during the decades 1960-70 and 1970-80 most of the sample countries had improved in respect of human development: only eighteen countries (e.g. Algeria, Australia, Bangladesh, Burundi, Ethiopia, Gambia, Liberia, Malawi, Malaysia, Pakistan, Paraguay, Rwanda, Sweden, Trinidad and Tobago, Upper Volta, Uruguay, Zaire, Zimbabwe) evidenced retardation during the sixties and sixteen countries (Argentina, Denmark, Ethiopia, Gambia, India, Israel, Malawi, Mozambique, New Zealand, Niger, Sierra Leone, Sri Lanka, UK, Upper Volta, Uruguay and Zimbabwe) retarded during the seventies in human development. The table also depicts that only half of the countries have shown improvement during the eighties. In fact the decade 1980 was a decade of disasters: the living standards of millions in Latin America even became lower than their standards of living in the early 1970s and in most of the Sub-Saharan Africa living standards had fallen to the levels last seen in 1960s. The period 1990-94 also have not shown any significant change in the scenario; forty-eight out of the ninety-two sample countries have shown decline in respect of human development.

It is of interest to compare the relative position of a country in respect of achievement indices and similar other composite indices measuring human development of a country. Table 4.2 presents rankings of the sample countries on the basis of the achievement index, weighted index formed with the same eight indicators (Wtd8), Physical Quality of Life Index (PQLI) formed by Morris, Human Development Index (HDI) of UNDP and Per Capita Real Gross Domestic Product (PCRGDP). The rank correlation coefficients (Spearman) between the above mentioned indices and PCRGDP, presented in Table 4.3 depict that the overall achievement indices has very high rank correlation with the Wtd8, PQLI, HDI and PCRGDP. It has the lowest rank correlation with PCRGDP for all the years.

Table 4.4 presents Spearman rank correlation coefficients between the overall achievement indices of different years. There are very high correlation coefficients between the achievement indices of all the years indicating no significant changes in the ranking of the countries in respect of overall well-being over the last thirty-five years.

Table
Rankings of the Countries:

Country	1960					1970				
	AI	W8	PI	HI	PC	AI	W8	PI	HI	PC
1	2	3	4	5	6	7	8	9	10	11
ALGERIA	53	51	55	62	32	68	68	64	63	40
ARGENTINA	15	15	26	21	20	16	16	26	26	22
AUSTRALIA	4	4	7	5	4	6	6	6	8	4
AUSTRIA	9	10	22	14	16	14	14	19	17	14
BANGLADESH	77	77	77	77	85	83	83	79	78	85
BARBADOS	29	27	25	20	29	27	27	31	18	26
BELGIUM	18	22	19	6	13	7	8	16	6	8
BENIN	91	91	87	87	77	87	87	85	88	81
BOLIVIA	76	71	73	58	64	62	62	70	65	60
BRAZIL	39	41	37	42	47	42	42	50	44	45
BURUNDI	72	76	84	85	76	82	84	89	89	88
CAF REP	80	85	90	90	74	81	81	87	85	78
CAMEROON	74	78	80	80	72	78	78	83	86	65
CANADA	5	5	9	10	3	5	5	8	12	3
CHILE	30	31	36	32	25	32	32	38	30	29
COLOMBIA	38	40	47	43	37	41	41	46	41	43
CONGO	67	64	53	44	66	61	61	49	56	54
COSTA RICA	42	37	34	27	34	31	31	18	28	38
CYPRUS	28	26	18	25	30	26	26	29	24	27
DENMARK	7	9	5	6	5	1	1	10	4	5
DOM REP	52	48	44	45	44	47	46	47	45	48
ECUADOR	51	46	48	44	56	50	50	48	46	62
EGYPT	48	54	67	59	73	56	56	63	61	69
EL SALVADOR	55	50	43	49	57	51	51	41	49	57
ETHIOPIA	79	75	76	75	88	86	86	78	83	87
FINLAND	20	20	21	15	14	19	19	12	14	10
FRANCE	11	13	14	8	11	12	12	7	9	7
FRG	10	11	16	12	6	8	7	14	16	6
GAMBIA	73	86	89	92	71	90	91	92	92	73
GHANA	60	61	61	60	42	64	64	65	64	50
GREECE	24	23	15	14	27	23	22	17	23	24
GUATEMALA	50	52	50	57	45	55	55	53	59	47

4.2
Different Indices

1980					*1990*					*1994*				
AI	*W8*	*PI*	*HI*	*PC*	*AI*	*W8*	*PI*	*HI*	*PC*	*AI*	*W8*	*PI*	*HI*	*PC*
12	13	14	15	16	17	18	19	20	21	22	23	24	25	26
63	63	53	66	40	57	59	51	59	45	47	48	48	56	43
21	21	31	26	26	22	14	38	29	23	24	23	32	30	27
4	4	6	9	8	6	22	7	7	16	6	3	10	12	13
12	12	9	14	10	15	18	19	14	15	15	13	11	13	9
84	84	74	82	84	83	84	75	82	68	80	80	76	78	71
29	28	32	21	29	30	28	25	17	24	30	27	22	21	29
5	5	25	13	9	3	1	27	10	9	2	9	9	5	5
81	82	71	78	86	81	81	76	87	77	76	78	82	84	69
60	60	66	62	56	66	66	55	71	64	59	57	58	55	59
39	39	48	44	38	38	42	53	50	36	39	41	50	49	40
83	83	85	86	87	82	82	81	86	89	85	84	83	85	85
80	80	91	83	81	71	70	82	81	83	77	76	78	77	75
71	71	78	74	63	69	69	67	67	63	79	89	80	66	64
10	10	10	10	2	7	24	3	5	3	10	4	5	8	7
31	31	38	32	33	32	26	36	28	32	32	36	29	29	30
40	40	43	42	41	36	35	33	38	43	37	40	35	38	41
62	62	58	59	58	70	71	68	65	57	68	69	71	69	66
32	32	14	27	36	34	30	28	23	41	40	38	34	39	38
26	26	26	29	27	28	33	16	19	23	19	18	23	23	20
1	1	11	4	6	9	6	13	18	4	8	12	19	19	26
50	50	45	49	47	46	46	52	49	52	45	50	46	47	49
51	51	51	45	48	48	45	48	47	44	43	43	44	40	45
54	54	55	64	55	59	61	65	69	61	56	54	64	68	49
55	55	44	50	65	54	53	59	56	60	54	53	53	52	58
87	87	82	88	90	84	83	87	73	91	87	86	86	86	91
18	18	7	11	12	17	21	1	1	11	18	15	14	15	17
13	13	9	6	7	10	9	21	8	6	7	10	7	7	8
6	6	15	17	4	5	19	22	13	5	2	5	15	18	10
91	91	92	92	66	86	88	90	89	76	83	83	87	88	77
65	65	68	67	70	67	68	67	64	88	67	66	66	64	62
20	20	16	28	22	20	7	23	25	26	21	22	24	24	25
57	57	54	59	50	60	60	61	60	53	61	62	60	62	53

(Contd.)

Country	1960					1970				
	AI	*W8*	*PI*	*HI*	*PC*	*AI*	*W8*	*PI*	*HI*	*PC*
1	2	3	4	5	6	7	8	9	10	11
GUINEA	89	90	81	88	61	91	90	90	87	72
GUYANA	36	35	33	26	39	38	38	23	27	46
HAITI	78	73	62	72	84	74	74	71	72	86
HONDURAS	59	58	54	53	59	57	57	56	55	61
HONG KONG	23	24	28	28	46	25	25	15	29	31
ICELAND	8	7	1	3	12	7	9	4	3	16
INDIA	68	66	65	63	78	70	70	67	66	80
IRAN	61	60	52	61	41	59	59	54	60	35
IRAQ	58	59	63	65	31	52	54	60	68	37
IRELAND	16	17	13	13	22	20	20	11	15	23
ISRAEL	12	8	20	23	21	10	10	22	21	19
ITALY	14	14	10	17	18	13	13	27	19	18
JAPAN	21	19	17	16	24	18	18	5	7	13
JORDAN	56	55	49	56	60	48	49	59	50	59
KENYA	71	72	69	73	82	69	69	62	67	82
KOREA REP	46	43	39	37	68	39	37	42	34	49
LIBERIA	64	70	66	76	62	72	73	61	73	64
MADAGASCAR	63	68	91	70	69	66	66	80	71	74
MALAWI	86	84	83	74	92	85	85	84	79	92
MALAYSIA	40	42	41	47	50	45	45	40	48	45
MAURITIUS	37	39	35	39	48	40	40	36	36	63
MEXICO	33	36	38	36	26	35	35	45	42	32
MOROCCO	65	63	58	66	70	63	63	55	70	56
MOZAMBIQUE	88	87	79	85	55	84	82	74	80	52
MYANMAR	69	62	60	50	90	60	60	66	52	89
NETHERLANDS	13	12	3	4	9	15	15	3	5	9
NEW ZEALAND	3	3	11	7	7	3	4	13	10	15
NICARAGUA	44	49	57	55	49	46	47	58	54	42
NIGER	87	88	84	89	83	88	88	82	90	79
NIGERIA	83	83	72	81	52	77	77	75	75	58
NORWAY	17	16	4	2	10	17	17	2	1	11
PAKISTAN	76	67	71	71	79	71	71	76	74	77
PANAMA	35	32	24	30	36	29	29	32	32	34
PAPUA NG	75	74	70	67	63	73	72	72	69	44

1980					1990					1994				
AI	*W8*	*PI*	*HI*	*PC*	*AI*	*W8*	*PI*	*HI*	*PC*	*AI*	*W8*	*PI*	*HI*	*PC*
12	13	14	15	16	17	18	19	20	21	22	23	24	25	26
88	89	89	89	71	92	92	91	92	81	89	89	89	81	61
41	44	30	24	57	53	54	45	40	58	53	45	47	43	68
75	74	60	76	83	75	78	71	77	79	71	72	72	75	79
58	58	56	56	60	61	58	44	58	66	58	56	55	53	65
25	25	8	19	20	24	8	9	24	12	29	33	20	22	4
22	7	3	3	14	7	11	3	14	14	1	1	2	1	15
73	73	67	71	79	72	72	63	72	67	66	67	67	65	73
59	59	57	61	44	55	55	60	62	28	52	55	51	51	39
44	47	49	60	30	43	39	46	44	40	57	60	61	61	54
22	22	20	18	23	21	23	10	22	25	22	21	18	16	22
14	14	22	23	19	18	4	17	20	22	17	20	21	20	19
3	3	18	16	16	4	3	15	15	19	3	7	8	6	12
19	19	2	1	11	19	19	2	2	10	20	19	1	2	3
49	46	47	48	59	42	38	40	51	47	35	39	42	42	46
69	70	70	63	82	68	67	66	63	79	64	64	59	60	72
36	36	34	33	41	29	13	32	30	37	25	29	26	27	28
72	72	64	77	69	79	80	83	83	72	82	85	84	81	78
68	69	71	69	77	77	76	77	68	78	81	81	81	83	88
86	86	84	85	89	87	87	88	84	85	88	87	85	82	87
46	45	40	51	34	39	43	34	45	35	36	34	36	44	32
37	38	46	41	51	41	47	42	43	51	41	35	39	46	23
34	35	36	38	31	33	36	39	35	27	33	32	40	35	35
64	64	61	68	54	62	62	64	70	59	60	63	65	70	52
85	85	81	79	72	88	86	84	85	75	91	91	88	87	81
56	56	65	58	88	58	56	57	54	78	62	61	62	59	84
15	15	4	5	13	12	12	12	6	13	13	14	6	4	11
11	11	13	8	17	11	29	18	12	18	12	8	17	14	18
48	48	52	43	52	44	40	50	39	49	55	58	57	57	67
78	88	86	90	76	91	91	89	91	84	90	90	91	92	83
90	78	76	75	53	80	79	78	79	72	74	73	70	74	74
9	9	5	7	5	1	2	4	9	1	4	6	4	3	6
74	75	72	81	75	76	77	74	80	62	70	74	75	76	60
30	30	33	31	37	35	34	30	31	38	38	37	31	31	37
76	76	75	73	62	73	73	70	74	55	65	65	63	63	57

(Contd.)

Country	1960					1970				
	AI	*W8*	*PI*	*HI*	*PC*	*AI*	*W8*	*PI*	*HI*	*PC*
1	2	3	4	5	6	7	8	9	10	11
PARAGUAY	32	34	40	35	53	36	36	35	39	53
PERU	43	45	59	48	33	43	43	52	47	36
PHILIPPINES	45	44	45	40	67	44	44	43	40	67
PORTUGAL	34	33	31	33	35	30	30	21	33	28
RWANDA	77	80	82	83	91	79	79	81	77	90
SIERRA LEONE	90	89	88	86	80	89	89	88	84	76
SINGAPORE	25	25	27	34	38	22	23	28	35	30
SPAIN	22	21	12	19	23	21	21	20	20	20
SRI LANKA	41	38	30	30	43	37	39	33	38	68
SUDAN	84	82	75	79	58	80	80	86	81	70
SURINAM	31	29	32	29	28	33	33	34	31	33
SWEDEN	2	2	2	1	2	4	3	1	2	2
SYRIAN AR	57	56	64	54	54	53	52	51	57	51
TANZANIA	85	74	74	82	86	67	69	69	58	84
THAILAND	49	47	51	41	75	49	48	44	43	66
TOGO	82	81	68	78	81	76	76	68	76	75
TRIN & TOB	27	28	29	22	19	34	34	30	25	21
TURKEY	54	57	46	51	39	54	53	39	51	39
UK	6	6	6	9	8	11	11	9	11	12
UP VOLTA	92	92	92	91	89	92	92	91	91	91
URUGUAY	19	18	33	18	17	24	24	25	22	25
USA	1	1	8	11	25	2	2	24	13	1
VENEZUELA	26	30	42	38	15	28	28	37	39	17
ZAIRE	62	65	78	68	87	75	75	77	82	83
ZAMBIA	66	69	86	69	65	65	65	73	62	71
ZIMBABWE	47	53	56	52	51	58	58	57	53	55

Note: (1)

AI : Achievement Indices
W8 : Weighted Indices comprised of eight variables
PI : Physical Quality of Life Indices
HI : Human Development Indices
PC : Per Capita Real Gross Domestic Product

1980					*1990*					*1994*				
AI	*W8*	*PI*	*HI*	*PC*	*AI*	*W8*	*PI*	*HI*	*PC*	*AI*	*W8*	*PI*	*HI*	*PC*
12	13	14	15	16	17	18	19	20	21	22	23	24	25	26
38	37	49	39	45	40	37	41	41	48	42	42	43	41	51
42	42	63	47	46	47	48	58	48	46	46	46	49	48	50
49	49	41	46	61	51	51	54	46	56	49	52	45	45	56
27	27	27	34	25	26	27	26	32	29	26	23	30	32	24
89	81	86	72	85	85	85	86	78	90	86	82	79	79	92
82	90	87	87	78	90	90	92	88	82	92	92	92	91	86
24	24	24	31	21	25	20	29	33	8	28	30	25	28	2
17	17	12	20	18	14	5	6	21	21	14	17	12	11	21
45	44	37	36	68	45	44	31	34	54	51	49	33	33	55
77	77	83	80	67	65	64	14	66	74	78	77	77	80	70
33	33	29	35	32	37	41	43	37	31	34	31	37	36	48
8	8	1	2	3	13	12	5	3	7	11	11	3	9	16
43	43	42	52	35	50	49	47	57	39	48	51	54	54	42
70	69	69	54	80	64	72	72	53	87	75	71	69	72	89
52	52	39	40	54	52	52	49	42	50	50	44	41	37	36
79	79	80	84	73	78	75	77	76	80	73	75	73	73	76
35	34	21	24	42	27	32	37	27	20	31	25	27	26	31
53	53	50	52	39	49	50	56	40	43	44	47	52	50	44
16	16	23	15	15	16	15	20	16	17	16	16	16	17	14
92	92	90	91	92	89	89	85	90	86	84	88	90	90	82
23	23	28	22	28	23	17	24	26	34	27	28	28	25	34
2	2	17	12	1	8	25	11	11	2	9	5	13	10	1
28	29	35	37	24	31	31	35	36	30	24	26	38	34	33
66	67	73	65	91	67	74	73	75	92	72	70	68	67	90
67	68	77	70	74	63	63	80	61	71	69	68	74	71	80
61	61	62	55	64	56	57	62	56	65	63	59	56	58	63

Note : (2) In the tables some of the country names have been abridged as follows:

CAF REP	:	Central African Republic
DOM REP	:	Dominican Republic
FRG	:	Federal Republic of Germany
KOREA REP	:	Korean Republic (South Korea)
PAPUA NG	:	Papua New Guinea
SYRIAN AR	:	Syrian Arab Republic
TRIN & TOB	:	Trinidad and Tobago.

Table 4.3
Rank Correlations Between Different Indices

(a) 1960

	AI	*W8*	*PI*	*HI*	*PC*
1	2	3	4	5	6
AI	1.00				
W8	0.99	1.00			
PI	0.96	0.96	1.00		
HI	0.97	0.97	0.97	1.00	
PC	0.89	0.89	0.87	0.87	1.00

(a) 1970

	AI	*W8*	*PI*	*HI*	*PC*
AI	1.00				
W8	1.00	1.00			
PI	0.96	0.96	1.00		
HI	0.98	0.98	0.97	1.00	
PC	0.91	0.91	0.89	0.88	1.00

(a) 1980

	AI	*W8*	*PI*	*HI*	*PC*
AI	1.00				
W8	0.99	1.00			
PI	0.95	0.96	1.00		
HI	0.97	0.97	0.97	1.00	
PC	0.93	0.93	0.91	0.89	1.00

(a) 1990

	AI	*W8*	*PI*	*HI*	*PC*
AI	1.00				
W8	0.98	1.00			
PI	0.94	0.93	1.00		
HI	0.97	0.95	0.94	1.00	
PC	0.94	0.92	0.90	0.91	1.00

(a) 1994

	AI	*W8*	*PI*	*HI*	*PC*
AI	1.00				
W8	0.98	1.00			
PI	0.94	0.93	1.00		
HI	0.97	0.95	0.94	1.00	
PC	0.94	0.92	0.90	0.91	1.00

Table 4.4
Rank Correlations Between Overall Achievement Indices of Different Years

	1960	*1970*	*1980*	*1990*	*1994*
1	2	3	4	5	6
1960	1.00				
1970	0.98	1.00			
1980	0.97	0.99	1.00		
1990	0.96	0.98	0.98	1.00	
1994	0.96	0.97	0.97	0.98	1.00

It has been expected that the initial achievement in an aspect plays significant role in determining the improvement of the country over the next decade or decades in that particular aspect. Table 4.5 presents relations between overall achievement indices (AI) at the initial point of time and the improvement indices (II) for the respective period, i.e., 1960 AI with 1960-94 II and 1960-70 II, 1970 AI with 1970-80 II, 1980 AI with 1980-90 II and 1990 AI with 1990-94 II. No significant relation has been observed between the initial achievement indices and the improvement indices in any one case which leads to the conclusion that improvement in well-being does not depend on achievement at the initial point of time.

Table 4.5
Correlations Coefficient Between Achievement Indices and Improvement Indices

Indicators	*Years*				
Ach. Ind.	*1960*		*1970*	*1980*	*1990*
Imp. Ind.	*1960-94*	*1960-70*	*1970-80*	*1980-90*	*1990-94*
1	2	3	4	5	6
AI	0.04	0.15	0.04	0.01	0.00

Note: None of the Correlation Coefficients are significant.

Concluding Remarks

Human well-being is a complex concept and measurement of it is still more difficult. In this study human well-being has been defined as a social well-being function in terms of achievement and improvement indices and attempt has been made to measure human well-being of the sample countries in terms of the achievement index and the change of the same over a certain period of time in terms of the improvement index. The study focuses a tri-polar picture of the picture of the World: the countries from North America, Western Europe and Australia-New Zealand zone at the pick of human development, the South and Central America and the Caribbean countries and countries from the East Asia are at the middle level, while the countries from South Asia and Sub-Saharan Africa are lagging behind the rest of the world in respect of human well-being. The Rank correlation results show there is no significant change in the scenario over the thirty-five years of the second half of this century.

References

1. Atkinson, A.B. and F. Bourguignon (1982), "The Comparison of Multidimensional Distributions of Economic Studies," *Review of Economic Studies*, Vol. 12, pp. 183 -201.
2. Atkinson, A.B. (1970), "On Measurement of Inequality," *Journal of Economic Theory*, Vol. 2, pp. 244-63.
3. Bairoch, P. (1975), *The Economic Development of the Third World Since 1900*, Methuen, London.
4. Bunge, Mario (1981), "Development Indicators," *Social Indicators Research*, Vol. 9, pp. 369-85.
5. Chakravarty, S.R. (1990), Ethical Index Numbers, Springer-Verlag, Berlin.
6. Chowdhury, O.M. (1991), "Human Development Index," *The Bangladesh Development Studies*, Vol. XIX, No. 3, pp. 125-27.
7. Cole, J.P. (1981), *The Development Gap*, John Wiley & Sons.
8. Das Gupta, Partha (1996), *An Inquiry into Well-being and Destitution*, Clarendon Press, Oxford.
9. Das Gupta, Partha and Weale, Martin (1992), "On Measuring the Quality of Life," *World Development*, Vol. 20, No. 1, pp. 119-31.
10. Desai, Meghnad (1991), "Human Development: Concept and Measurement," *European Economic Review*, Vol. 35, pp. 350-57.

11. Drewnoski and Scott (1966), "The Level of Living Index," UNRISD, Geneva.
12. Dreze, Jean and Sen A.K. (1989), *Hunger and Public Action*, Clarendon Press, Oxford.
13. Dreze, Jean and Sen A.K. (1990), *The Political Economy of Hunger*, 3 Volumes, Clarendon Press, Oxford.
14. Dreze, Jean and Sen A.K. (1995), *India Economic Development and Social Opportunity*, Oxford University Press, Calcutta.
15. Dreze, Jean and Sen A.K. (1997), *Indian Development: Selected Regional Perspectives*, Oxford University Press, Calcutta.
16. Estes, Richard J. (1990), "Development under Different Political Systems," *Social Development Issues*, Vol. 13, No. 1, pp. 5-19.
17. Estes, Richard J. (1993), "Toward Sustainable Development: From Theory to Practice," *Social Development Issues*, Vol. 15, No. 3, pp. 1-29.
18. Estes, Richard J. (1995), "Social Development Trends in Africa, 1970-1994: The Need for a New Paradigm," *Social Development Issues*, Vol. 17, No. 1, pp. 19-47.
19. Estes, Richard J. (1996), "Social Development Trends in Asia, 1970-1994: The Challenges of a New Century," *Social Indicators Research*, Vol. 37, pp. 119-48.
20. Estes, Richard J. (1996), "Social Development Trends in Latin America, 1970-1994: In the Shadows of the Twenty-first Century," *Social Development Issues*, Vol. 18, No. 1, pp. 25-52.
21. Estes, Richard J. (1997), "Social Development Trends in Europe, 1970-1994: Development Prospects for the New Europe," *Social Indicators Research*, Vol. 42, No. 1, pp. 1-19.
22. Fishlow, Albert (1995), "Inequality, Poverty and Growth: Where Do We Stand?" Proceedings of the World Bank Annual Conference on Economic Development held in May 1995.
23. Gerson, E.M. (1976), "On Quality of Life," *American Sociological Review*, Vol. 41, pp. 793-806.
24. Haq, Mahbub ul (1996), *Reflections on Human Development*, Oxford University Press, Calcutta.
25. Haq, Mahbub ul (1996), *Human Development Paradigm for South Asia*, Institute of Social Sciences, New Delhi.
26. Haq, Mahbub ul (1997), *Human Development in South Asia*, Oxford University Press, Calcutta.
27. Hicks, N.L. (1982), "Sector Priorities in Meeting Basic Needs: Some Statistical Evidence," *World Development*, Vol. 7, pp. 567-80.
28. Hicks, N.L. (1979), "Growth vs. Basic Needs: Is There a Trade Off?", *World Development*, Vol. 7, Nos. 11/12, pp. 985-94.
29. Hicks, N.L. (1979), "Is There a Tradeoff between Growth and Basic Needs?", *Finance and Development*, June, Vol. 17, No. 2, pp. 17-20.

30. Hicks, N.L., and Paul, Streeten (1979), "Indicators of Development: The Search for a Basic Needs Yardstick," *World Development*, June, Vol. 7, No. 6, pp. 567-80.
31. Hirschberg, J.G., Maasoumi E., and Slottje D.J. (1991), "Cluster Analysis for Measuring Welfare and Quality of Life Across Countries," *Journal of Econometrics*, Vol. 50, pp. 1-13.
32. Kakwani, N.K. (1993), "Performance in Living Standards," *Journal of Development Economics*, Vol. 41, pp. 307-36.
33. Kelley, Allen C. (1991), "The Human Development Index: Handle with Care," *Population and Development Review*, Vol. 17, No. 2, pp. 315-24.
34. Kolm, S.C. (1969), "The Optimal Production of Social Justice," in Margolis, J., and Guittan, H. (eds.), *Public Economics*, Macmillan, London.
35. Kolm, S.C. (1977), "Multidimensional Egalitarianism," *Journal of Econometrics*, Vol. 91, pp. 1-13.
36. Larsen, D.A., and Wilford, W.T. (1979), "The Physical Quality of Life Index: A Useful Social Indicator," *World Development*, Vol. 7, pp. 581-84.
37. Leipziger, D.M., and Lewis, M.A. (1980), "Social Indicators, Growth and Distribution," *World Development*, Vol. 8, pp. 299-302.
38. Maasoumi, E. (1986), "The Measurement and Decomposition Analysis of Inequality in the World System," *American Sociological Review*, Vol. 53, pp. 838-52.
39. Majumder, Amita, Mazumdar, Krishna and Chakrabarti, Snigdha (1994), "Patterns of Inter- and Intra-regional Inequality: A Socio-Economic Approach," *Social Indicators Research*, Vol. 34, pp. 325-38.
40. Majumder, Amita and Chakravarty, Satya R. (1996), "Achievement and Improvement in Living Standards," *Journal of Development Economics*, Vol. 50, pp. 189-95.
41. Majumder, Amita and Chakravarty, Satya R. (1996), "Achievement and Improvement in Living Standards — An Empirical Analysis," *Social Indicators Research*, Vol. 37, pp. 269-80.
42. Mazumdar, Krishna (1995), "Classification of Countries: A Socio-Economic Approach," *Social Indicators Research*, Vol. 34, 261-73.
43. Mazumdar, Krishna (1996), "Level of Development of a Country: A Possible New Approach," *Social Indicators Research*, Vol. 38, No. 3, pp. 245-78.
44. Mazumdar, Krishna (1996), "An Analysis of Causal Flow Between Social Development and Economic Growth," *American Journal of Economics and Sociology*, Vol. 55, No. 3, pp. 361-83.
45. Mazumdar, Krishna (1997), "Pairwise Comparisons of Social Development of Selected Countries: 1960 to 1994: An Application of D^2-Statistics," *Social Indicators Research*, Vol. 44, pp. 155-94.

46. Mazumdar, Krishna (1998), "Measuring Well-beings of the Developing Countries," *Social Indicators Research*, Forthcoming.
47. McNamara, R. (1971), "Address to the Board of Governors of the World Bank," Washington, D.C., The World Bank, 1971, September 27.
48.. Mehra, Y.P. (1977), "Money Wages, Prices and Causality," *Journal of Political Economy*, Vol. 85, pp. 1227-44.
49. Morawetz, D. (1977), *Twenty-five Years of Economic Development*, World Bank, Washington, D.C.
50. Morris, M.D. (1979), *Measuring the Condition of World's Poor: The Physical Quality of Life Index*, Pergamon Press, New York.
51. Nussabaum, Martha and Sen, A.K. (1993), *The Quality of Life*, Clarendon, Oxford.
52. Ram, Rati (1979), "International Income Inequality 1970 and 1978," *Economics Letters*, Vol. 14, pp. 187-90.
53. Ram, Rati (1980), "Physical Quality of Life Index and Inter-country Inequality," *Economics Letters*, Vol. 22, pp. 195-99.
54. Ram, Rati (1982), "Composite Indices of Physical Quality of Life, Basic Needs Fulfilment, and Income: A 'Principal Component' Representation," *Journal of Development Economics*, Vol. 11, pp. 227-47.
55. Ram, Rati (1982), "International Inequalities in the Basic Needs Indicators," *Journal of Development Economics*, Vol. 11, pp. 113-17.
56. Ram, Rati (1984), "Another Perspective on Changes in International Inequality from 1950 to 1980," *Economics Letters*, Vol. 16, pp. 191-96.
57. Ram, Rati (1985), "The Role of Real Income Level and Income Distribution in Fulfilment of Basic Needs," *World Development*, Vol. 3, No. 5, pp. 589-94.
58. Ram, Rati (1986), "Causality Between Income and Government Expenditure: A Broad International Perspective," *Public Finance*, Vol. XXXXI, No. 3, pp. 383-414.
59. Ram, Rati (1986), "Government Size and Economic Growth: A New Framework and Some Evidence from Cross-Section and Time-Series Data," *The American Economic Review*, March, Vol. 76, No. 1, pp. 91-202.
60. Ram, Rati (1987), "International Inequalities in Income and Index of Net Social Progress," *Economics Letters*, Vol. 24, pp. 295-98.
61. Ram, Rati (1989), "Level of Development and Income Inequality: An Extension of Kuznets-Hypothesis to the World Economy," *Kyklos*, Vol. 42, Fasc.1, pp. 73-88.
62. Ram, Rati (1992), "Inter-country Inequalities in Income and Basic Needs Indicators: A Recent Perspective," *World Development*, Vol. 20, pp. 899-905.

63. Rodgers, G.B. (1979), "Income and Inequality as Determinants of Mortality: An International Cross-sectional Analysis," *Population Studies*, Vol. 39, pp. 343-51.
64. Rostow, W.W. (1960), *The Stages of Economic Growth*, Cambridge University Press, Cambridge.
65. Sen, A.K. (1958), *Commodities and Capabilities*, North Holland, Amsterdam.
66. Sen A.K. (1970), *Collective Choice and Social Welfare*, Holden Day, San Francisco.
67. Sen, A.K. (1973), *On Economic Inequality*, Oxford University Press, London.
68. Sen, A.K. (1981), *Poverty and Famines*, Oxford University Press, Oxford.
69. Sen, A.K. (1981), "Public Action and Quality of Life in Developing Countries," *Oxford Bulletin for Economics and Statistics*, Vol. 43, No. 4, pp. 287-319.
70. Sen, A.K. (1983), "Development Which Way Now?", *The Economic Journal*, Vol. 93, pp. 745-62.
71. Sen, A.K. (1987), *The Standard of Living*, Cambridge University Press, Cambridge.
72. Sen, A.K. (1992), *Inequality Re-examined*, Harvard University Press.
73. Shin, Doh C. (1980), "Does Rapid Economic Growth Improve the Human Lot?", *Social Indicators Research*, Vol. 8, pp. 199-221.
74. Shorrocks, A.F. (1978), "Income Inequality and Income Mobility," *Journal of Economic Theory*, Vol. 10, pp. 376-93.
75. Sims, C.A. (1972), "Money, Income and Causality," *The American Economic Review*, September, Vol. 62, pp. 540-52.
76. Slottje, D.J. (1991), "Measuring the Quality of Life Across Countries," *The Review of Economics and Statistics*, Vol. 73, pp. 684-93.
77. Spout, Ronald V.A., and Weaver, J.H. (1992), "International Distribution of Income: 1960-87," *Kyklos*, Fasc. 2, pp. 237-58.
78. Srinivasan, T.N. (1977), "Development Poverty and Basic Human Needs: Some Issues," *Food Research Institute Studies*, Vol. 16, No. 2, pp. 11-28.
79. Stewart, F. (1985), *Basic Needs in Developing Countries*, Johns Hopkins University Press, Baltimore, MD.
80. Streeten, P. (1977), "The Distinctive Features of a Basic Needs Approach to Development," *International Development Review*, Vol. 3, pp. 8-16.
81. Streeten, P. (1981), First Things First, London, Oxford University Press. Summers, R., and Heston, A.W. (1984), "Improved International Comparison of Real Product and its Comparison: 1950-1977," *Review of Income and Wealth*, Vol. 30, pp. 207-62.

82. Streeten, P. (1984), "Basic Needs: Some Unsettled Questions," *World Development*, Vol. 12, No. 9, pp. 973-78.
83. Summers, R., and Heston, A.W. (1984), "Improved International Comparisons of Real Product and its Comparisons 1950-1977," *Review of Income and Wealth*, Vol. 30, pp. 1-25.
84. Summers, R., and Heston, A.W. (1988), "A New Set of International Comparisons of Real Product and Price Levels: Estimates for 130 Countries, 1950-1985," *Review of Income and Wealth*, Vol. 34, pp. 1-25.
85. Summers, R., and Heston, A.W. (1991), "The Penn World Table (Mark V): An Extended Set of International Comparisons,1950-1988," *Quarterly Journal of Economics*, pp. 327-68.
86. Theil, H. (1989), "The Development of International Inequality," *Journal of Econometrics*, Vol. 42., pp. 144-55.
87. Waldman, R.J., "Income Distribution and Infant Mortality," *Quarterly Journal of Economics*, pp.1283-1302.
88. Ward, M. (1984), "Changing Patterns of Inequality in a Changing Global Order," *Kyklos*, Vol. 35, pp. 115-34.
89. Wheeler, D. (1980), "Basic Needs Fulfilment and Economic Growth: A Simultaneous Model," *Journal of Development Economics*, Vol. 17, pp. 435-51.
90. Wiedermann, Paul (1984), "Comparing the Process of Socio-economic Development in Non-market Economies: The EEC and CMEA," *Cambridge Journal of Economics*, Vol. 8, pp. 311-30.
91. Williams, D., Goodhart C.A.E., and Gowland D.H. (1976), "Money, Income and Causality; The U.K. Experience," *American Economic Review*, Vol. 66, pp. 417-23.
92. United Nations Development Program, Human Development Reports, different issues.
93. World Bank: World Tables, different issues.
94. World Bank: World Development Reports, different issues.

CHAPTER 5

Welfare Economics: A Post-Modern Response

Debaprasad Bandopadhyay

> ".... [w]ithout the inhuman influence of the Government, there is no way out in our hands to eradicate our sense of lacks — we loose our country by fixing such an idea in our mind." — Rabindranath

No Buffer Zone Remains

No buffer zone that is beyond the gazé of Panopticon remains. In every space, in every domain the presence of omnipotent market-sponsored state is felt. Even the counter-zone of public action is within the grasp of state as state now offers us each and every "right" that was once totally unimaginable for the past sovereign! Foucault remarked, " .... and beyond all the oppressions and "alienations", the "right" to rediscover what one is and all that one can be, this "right" .... was the political response to all these new procedures of power which did not derive, either from traditional right of sovereignty." [1]

The word "Revolution" is now either a commodity available in the market by producing credit card or it is sanctioned by the state. The haunting question, now, in the midst of extreme persecutory paranoia, whose agent am I? Who am I working for ??? The state, the market and my action against both these two is within the design of an enlightened epistemology called "Welfare Economics" (WE)—it is a political response to the public action and legitimacy crisis of state as opposed to traditional right of sovereignty.

Knowing Inner Domain

When Michel Foucault, in course of defining "sexuality" in an interview, was talking about different permutations and combinations of acts-pleasure-desire in different epochs of History, he said "And I could say that the modern 'formula' is desire, which is theoretically underlined and practically accepted, since you have to liberate your own desire. Acts are not very important, and pleasure—nobody knows what it is." [2]

Nobody except the Welfare Economist does know the distinctive features of "pleasure" as what it is! A welfare economist, with his/her econometric tools and game theory, is now ready to serve Foucault regarding the nature of pleasure. Though, s/he calls it "utility"—a term that is derived, it is needless to say, from the Utilitarian Philosophy of the past century (to understand the politics of Utilitarianism, please see Eric Stokes's excellent work "English Utilitatrians in India" [19591]. Benthamian connotation of the term along with the Benthamian distinction between pleasure and happiness are deployed in the dominant and revived system of Welfare Economics (WE).

Thus, sexuality, in the Foucauldian sense of the term, is divided in the three domains of *dispotif* acts are found in the simulated hyper-reality of cyberspace, desire in the fetish consumer's market and pleasure has sprang out of these two and is being analysed in the table of welfare economist. Bentham invented hedonistic/felicific calculus to measure pleasure; welfare economist extends that calculus with his/her econometric tools. In this way, an enlightened epistemological field is fulfilling the desire of power by equating state and statistics. Statistics is used here as an intervening tool to penetrate and to objectify the desiring body of the welfare state's subject. Thus it also fulfils the requirement of the panopticon-state. Anything that was hidden and covert in the sovereigns' domain that is supposed to be exposed by the deployment of WE- technique. Therefore, pleasure, in the guise of utility is incorporated in the domain of WE along with its subsidiaries like health and education. All the ideological state apparatuses (Schools for official literacy, hospitals for controlled and conditioned behaviour) in the guise of welfare, subjectify themselves under the welfare state. Nothing can escape Panopticon's gaze: health or education or death!

Death Industry

Yes, death! As WE is mostly concerned with "life-expectancy" or enhancement of "life- style," it is also concerned with "death-rate" that reflects the supposed "development." However, it ignores the fact that the "life expectancy" as well as "physical quality of life" depends largely on the *death industry* (*i.e.* war industry). All the so-called developed nations depend on the production of the deadly weapons to snatch away the lives of other. It is "living in the way of killing," as Foucault remarked: "modern man is a political animal whose politics places his (*sic*) existence as a living being in question."[3] However no such question arises in WE as its first premise is ideal living being in an ideal living condition that may be "distorted" "corrupted" due to the "failure of state." This maximisation of state and its ideological apparatuses are subscribed by the anatomo-bio-politics of WE as WE is concerned with docile body's health, education and choice. What sort of health, education and choice are these?

(a) Is it health maintained by the medical police or medical bureaucrats and that is disturbed as well as polluted by the large-factory products?

(b) Is it official universal literacy, instigated by the enlightenment-project that ignores the indigenous knowledge base?

(c) Is it choice and consent that are manufactured and engineered by the ad-management? Ultimately, whose choice is it? Is not majority voting is merely a "minority dollar voting" in the democracy?

The success of WE-epistemology makes us remember the "power over life"-hypothesis of Michel Foucault. As Foucault showed that, in the eighteenth century, the proliferation of demographic techniques, taking cue from the classical period, to "know the body" lead to the administration and subjection of the docile body. The procedures of power here get a chance to know and penetrate the body through, what Foucault called as "anatomo-politics." The Game theory, one of the technical weapons used by WE, has a presupposition: man is a perfect machine with an inbuilt computer that has a "freedom" of choice. This is the basic premise of anatomo-politics of the human body. What Foucault explained in this regard may be useful to the reader, who wants to analyse critical discourse of WE in the light of anatomo-politics, which is formed "centred on the body as machine: its disciplining, the ***optimisation of its capabilities***, the extortion of its forces, the parallel increase of its ***usefulness*** and its docility, its integration into systems of efficient ***economic controls*** . . . ."[4] (Emphasis added). On the other hand, the procedures of power also penetrate the human species by deploying universal mechanics. These attempts to intervene with regulatory control over the species are, according to Foucault, the "bio-politics."

In the context of proliferation of death-industry as well as the body-penetrating paradigm of WE, I cannot but quote Foucault, "The Atomic situation is now at the end point of the process. The power to expose the whole population to death is the underside of the power to guarantee an individual continued existence."[5] Though it may seem to be paradoxical, it is the power that, in the beautiful guise of WE, guarantees our physical quality of life. Thus WE legitimises the statist "right to take life or let live."[6] This makes me remember Tagore's *Raktakaravi*: a frog survived for three thousand years, but s/he was not alive. This distinction between "survival" and "living" made by Tagore takes us to a crucial question of our existence as a living being. As we are continuing to survive (though in WE's Newspeak, it is dubbed as "to live") in the midst of nuclear holocaust as well as drastic environmental disorder, that entails the total extinction of human being. One cannot but to be a sceptic, when one hears the voice of welfare from the same domain that at a time propagates war and welfare. In fact, war and welfare are the two sides of the same coin. It is the political response to the Third World discontent as well as the demand of "right to live" from the part of those countries who are capable to dictate UNDP to create Human Development Index (HDI). UNDP is the organ of that international institute who has nothing to do but to advise "other" countries to sign NTBT.

What about the shadow play in the discourse of WE? WE-specialist is bothered about the unpaid area, what Pigoue defined as shadow zone (that are not quantified in GDP, GNP etc.) of economics. Thus HDI came into being. However, WE-specialist is also concerned with the entities that is countable as well as quantifiable by means of econometric tools, therefore HDI can be formally countable. The earlier version of Economics did not count the fact that non-professional act has also a solid contribution in the "development," therefore WE jumps into the field to incorporate everything under the gaze of Panopticon.

HDI is a perfect example of state-statistics nexus. WE handles its carefully. On the one hand it tries to know the docile body by measuring life expectancy, death rates of pregnant, per capita physicians, number of daily newspapers, literacy rates etc. for the purpose of welfare. On the other hand, WE, with its disciplinary technology, objectifies the body with a supposed optimal standard. It makes me remember of a giant in the Greek mythology, Damastes or otherwise Prokrustes, who laid all human beings on his bed and then "lop them or rack them out to make fit it." WE creates such Procrustean bed through its "normalisation" process. It is the end product of scientia sexualis that penetrates, normalises the human body with the help of the state. It establishes the body-power relationship in its critical discourse.

Ecological Entitlement

Anil Agarwal, in one editorial-page comments, in one of the 1998 November issue of the *Business Standard*, alleged the ecological entitlement is grossly absent in the particular and contemporary version of WE. If developmental planning depends on the capability of buying products (that also include health and education), ecological factors are crudely marginalized. It is not even a variable in the epistemology of WE.

Though Agarwal did not elaborate the notion "ecological entitlement," it is a key notion for this time. What is this in fact? Let me elaborate it:

- There is "something" which we call "natural" resources in this third and green planet.
- These resources are not, quantitatively, too much so that one can distribute these equally and proportionately for the consumption of the whole population.
- Therefore, it is necessary to "snatch away" such resources for the private consumption by the way of legal or social codes so those very "fittest" few can

utilize it. After all, anarchist says, "Private Property is a theft' and WE-specialist says "entitlement."

- However, there is a vicious circle within these legal code of entitlement: legal code is not enough to satisfy the ever grown consumption of "natural" resources. So, it is better to "avoid" legal, social or even religious control to fit oneself for the consumption of goods produced from "natural" resources.
- Any "deviation" from the construct of codes is called "corruption." Due to this, corruption, ideal notion of "state" is at stake. Corruption negates state *per se*.
- However, from the perspective of "ecological entitlement," all the codes that legitimise the deviation of nature in the form of private property as well as the violation of codes—are considered as corruption or pollution, *i.e.* corruption is equal to pollution.
- Sounds "essentialist?" Then "ecological entitlement" is a paradox because "ecological entitlement" is no one's entitlement and it is entitlement for everyone. Supposed any legal and social right does not bind "nature" and it is also bound by the right to non-corrupt as well as non-pollute it.
- Thus demarcation of nature and culture is being confused here. Deviation from nature is pollution and deviation from culture (legal or social) is corruption. Who knows, what is nature and what is culture?

As WE is not concerned with this ecological entitlement, the issue of health is tackled with the proliferation of medical bureaucrats' prescriptions and education is tackled with the academic bureaucrats. Proliferation of both these two *via* ideological state apparatuses confirms the triumph of state ideology. Massive industrialization without ecological entitlement and market exchange-entitlement in the guise of its pseudo-philanthropist plea for "development" is the key of WE.

How Development?

WE-specialist is happy with the results only. S/He avoids "how" questions. *How* could we get education and keep ourselves healthy, is not WE-specialist's cup of tea. Let us think that with the behavioural management, academic and medical bureaucrats succeed to implement certain well-defined closed model of education and health that enhance their developmental index. Does it entail that the country achieves the supposed development?

To illustrate, I want to quote Chomsky:

> "Of course one can design a restricted environment in which such control and such patterns . . . can be demonstrated, but there is no reason to suppose that any more is learned about the range of human potentialities by such methods than would be learned by *observing humans in prison or an army or in many a schoolroom.*"[7] (Emphasis added)

What do WE-specialists find "by observing humans in prison or an army- or in many a schoolroom?" Do they really find out the human potentialities in these domains? Nothing can be learned except the bourgeois behavioural manipulation of the docile bodies as found in the famous verse libere of Tagore, "Totakahini." WE develops a restricted environment, where WE-specialist demonstrates the hierarchy of development!

Apart from the statist ideology, WE is also for the liberated market. WE pronounces market and state in a same breath. The simultaneous handling of market economy and state triggers many problems. If state cannot control the liberated market (if there are controls, then it is not "liberated!") It seems paradoxical to some people as they think that one cannot at a time preserve state's autonomy and market autonomy. According to them one of these two must be minimized. Advocators of WE, of course, think it otherwise. They advocate liberal market economy with free flow of goods and, peculiarly enough with full awareness regarding the stakes of commodity fetishism. These paradoxes reveal that the advertisement of philanthropic state entails the legitimisation of state by WE-enthusiasts. In fact, they are camouflaging all pervading market in the name of state.

One cannot handle, on the other hand, state-sponsored excessive coercion by means of death-industry and welfare in the same hand without refuting the former. The producers of large death-industry, paradoxically enough, categorised as "developed" and the consumer-countries are under/un-developed (in the WE newspeak, they are "developing" countries). The per capita energy consumption is much more in the so-called developed countries than that of "undeveloped." In what and whose cost such luxury is entertained? The obvious answer is colonialism which is absent in the discourse of WE.

In fact, state needs such paradigm to rationalise and legitimise its existence. As for example, state needs a referee, when "democratic" franchise (where minority wins by spending dollars to appropriate the consumers' choice of brands) is no longer faithful to the people. Thus emerged T.N. Seshan. State-sponsored TV showed the manipulations in the post-voting day *via* Nalini Singh. It also shows *andha kanun* (blind law)-like films to pacify the revolutionary nerves of the discontent dissenters. In the academic sphere, such an epistemology is needed to allay discontents. In fact WE-specialists rationalise market by legitimising the state.

Literary Facts

All the attacks on WE may seem wordy. So, we need empirical facts and figures following the path of enlightened science. I like to depend on "imagined" fictions in their different forms rather than that of "real" historical facts in this regard, quite contrary to modernist structural writings. This difference does not stand as Spivak[8] (1997:76) aptly said that the difference is "in degree rather than in kind."

To understand the condition of the subaltern-space due to WE-type of epistemological intervention, let us take an example of such intervention from a Bangla novel, Satinath Bhaduri's "DhoRay corit manoS." The Author describes the situation of Tatmatuli, after the census had been done on that demography:

> "At that time, almost for a month, sparrows have not been seen. All are talking about a severe disease that was supposed to come. Furthermore, (they) had calculated people after allotting numbers in households (census). Every one is scared. Then that happens what was thought earlier. Jirania, TatmaTuli, dhaNORTuli—what an epidemic! What a disease! 'Bay ukhRanor bEram'— fever,

jhOTde bimar, pOTde khOtom (sudden fever, sudden death)."

It may be, from the point of view of enlightened science, merely a case of *post hoc ergo propter hoc* — a co-incidental fallacy. However, when, as a watchdog, the state is trying to penetrate the body of the subject with its demographic tools, subjects feel certain uneasiness. This psychic un-pleasure leads to some somatic disorders. The paradox of this situation is that welfare state is supposed to provide pleasure in the body of the subject and the subject rejects it in the way of disease. These consequences are beyond the domain of enlightened science, the modernist paradigm of which is followed by WE.

Tarashankar Bandopadhyay's famous novel *Ganadevata* depicts the situation of ordinary people in the context of changing scenario in the late colonial period under the British Raj. Debu Ghosh, a literate farmer, who is often referred to as/ponDit/ "scholar" by the villagers, was called as /tuy/"second person singular-honorific" by the Government land-surveyor, Kanungo. Debu in his return-address, also used /tuy/ to refer Kanungo. The villagers as well as Debu were not happy with the land-survey and Debu expressed his discontent at the time of the survey. Mingling with this fact and the incidence of referring Kanungo as /tuy/ lead to the arrest of Debu. Thus, the anatomo-bio-political intervention in the domain of land leads to the imprisonment of Debu's docile body.

The incidence of imprisonment due to referring back in-honorific and to resist survey showed the strength of anatomo-politics deployed by the state. It is, in fact, a part of statist design, that designates land and life.

Though state guarantees security in life through life insurance, it has its own stake. In the movie *The Circus*, Chaplin was bound to walk on the rope as the professional rope-walker was not available for that purpose. Chaplin prepared himself with a hidden wire-support to execute the job so that he would not have a chance of falling from the rope. Incidentally, that life-saving wire-support was tied off from his body. When, unknowingly as well as merrily, he was walking on the rope, the fellow-players of the circus reported it to the manager. Manager just uttered, ***"He is insured,"*** thus there would be no problem, if he fell. This is one example of secured human existence, guaranteed by the state or private companies.

Is It Anti-Modernism?

The whole commentary above may seem to be an anti-modernist agenda that wants to negate the scientific endeavour of modern state for the well-being of the subjects. This type of responses that negate Western enlightenment, are not in the good book of WE-specialist. For example, in two lectures (Abha Maity and Satyajit Ray Memorial lecture), Amartya Sen tried to rescue WE-metanarrative (a derivative of enlightenment project) by anticipating post-modern non-formal and plural responses. To him, science is always science; there is no geographical particularism in the construction of global science. The cultural plurality vanishes by the introduction of gross cultural diffusionism in Sen's discourse. And anything goes against the print capitalist construct of "Nation State" he was ready to rescue it. Thus the free will of enlightenment project is imported from "above" for subjugating the "free will" of below.

In fact, WE is a post-industrial epistemology that confirms, as a supplier, the legitimised existence of simulated sovereign State, (which is a hyper-reality) for the sake of free-flowing market economy, the dominant form of which is death industry.

References

1. Foucault, M. (1990), *The History of Sexuality,* (Vol. 1), New York, Vintage, p. 145.
2. Rabinow, P. (ed.) (1984), *The Foucault Reader*, New York, Pantheon Books, p. 359.
2. *Op. cit.*, 1, p. 143.
3. *Op. cit.*, 1, p. 139.
4. *Op. cit* , 1, p. 137.
5. *Op. cit.*, 1, p. 136.
6. Chomsky, N. (1972), *Language and Mind*, p. 114.
8. Mahasveta Devi (1997), *Breast Stories,* (Tr. Spivak Chakrovorty), Kolkata, Seagull, p. 76.

CHAPTER 6

Sen's Sense of Development: A Humanitarian Outlook

Anindya Bhukta

Amartya Sen received the Nobel Prize in economics for the year 1998. In its Nobel citation the Royal Swedish Academy of Sciences emphasises his contribution, particularly, to welfare economics. But his contribution to development economics is no less important. In fact, as an economist, Prof. Sen started his career with development economics as his subject of study. The thesis which earned him the Ph.D. degree in 1959 was entitled 'Choice of Techniques.' In this work he deals with the problem of choosing the suitable production technique in an overpopulated developing country. When published in book form in 1961, the thesis brought reputation for him also. But as a development economist Sen will not be remembered for this book. In fact, the concept of development got a new birth in the able hands of Prof. Sen. He added a human flavour to the concept of development. But this happened in later years.

After the publication of 'Choice of Techniques' Sen's interest turned to welfare economics, Prof. Sen resumed his writing on development economics almost a decade after. But, in the mean time a humanitarian outlook developed in Sen's approach.

The subject of development economics developed shortly after the Second World War. Initially it appeared to be something of a bastard child of growth economics, because at least in one respect, namely an overarching preoccupation with the growth of real income per head, the subject showed its resemblance with growth economics. Thereafter for a pretty long time the word 'development' was treated as synonymous with 'growth in real per capita income.' The credit of Amartya Sen lies in his continuous endeavour to make development economics free from this age-old contention.

Development, generally, is characterised as either expansion of availability of goods and services, or increase in utilities, or meeting basic needs. However, meeting basic needs can never be a good index of development. There are so many low-income countries where the basic needs of the people are already met, but a large section of people there are suffering from inadequate supply of health-care facilities, medical treatment, pure drinking water and so on. Literacy rate there is very low, very low is their average life-expectancy at birth. May it be that the basic needs of the people are satisfied, but the hard truth is that they are not developed in the true sense of the term.

What is then real development? Can it be enjoyed with more goods and services? The common concern to economic development is that it simply means expansion of availability of goods and services in the society, and that real GDP per capita is a good index of economic development as it considers both GDP in the aggregate and the population stock of the economy. When development economists choose per capita real GDP as development index they did not ignore the possibility of distributive inequality in the society. But they expressed their hope that the benefits of development will percolate to the bottom strata of the society. The critics argue that this expectation does not work. They question the trickle down theory of development because of widespread primary poverty in the developing world (S.N. Reddy *et al.*, 1998). And whenever one questions the trickle down theory, it turns out to be a question of effectiveness of real GDP per capita as development index.

According to Prof. Sen, goods and services, no doubt, are valuable, but they are not valuable in their own. Their value rests on what they can do for people, or rather, what people can do with these goods and services (Sen 1984a). The question essentially relates to the concept, what Sen terms, 'capability.'

Development, or Human Development?

Amartya Sen has the habit of writing on various aspects of economics (and on other subjects as well). His interest in economics ranges from planning to project evaluation, from agricultural economics to monetary economics, from development economics to welfare economics and so on and so forth. But in all these writings his central focus always is, human being, more specifically, welfare of mankind. Probably this welfare attitude of Prof. Sen led him in search of an index which describes development not only in material terms, but in terms of things beyond that.

However, Amartya Sen is not pioneer in this line of thinking, though he is pioneer in establishing this line on a strong foothold and also in changing the direction of development economics of today almost single-handedly. In his recent monograph 'Development as Freedom' Prof. Sen writes: "The focusing on the quality of life and on substantive freedoms, rather than just on income or wealth, may look like something of a departure from the established traditions of economics, and in a sense it is. But in fact these broader approaches are in tune with lines of analysis that have been part of professional economics right from the beginning."

In fact, even in the writings of classical political authors the focus of development economics was on the growth of incomes. However, though classical authors, *e.g.*, Adam Smith and J.S. Mill, wrote a great deal on the growth of income, they saw income as one of several different means to important ends. These classical authors were deeply concerned with the recognition that we have reasons to value many things other than income and wealth, which relate to the real opportunities to lead the kind of life we would value living (Sen *et al.*, 1995).

The question now: what are these 'many things other than income and wealth?' This was not explicitly answered by the classical political authors. Being indoctrinated in humanism during his intensive occupation with welfare economics in 1960s, Prof. Sen started offering answers to this question when he resumed his writing on development economics in the early 1970s. According to Amartya Sen development should not be viewed from economic angle only, rather it should be viewed from a humanitarian angle. In other words, the term 'development' does not imply mere 'economic advancement,' rather it implies 'human development' in Sen's sense. Increase in income and wealth can ensure economic progress, but it may not entail human development as a whole. Initially Prof. Sen believed that it was the quality of life which was the main determinant of human development. Later on he started putting emphasis on various types of freedom for the development of mankind.

Entitlements and Capabilities

Sen has argued that the real limitation of traditional development economics arose not from the choice of means to the end of growth, but from the insufficient recognition that growth was no more than a means to some other objectives (Gupta, 1999). The basic objective of people is to lead a happy and healthy life, and economic development is only a means to achieve this goal. Sen, in his development study, thus puts first and foremost emphasis on the betterment of living standard.

What is meant by 'betterment of living standard?' Obviously, if a person is entitled to primary education, health care service, proper sanitation facility, free access to safe drinking water etc., he can enjoy a better living standard. However, well-being, according to Prof. Sen, must assess amongst other things, the freedom to achieve along with actual achievements (Sinha, 1999). The quality of life of a person can never depend solely on what he achieved. For example, sometime at the end months of the year 1999 it was learnt through media that a blind youth in West Bengal, who had succeeded in the School Service Examination was refused to join a school as a teacher because of his lost sight. Thus the unfreedom of this youth to get a job finally made his quality of life very poor though he actually achieved the eligibility criteria of getting the job. Besides actual achievements, freedom to achieve is, therefore, very much important in assessing one's well-being. It is in this context Prof. Sen introduces the concept of capability. According to Sen, the ultimate objective of economic development should be the generation of capability. The process of economic development has to be concerned with what people can or cannot do (Sen, 1983).

What is Capability? 'Capability' refers to the alternative combinations of functioning from which a person can choose (Sen, 1985). Functionings are, however, personal features. They tell us what a person is doing, capability to function reflects what a person can do (Sen, 1984).

According to Sen, what creates welfare is not goods as such, but the activity for which they are acquired. Goods create 'functional opportunities' for individuals. The set of such functional opportunities can then be used to define an individual's actual opportunities or 'capabilities' (Nobel Citation in Economics, 1998, Royal Swedish Academy of Sciences). In accordance with this view income is also significant because of the opportunities it creates. But what, in fact, Sen tries to point out is that capability or actual opportunity or freedom to achieve on which depends the quality of life of a person depends on a number of factors other than real GDP per capita. Capability is thus a broader concept of development index.

It is in this context, Prof. Sen introduces another concept, namely the concept of 'entitlement.' There is a significant relation between these two concepts—capability and entitlement.

The set of all bundles of commodities from which a person can choose one bundle can be called the person's 'entitlement' (Sen 1984a, *op. cit.*). A person in any society has certain endowments (labour, power, financial assets, skills) which she/he can directly use to obtain goods and services she/he desires or can trade them or the outputs produced with their help, in a formal or informal exchange with others to procure her/his preferred bundle of goods and services (Bagchi, 1998). Thus arises the idea of, which Sen terms, 'exchange entitlements.' But not all entitlements consist of such endowments. The entitlement of a person also includes what can be obtained through claims against the state, *e.g.*, the entitlement to unemployment benefit or to social subsidy. Sen has included in the concept of entitlement items like nutritious food, medical and health care, employment, security of food supply in terms of famine etc. (Brahmananda, 1998). These entitlements enable the people to consume goods and services which raise their capabilities (Roy, 1999).

Entitlement is thus the precondition of capability. According to Sen, "The generation of capabilities relates to entitlements, in the form of command over goods and services." In his article 'Goods and People' Prof. Sen writes, "While income is a good intermediate variable in studying food entitlement, it often provides an unhelpful perspective in dealing with entitlements to other goods and services, including those complementary to food." He thus advocates income to replace by 'capability' as the development index. He defines the 'process of economic development' as a 'process of expanding the capabilities of people.' However, according to Sen, 'given the functional relation between entitlements of persons over goods and their capabilities' economic development can also be characterised in terms of 'expansion of entitlements.'

Development as Freedom

In his recent monograph 'Development as Freedom' Prof. Sen explains development 'as a process of expanding the real freedoms that people enjoy.' He writes—"Development requires the removal of major sources of unfreedom: poverty as well as tyranny, poor economic opportunities as well as systematic social deprivation, neglect of public facilities as well as intolerance or overactivity of repressive states."

In Hindu societies widows are deprived of many freedoms. They are not entitled to take non-vegetarian food items, to wear coloured garments, to participate in auspicious ceremonies etc. These unfreedoms make them incapable of leading a healthy and joyful life. Their development is restricted by these social deprivations.

The social deprivations of Hindu widows in our illustration thus are taken into consideration in the new alternative approach of evaluating development in terms of various freedoms. In fact, had we assessed the development status of the Hindu widows in terms of quality of life (on which Sen emphasises earlier) we would get the same result, *i.e.*, these deprivations make their lives very poor. Hence, freedom as a development index is, in fact, a broader concept which includes all the earlier indices.

Indeed, we would fail to understand the deprivation of people unless and until we look at the restrictions that bind their lives and opportunities, the freedom that they lack. Development, in the alternative approach, thus defined as 'the process of acquiring and securing the freedoms that we have reason to value.' They make our lives richer and more enjoyable and unfettered, and they allow us to be fuller social persons, exercising our own volitions and interacting with—and influencing—the world in which we live (Sen, 1999).

In this alternative approach to development, expansion of freedom is viewed both as the primary end and as the principal means of development. When we say that the primary objective of development is to acquire freedoms of different kinds, the role of freedom will be 'constitutive' *i.e.*, achievement of freedom here constitutes development. On the other hand, if we say that freedom is the principal means of development what we actually mean is that development can be reached through the achievement of various types of freedom. The role of freedom in this case will be 'instrumental,' *i.e.*, freedom acts as an instrument to development.

The constitutive role of freedom relates to the importance of substantive freedom in enriching human life (Sen, 2000). The substantive freedoms include elementary capabilities like ability to avoid starvation, undernourishment, escapable morbidity, premature mortality, to deliver uncensored speech, to enjoy political participation and so on. In this constitutive perspective development is viewed as the process of expanding human freedoms.

The instrumental role of freedom, on the other hand, concerns the way different kinds of rights, opportunities and entitlements contribute to the expansion of human freedom in general, and thus to the promotion of development. Prof. Sen points out several distinct but interrelated components of instrumental freedom. They are economic entitlement, political rights, social opportunities, transparency guarantees and protective security.

These five categories of instrumental freedoms are defined by Prof. Sen in the following ways. Economic entitlements refer to the opportunities that individuals respectively enjoy to utilise economic resources for the purpose of consumption, or production or exchange. The opportunity to enter and use markets belongs to this category. Broadly conceived, political freedoms (including civil rights, include the opportunities that people have to determine who should govern and on what principles, and also include the possibility to criticise and scrutinise authorities, to have freedom of political expression and an uncensored Press, to pursue multi-party politics and so on. Social opportunities refer to the arrangements that society makes for education, health care and so on, which influence the individual's substantive freedom to live better. Transparency guarantees deal with the need for openness — the freedom to interact with visibility and lucidity — that people can expect. Lastly, protective security includes fixed institutional arrangements such as unemployment benefits and statutory income supplements to the indigent as well as *ad hoc* arrangements such as famine relief or emergency public employment to generate income for destitutes.

These instrumental freedoms not only directly promote the capabilities of people, but also they supplement and even reinforce one another. For example, when a society makes arrangement for basic public education and health care it will, in the first instance directly promote economic development and then, in the second, play an indirect role in reducing mortality rates. Reduction of mortality rates, in turn, can help to reduce birth rates, reinforcing the influence of basic education on fertility behaviour (Sen, 2000). The interconnections and complementarities among these instrumental freedoms have another significance. Public policy to foster human capabilities and substantive freedoms in general can work through the promotion of these interrelated freedoms.

Let me now conclude this article with a quotation from Sen. In a recent essay entitled 'Alternative approaches to development,' Amartya Sen writes: "Once we depart from the old characterisation of development in terms of increasing national income or the GNP per head and take an adequately broad alternative view of development, we can see that development studies as a subject is relevant for analysing the predicament of the deprived sections of the people."

References

Bagchi, A.K. (1998), Amartya Kumar Sen and the Human Science of Development, *Economic and Political Weekly*, Vol. 33, No. 49, pp. 3139-50.

Brahmananda, P.R. (1998), Amartya Sen and the Transformation of the Agenda of Welfare Economics, *The Indian Economic Journal*, Vol. 46, No. 2, pp. 1-25.

Gupta, Subrata (1999), Aspects of Sen's Economic Ideas: *West Bengal*, January 1 and 16, pp. 57-64.

Reddy, S.N., Rajasekhar A., and Reddy P.K. (1998), A.K. Sen's Contribution to Human Development, Conference Volume, IEA, pp. 73-76.

Roy, H.N. (1999), Amartya Sen: The Man and the Economist: *West Bengal*, January 1 and 16, pp. 67-74.

Sen, Amartya (1983), Development: Which Way Now? *Economic Journal*, Vol. 93, December, pp. 745-62.

Sen, Amartya (1984a), Goods and People: Essay 20 in the book *Resources, Values and Development*, Blackwell Publishers Ltd., Oxford.

Sen, Amartya (1984b), Rights and Capabilities, Essay 13 in the book *Resources, Values and Development*, Blackwell Publishers Ltd., Oxford.

Sen, Amartya and Jean Dreze (1995), *India: Economic Development and Social Opportunity* (Chapter 21), Clarendon Press, Oxford.

Sen, Amartya (1999), Alternative Approaches to Development, *The Statesman*, Festival 1999, pp. 103-13.

Sen, Amartya (2000), *Development as Freedom*, Oxford University Press.

Sinha, Anup (1999), Professor Amartya Sen's Ideas on Economic Development, *West Bengal*, January 1 and 16, pp. 55-56.

CHAPTER 7

Gender Inequality in the Education System of India

Abhijit Kumar Pal & Surendranath Banerjee

Education for women's equality is a vital component of the overall strategy of securing equity and social justice in education. The National Policy on Education (NPE, 1986) was very strong and forthright statements on the intervening and empowering role of education. *Inter alia*, they laid special emphasis on the removal of disparities, with the provision of special support services and removal of factors which result in gender discrimination at all levels of education and also to equalise educational opportunity by attending to the specific needs of those who have been denied equality so far. The Programme of Action (POA, 1992) also clearly spelt out the actions which need to be taken to promote education for Women's equality, which can hardly be improved upon.

The removal of women's illiteracy and obstacles inhibiting their access to and retention in elementary education, according to the NPE and POA, should receive overriding priority, though provision of special support services, setting of time targets and effective monitoring. Major emphasis should be laid on women's participation in vocational, technical and professional education at different levels. The policy of non discrimination should be pursued vigorously to eliminate sex stereo-typing in vocational occupations. Education should also be used as an agent of basic change in the status of women.

But, in spite of all these plans, programmes and provision of special support services for removal of factors which result in gender discrimination at all levels of education, the actions which need to be taken to promote women's education can hardly be improved upon. There is, however, a wide gap between the policy statement and its implementation. The present study aims to focus the present situation of gender disparity in Indian education system.

Methodology

For the present study various statistics, reports and policies, *e.g.*, National Policy on Education — 1986, The Programme of Action (1992), NPERC Report (1990), Report of the CABE Committee on Policy, Annual Report of Department of Education, Ministry of Human Resource Development, Current Educational Statistics (1989-99) etc., have been consulted. Various research findings of the present author and also the different project reports on Education, of the Psychology Research Unit, Indian Statistical Institute have also been taken into consideration to highlight the present position.

Results and Discussion

1. Position of Women's Education During 1986

At the time of formulation of National Policy on Education (1986), the position of women's education is shown in Table 7.1.

According to 1981 census only 29.8 per cent females of the whole country were literate as compared to 56.5 per cent male literates. So, at that time a huge female population of the country more than 70 per cent were illiterates. Illiterate women were predominant in the rural areas, about 78.2 per cent in comparison to 43.6 per cent in the urban areas. The illiteracy rate was as high as 90 per cent among SC women and 92 per cent among ST women during that period.

Regional disparities in the state of women's literacy were also pronounced. According to 1981 census, while the illiteracy among women in Kerala was 34 per cent, it was as high as 89 per cent in Rajasthan and 86 per cent in Bihar.

During 1981 about 42 per cent of boys in the age group of 6-14 years at all India level were not attending schools, while 62 per cent of girls of the same age group did not go to schools. The percentage of girl's enrolment to total enrolment in Primary, Middle, Secondary/Hr. Secondary and Higher education level during 1985-86 were 40.3 per cent, 35.6 per cent, 30.3 per cent and 33 per cent respectively. This gender disparity is further accentuated if we look the rural population separately. When 47 per cent of rural boys in the 6-14 years age group did not attend school during this period, the proportion of rural girls outside the ambit of formal education was as high as 70 per cent. Even in urban areas, more than one-third of the girls were outside the school system. Enrolment rates were poorest among girl children belonging to minority communities SC, ST and other educationally backward communities, who suffer from social and economic discrimination.

Table 7.1
Showing the Literacy Rates, Enrolment (Percentage) and Drop-out Rates During 1981-82 and 1985-86

Contents	*Years*					
	1981 (census)			*1991 (census)*		
	Persons	*Male*	*Female*	*Persons*	*Male*	*Female*
Literacy rates (all areas)	43.67	56.50	29.85	52.20	64.20	39.20
—do—(rural)	36.10	49.70	21.80	44.50	57.80	30.30
—do—(urban)	67.30	76.80	56.40	73.10	81.00	63.90
—do—(SC)	21.38	35.27	10.93	37.41	49.91	23.76
—do—(ST)	16.35	26.54	08.04	29.60	40.65	18.19
		1981			*1985-86*	
Enrolment (Percentage)		*Male*	*Female*		*Male*	*Female*
Primary (I-V)		57.85	38.67		59.62	40.35
Middle (VI-VIII)		55.39	32.92		57.37	35.63
Secondary/Hr. Secondary (10+2)		51.62	29.65		53.29	30.37
Higher Education (degree & above)		48.37	26.73		50.53	33.05
Rural (6 - 14 years)		53.50	30.93		58.29	32.61
Urban (6 - 14 years)		74.66	65.52		81.52	68.39
Dropout Percentage	*Persons*	*Male*	*Female*	*Persons*	*Male*	*Female*
Primary (I - V)	58.7	56.2	62.5	47.61	45.84	50.27
Middle (I - VIII)	72.7	68.0	79.4	64.42	60.70	70.04

Source: Selected Educational Statistics, 1997-98.

The percentages of drop-out of girls during 1980-81 and 1985-86, were 62.5 per cent, 50.27 per cent respectively in the primary level and were as high as 79.4 per cent and 70.04 per cent respectively in the middle school level.

Table 7.2
Showing the Proportion of Girls' Enrolment in Different Courses of Higher Education and Proportion of Women Teachers During 1985-86

Level and Courses	*Girls' Enrolment (proportion) 1985-86*
Higher education (degree and above)	33.01
Arts courses	55.05
Science courses	20.11
Engineering courses	06.02
Level	*Proportion of women tachers 1985-86*
Primary school	26.3
Middle school	32.2
High/Higher secondary	31.2

Source: Programme of Action, 1992.

During 1985-86 the representation of women in higher education was as low as 33 per cent. Data show, that of all women enrolled in higher education only 55 per cent were in arts courses, only 20 per cent in science courses and only 6 per cent were enrolled for engineering courses in the whole country.

The proportion of women amongst teachers engaged at Primary, Middle and High/Higher Secondary levels in 1985-86 was as low as 26.3 per cent, 32.2 per cent and 31.2 per cent respectively. Also at the higher levels of decision-making process in the education system women were poorly represented.

2. *Present Position of Women's Education*

In spite of the directives of National Policy on Education (NPE, 1986) and its Programme of Action which clearly emphasized on women's education, very little improvement has been noticed which is shown in the Table 7.3 below.

Table 7.3
Showing the Position of Women in Education During 1991 and 1997-98

Contents	*Years*					
	1991			*1997-98*		
	Male	*Female*	*Total*	*Male*	*Female*	*Total*
Literacy (Percentage)	64.2	39.2	52.2	64.13	39.29	52.21
Enrolment (Percentage)						
Primary level	65.00	41.91		78.65	43.62	
Upper primary level	58.52	38.29		65.39	40.15	
High/Higher secondary	55.81	33.84		61.24	37.13	
Higher education (degree and above)	52.35	32.37		58.56	34.82	
Drop-out (Percentage)						
Primary level	40.13	46.05	42.65	38.23	41.34	39.58
Middle school level	59.15	65.19	60.92	50.72	58.61	54.14

Level	*Proportion of women teachers*	
	1991	*1997-98*
Primary school	29.92	34.34
Middle school	33.82	36.05
High/Higher secondary school	32.58	35.24

Source: Selected Educational Statistics 1997-98.

According to the 1991 census female literacy rate was 39.2 per cent compared to 64.2 per cent for males. The number of female illiterates were 70 million more than male illiterates, even though the female population at that time, was 32 million less than the male population. There were significant rural-urban disparities among women, rural female literacy was less than half of urban female literacy. But if we consider the female literacy during the year 1997-98, the figure remains almost same as in 1991 figure, only 39.29 per cent compared to 64.13 per cent for males.

From the available data it is revealed that according to 1991 census the enrolment of the girl students in primary, upper primary, high/higher secondary and degree and above level students were 41.91 per cent, 38.29 per cent, 33.84 per cent and 32.37 per cent respectively against the corresponding enrolment for boys were 65 per cent, 58.52 per cent, 55.81 per cent and 52.35 per cent respectively during the same period. Where as during 1997-98 the said figures for girls enrolment is 43.62 per cent, 40.15 per cent, 37.13 per cent and 34.82 per cent respectively against the corresponding boys enrolment of 78.65 per cent, 65.39 per cent, 61.24 per cent and 58.56 per cent respectively.

The percentage of drop-out of girls according to 1991 census was 46 per cent in the primary level and as high as 65.2 per cent in the middle school level. During 1997-98 the corresponding figures are 41.34 per cent and 58.61 per cent respectively. Moreover there are ecological disparities in female education. A striking finding is that for every 100 girls in class I in rural areas, there are only 40 in class V, 18 in class VIII, 9 in class IX and only 1 in class XII. The corresponding figures for urban areas being 82, 62, 32 and 14. If ten to twelve years of general education is the basic requirement for entrance into technical and professional education rural girls would therefore stand excluded. An overwhelming proportion of vocational, higher and technical education facilities are located in urban or semi-urban areas. Participation of girls in this sector continues to be low and gender stereotyped. Similarly proportion of women in engineering and agricultural based courses is woefully low.

According to 1991 census, the percentages of female teachers at the primary, middle and high/higher secondary schools were 29.92 per cent, 33.82 per cent and 32.58 per cent. Whereas during 1997-98 these percentages are 34.34 per cent, 36.05 per cent and 35.24 per cent respectively. So, the increase of women teachers in each level during these years is only marginal.

Conclusion

Political independence had hardly made for much of a difference. Since independence, several commissions and committees have been constituted at the National level for examining the working of the educational system and for suggesting measures for reform of the gender disparities. Notwithstanding their recommendations, the essential character of our education has remained more or less unchanged. Economic growth, defined in terms of rate of growth in per capita income has by and large been listless over the past five decades. There has been fierce competition between the classes to corner the opportunities this limited growth has thrown up. Those who have been socially and economically most powerful in the patriarchal society of the country, have consistently tried to pre-empt others from sharing the resources allocated for education. The Government policies, organisational changes and the curriculum reforms introduced over the years have been elite and cosmetic in nature. No radical alternative has been given a trial; even the basic education proposed by Mahatma Gandhi, based on the principle of learning by doing, has not been seriously tried anywhere. The Nobel Laureate Prof. Amartya Sen rightly described, "The inequality among human beings (gender) proved to be a hydra-headed monster and its description could not be reduced to its measures usually deployed by economists. Human beings need not only food, shelter and clothing, they also need education freedom to choose and access to all facilities provided by society for self-improvement. On the other hand, most existing societies have fostered institutions which systematically deny such facilities to a particular gender in order to make them as the weaker gender of the society." So, it is a pity that, we have to proceed to the twenty-first century with this huge number of illiterate women population.

References

Banerjee, Surendranath (1996), "Impact of Certain Socio-economic Factors on Primary Education," *Socio-economic Transformation in India*, Kanishka Publishers, Distributors, New Delhi.

Banerjee, Surendranath (1999), "Gender Disparities in the Educational System in India," *Socio-economic Reforms in India*, Kanishka Publishers, Distributors, New Delhi.

Banerjee, Surendranath (1999), "Problems of Primary Education and Economic Development in India" (Accepted for publication), *Socio-economic Development in India*, Kanishka Publishers, Distributors, New Delhi.

Government of India, Ministry of Human Resource Development (1992), "National Policy on Education 1986 (with modification in 1992)," Department of Education, New Delhi.

Government of India, Ministry of Human Resource Development (1992), "Programme of Action 1992," Department of Education, New Delhi.

Government of India, Ministry of Human Resource Development (1997), "Annual Report 1996-97," Department of Education, New Delhi.

Government of India, Ministry of Human Resource Development (1999), "Selected Educational Statistics 1997-98," Department of Education Planning, Monitoring and Statistics Division, New Delhi.

Sen, Amartya and Dreze, Jean (1995), "India: Economic Development and Social Opportunity," Clarendon Press, Oxford.

CHAPTER 8

Words and Actions: Leadership and Development in the Dusty Rear

Bhola Nath Ghoṣh

Introduction

Most of the newly independent and developing nations of the world are committed to a policy of planned economic and social growth. In many of them the process of modernisation is being pushed at an accelerated pace. One of the important prerequisites for this planned changes is the availabilities of a type of leadership possessing specific qualities, like mobilising not only those who are at the top but also at the grass-root level.

In a society, the privilege of formulating policies, taking decisions and making "laws" is generally enjoyed by a small group. Depending on the type of society, this group comes from aristocratic or wealthy and of influential families. It may also consist of individuals whose personal qualities seem to raise them to such leadership positions.

There are different schools of thought about the nature and characteristics of leadership in the rural areas and its impact on development issues. Here, we are concerned about the problem of rural leadership in effecting rural development and the pattern of changes both in leadership as well as in nature of development.

There are various definitions of "leadership" and rural "development." Although they differ in verbatose and in styles, there is an element of commonality among the definitions given by eminent scholars. We have however chosen a definition most suitable for our kind of study on Rural 'leadership' and rural 'development' on the following lines.

By leadership we would mean, a process of influence group activities towards goal-setting and goal-achievement. This is however, quite similar to the definition given by Stogdill. We have only marginally changed the content of Stogdill's (1950) definition to suit the purpose in the specific area of our study.

By rural development, we would mean a strategy designed to improve the economic and social life of a specific groups of people especially of the rural poor. It involves extending the benefits of development to the poorest among those who seek livelihood in the rural areas. This group includes small farmers, tenants and landless. The objectives of rural development, however, extend beyond any particular section. This encompass improved productivity, increased employment and thus higher income for target groups, as well as minimum acceptable levels of food, shelter, education and health.

Local leadership is an effective mechanism for mobilisation of the villagers and also the building up of organisations of them. An effective leadership can build up a group of followers and can transmit through them any idea or carry out any action and thereby diffuse the same to a larger section of the society. Thus, the gap between the idea for social change and the actions needed to implement them need be bridged.

It is obvious that leadership-role is associated with certain special responsibilities and initiatives as distinct from the role of an average person.

What leaders do and fail to do affects the group to which they belong to and also the people under their influence.

In the developmental context, the leaders have varied roles.

Leadership helps in crisis management. It is only the leader who in crisis situations can organise the isolated and dissenting members into a co-operative group.

If rural development programmes are treated as a movement for socio-economic change then leadership can be treated as the most effective instrument of interest identification, interest articulation, interest aggregation of the people.

Leaders also act as reference individuals in the acceptance of innovations and techniques for development. Above all, they can act as agents of modernisation, social change and social mobility. So, for speedy and smooth implementation of a development programme there is need for identification and proper utilisation of the local leaders.

The Problem

The problem we are concerned with addresses the following questions, namely,

- *(a)* whether the change in the pattern of leadership effectively corresponds to the change in the pattern of rural development.
- *(b)* whether the attributes of leadership underwent any change while there had been new orientations in development goals, and
- *(c)* whether a rural leader of the past would have been able to tackle the development issues at the present?

We decided to confine our attention to the rural situation alone and tried to interface the twin issues resulting in change in the rural societies. The various aspects of leadership issues and development issues had to be examined in order to understand the evaluation of rural leadership in response to the need for rural development.

This chapter intends to summarize the major findings of the larger report to be published very soon.

We examined all the approaches of identifying leaders by eminent predecessors and tried to learn from those.

We not only counted the political and social leaders but also leaders of different other facets. The essence of the whole process of identification was actually on the basis of the following.

Our focus was: who leads in which issues and how does he do it?

Leadership, is not a technique *per se* but an art by itself. While doing so we have not ignored the basic questions of leadership, namely the factors of motivations, the driving force and the orientations whichever are necessary to lead others.

In this study, various sociological tools like pre-ordained pre-tested schedules, questionnaires for interviews etc. were used. Unrestrained dialogue with the leaders, followers and different villagers were undertaken to gain insight into the process of evolution of rural leadership as well as the rural development issues.

In order to understand the individual leaders as a part of the process of leadership evolution, we undertook several case studies of different leaders having different facets like political, social and matabbar etc.

The Locale

The villages studied in connection with the enquiry of the rural leaders are located within Mohammad Bazar Block of Birbhum district in West Bengal. The names of the three villages are Kabilpur a developing, Seorakuri developed and Latapakur an underdeveloped village. These 29 leaders come out of the three villages are presented in Tables 8.1 and 8.2.

From these villages 29 leaders were identified having different facets. We did not ignore any leader for having a particular facet or age, sex, community, class or type.

The Findings

The major findings of the aforesaid empirical study may be briefly presented as follows. The details are given at Table 8.3.

The class background of the rural leaders had undergone a change from rich to poor in the last two decades. Marginal farmers and landless labourers seem to have shared some power and position with the rural gentry who still constitute around two-fifth of the army of leadership. Case studies point out and survey data confirm that even though in minority the real power is still in the hands of the rural gentry.

Leaders mainly are male and grown up young men or middle-aged. There has been no proportionate representation of leadership from among women and people belonging to their early youth (below twenty-five years) although there is universal suffrage above eighteen irrespective of sex.

Majority of rural leaders come from among high and middle caste Hindus. Lower caste Hindus (SC) and Muslims' (Religious minority) throw much less leaders even compared to tribals (ST).

Table 8.1
Identification of Leaders by Their Ethnic and Family Background

Sl. No.	Name of leader	Village (v)	Sex	Age	Caste/ Tribe	Marital status	Education level	Family size	Type of family	Main trait
(1)	(2)	(3)	(4)	(5)	(6)	(7)	(8)	(9)	(10)	(11)
1.	M.C.	Seorakuri (S)	M	32	Brahmin	M	X	9	Joint	Political
2.	U.C.	"	M	34	Brahmin	M	X	9	Joint	Political
3.	B.S.	"	M	38	Santhal (ST)	M	VIII	5	Nuclear	Political
4.	G.G.	"	M	60	Goala	M	X	8	Joint	Murabbi
5.	T.M.	"	M	50	Sadgop	M	VIII	9	Joint	Political
6.	A.M.	"	M	35	Muslim	M	IV	6	Joint	Religious
7.	M.M.	"	M	30	Muslim	M	VIII	6	Joint	Religious
8.	H.S.	"	M	42	Santhal (ST)	M	II	5	Joint	Social
9.	B.M.	"	M	28	Sadgop	M	M.A.	7	Joint	Babu
10.	B.M.	"	M	55	Sadgop	M	VIII	9	Joint	Matabbar
11.	S.M.	"	M	38	Dome (SC)	M	IX	6	Nuclear	Social
12.	S.D.	"	F	30	Kayastha	UM	H.S.	5	Nuclear	Social
13.	L.S.	Latapakur (L)	F	30	Santhal (ST)	M	S.F.	6	Joint	Social
14.	L.B.	"	M	34	Santhal (ST)	M	—	6	Joint	Political
15.	S.M.	"	M	35	Santhal (ST)	M	—	6	Nuclear	Political
16.	C.M.	"	M	48	Santhal (ST)	M	—	8	Joint	Tribal chief

(Contd.)

Sl. No.	Name of leader	Village (v)	Sex	Age	Caste/ Tribe	Marital status	Education level	Family size	Type of family	Main trait
(1)	(2)	(3)	(4)	(5)	(6)	(7)	(8)	(9)	(10)	(11)
17.	N.M.	Kabilpur (K)	M	60	Sadgop	M	S.F.	6	Nuclear	Matabbar
18.	K.M.	"	M	55	Sadgop	M	S.F.	7	Nuclear	Matabbar
19.	A.G.	"	M	52	Brahmin	M	B. Com.	4	Nuclear	Political
20.	N.G.	"	M	50	Brahmin	M	M.A., B.T.	4	Nuclear	Dada
21.	R.B.	"	M	42	Brahmin	M	M.A.	6	Nuclear	Political
22.	L.B.	"	M	52	Bagdi (SC)	M	—	4	Nuclear	Social
23.	S.P.	"	M	36	Sadgop	M	VIII	6	Nuclear	Political
24.	T.G.	"	F	25	Brahmin	UM	B.Sc., B.A.	4	Nuclear	Social
25.	M.M.	"	M	58	Sadgop	M	VI	8	Joint	Political
26.	S.H.	"	M	36	Santhal (ST)	M	VI	8	Joint	Political
27.	F.B.	"	M	51	Bagdi (SC)	M	IV	8	Joint	Political
28.	L.M.	"	F	32	Santhal (ST)	M	VIII	5	Nuclear	Social
29.	J.M.	"	M	58	Sadgop	M	M.A.	10	Joint	Traditional

Table 8.2
Identification of Leaders by Occupation, Income, Land Ownership, Political Affiliations and Positions

Sl. No.	(v)	Occupation: Primary	Occupation: Secondary	Family occupation	Individual income per year (in Rs.)	Landsize (in bigha) Individual: Ownership	Landsize (in bigha) Individual: Operational	House type	No. of rooms in family home	Political party affiliations	Panchayat position held in since
(1)	(2)	(3)	(4)	(5)	(6)	(7)	(8)	(9)	(10)	(11)	(12)
1.	s	business (b) paddy	—	Cultivation (c) +contractor (cr) + business (b)	25,000	6	6	Kachha —tin	5	M	1987 (Pradhan)
2.	"	cr	—	- do -	25,000	6	6	"	5	M	—
3.	"	Industrial labour (Ind.l)		Ind. l +Pig rearer (pr)	4,800	1	1	Kachha —shed	3	M	1983, 1987
4.	"	Cultivator	Primary teacher (Pt)	c+Pt+milk selling (MS)	36,000	17	17	Pucca	4	C	—
5.	"	- do -	b (grocery)	c+b+ money lending (ml)	36,000	30	30	"	4	C	1978, 1983
6.	"	Gobar gas technician (tech)	—	tailoring + share cropping (sc) + tech	6,000	2	6	Kachha —shed	2	C	—
7.	"	b (cycle repairing shop)	—	cattle grazing + b (cycle reparing, vegetable)	3,600	—	—	"	2	—	—
8.	"	Ind.l	—	Ind.l +pr.	3,600	—	—	"	2	M	—
9.	"	Secondary teacher (St)	c	St + c + b	40,000	17	17	Pucca	3	C	—
10.	"	c	—	c + ml + wood seller	48,000	15	15	"	4	—	—

(Contd.)

(1)	(2)	(3)	(4)	(5)	(6)	(7)	(8)	(9)	(10)	(11)	(12)
11.	S	Service	—	S + vegetable seller	3,600	2	2	Kachha —shed	1	—	—
12.	"	S	—	S + b (coal and food grains)	4,800	—	—	Pucca	3	—	—
13.	L	Pt	c	Pt + c + S	18,000	6	6	Kachha —shed	2	—	—
14.	"	c	Agl.	c + Agl. + Ind.l	6,000	5	5	"	2	M	1978, 83, 87
15.	"	c	—	c + pr.	15,000	16	16	"	2	M	—
16.	"	c	Agl.	c + Agl. + sc	5,000	3	6	"	2	—	—
17.	"	c	b	c + b + ml.	60,000	36	36	Pucca	4	C	—
18.	"	c	b	c + b + ml.	60,000	36	36	Pucca	4	C	—
19.	"	c	s	c + s	12,000	10	10	Kachha —tin	3	—	—
20.	"	St	c	St + c + s	36,000	9	9	"	3	FB	1983, 1987
21.	"	S	c	S + c	12,000	18	18	"	3	FB	—
22.	"	Agl.	Sc	Agl. + sc + cattle grazer	3,000	—	2	Kachha —shed	1	ML	—
23.	"	c	—	c	6,000	4	4	Kachha —tin	2	M	1987
24.	"	Unemployed	—	c + s	Nil	—	—	"	3	—	—
25.	"	c	—	c	12,000	18	18	"	5	—	—
26.	"	c	b (grocery)	c + b + s	5,000	3	3	Kachha —shed	3	M	1987
27.	"	Agl.	—	Agl. + Daily lab.	5,000	1	1	"	2	FB	1983
28.	"	Agl.	c	Agl. + c + sc	3,000	3	5	"	2	M	—
29.	"	St.	c	St + c	48,000	25	25	Pucca	4	—	—

Table 8.3
Rural Leaders at a Glance

(n=29)

	Community		
	Hindu	Higher caste	20.68
	Hindu	Middle caste	30.48
	Hindu	Lower caste	10.34
	Tribe		27.58
	Muslim		6.89
2.	Class	Large > 15 (in bigha)	34.48
		Small < 15 ≥ 7.5 (in bigha)	6.89
		Marginal < 7.5 (in bigha)	41.37
		Landless 0	17.24
3.	Annual income	Upto Rs. 12,000	58.62
	(Rs.)	12,001 - 25,000	13.79
		Above 25,000	27.59
4.	Age	≤ 25	3.44
		26 - 50	65.51
		> 50	31.03
5.	Sex	Male	86.20
		Female	13.79
6.	Education	Illiterate	13.49
		Primary	10.34
		Secondary	51.72
		Above secondary	24.13
7.	Primary	Cultivation	41.38
	occupation	Service	10.34
		Labour	17.24
		Teacher	13.79
		Others	17.25

(Contd.)

8.	Source of livelihood	Single source	6.90
		Double source	41.38
		Triple source	51.72
9.	Marital status	Married	93.10
		Unmarried	6.90
10.	Family size	≤ 5	27.58
		6 - 8	55.16
		> 8	17.23
11.	Family type	Joint	72.41
		Nuclear	27.58
12.	House type	Kachha shed	44.82
		Kachha tin	27.58
		Pucca	27.58
13.	Type	Formal	27.58
		Informal	72.41
14.	Political affiliation	CPI (M)	31.03
		Congress	20.68
		Forward block	10.34
		CPI (ML)	3.44
		Non-party	34.48
15.	Main trait	Political	41.37
		Social	24.14
		Matabbar	10.34
		Others	24.15
16.	Facets	Single	27.58
		Multiple	72.42

So, the roles of caste and religious factors in connection with the emergence or imposition of leadership cannot just be wished away.

Majority of leaders come from among people of low educational level which however, may be explained with the level of literacy and education of the population inhabiting the villages.

Contrary to general belief that a leader is made or imposed by political parties or any village institutions, the findings show that about one-third of the leaders emerged outside the influence of political parties or organised village institutions. It may, therefore, be said that non-party or extra-party leaders play important role in rural life.

Joint families of moderate size (neither too big nor too small) allow the leader enough time which could be devoted to outside work. Families of very small size cannot afford to release its member in terms of responsibility and those of very big size in terms of the time spent on family work.

The present class basis of the political parties in the rural areas were examined which showed that while Naxalites base themselves solely on landless labour, CPI(M) has significant control over the small and marginal farmers. The class basis of Congress is still the rural gentry whereas Forward Block has no particular class basis. Forward Block picked up leaders from whichever class it has possible.

The position of informal leaders irrespective of their support to any or all political parties holds a unique character. Almost seven-tenth of the leaders have emerged from among the rural folks which underlines the importance of the informal leaders in rural situation. That is to say that imposition of leadership in rural situation cannot and should not be taken as granted.

Cultivation remaining the main-stay of rural income and hence primary occupation of the people in general, it is obvious that majority of leaders should be mainly engaged in the primary sector, agriculture. But the tertiary sector is trying to catch up and rise to the occasion in the sense that teachers, service-men and business people are trying to assume the rural leadership. These elements would remain indifferent to politics in general and sharing of power with rural gentry in particular. But with the introduction of panchayat election on the basis of universal franchise, these elements are also taking active parts in politics.

With the present income situation of the rural households, it is being gradually impossible for the villagers to depend solely on cultivation and so secondary occupations have been necessary to meet both ends of a rural family. That is why, the majority of the leaders' households had secondary occupations and hence multiple sources of income.

All types of leaders, be they formal or informal, possess multiple facets. Fourteen distinct roles were identified by us which were played by twenty-nine leaders. Again most of the leaders have more than one trait and as many as seven traits were identified. What we observed was that most such aspects are socio-centric and the traits were political. There is, however, no strict dichotomy. In some cases there are close relationship between social and political responses of the leaders and in most cases differentiations is little or none at all. Contextual variables such as degree of development in the village or rate of literacy sometimes seem relevant for the existence of dichotomy as stated above. With increasing development and modernization the dichotomy between social and political issues become apparent. From the data we could not conclude that the dichotomy is real which suggest that further probe would be necessary for making any generalization.

The data showed a continuum between traditional (conscience keeper, tribal chief etc.) and modern (political, social etc.) having evidences that there was no outright rejection of traditional in favour of political values. Attitudinal responses of the leaders also support the same.

Interfaced with developmental issues, be it improvement of physical condition of the village, income generation projects, social welfare, social institutional and political, most leaders played multiple roles. The top-most priority was often dictated by concrete village situation at day-to-day level which may be termed internality where other priorities were the result of extranality like political decision etc. The data conclusively showed the importance of social issues is still primary in the rural areas. Case studies also reveal that a leader starts by participating in social activities. Transformation of a leader from social to political arena is not automatic or usual. The existence of non-political or apolitical leaders in rural area supports this contentions.

Most leaders rate economical issues as highest priority, whereas other issues specially environmental issues still occupy low priority.

Leaders' capability to lead starts by leading one-self. So awareness and exposure responsible for achievement of leadership quality are subjected to scrutiny in our sample also. The data show very low level of exposure of the rural leaders in terms of mass media, outsiders and outside world. It is, therefore, apparent that leadership qualities would not quite flourish among the rural leaders due to their lack of access to objective information and experiences of their counterparts in other rural areas or urban settlements.

From the inquiry into the socio-political and psychological attitudes of the rural leaders and also about the values which they cherish, we can lay down some broad findings as follows:

> Attitudes towards different social questions of different leaders do not as a rule tally with their ideologies. But there is evidence of liberal views among most leaders political and non-party political, formal and informal regarding various social questions.

The political parties do not try to hurt the traditional value system and some fall prey to obscurantism and prejudices. The level of consciousness of leaders must therefore be upgraded in order that there can be progressive change.

It has been further observed that ideologies have great impact on shaping the social attitudes of the leaders. Commitment does not come by itself. It depends on degree of grasping the ideas. Political parties' class basis are often not consistent with the ideologies they preach and there is therefore a great difference between the leader's precepts and their individual practices.

A result cannot be explained by a constant since causes and effects are always variables. An effect cannot be explained by something that has not varied. The key to the understanding of a cause is variations. Leadership is an effect and the physical (environmental), spiritual (ideological) and social background (related to wealth, caste, age, sex, education etc.) are the causes that produce the effect.

Leadership is a life-process. To the question whether leader is born or made there cannot be an either/or answer. The spirit of being distinguished is common. Both in cases of inheritance (X's son or Y's daughter), and achievement (aspiration for power, affection from the people, respect from others etc.). The common factor is the spirit of distinction. Leaders' case studies unambiguously showed that the motivation behind leading others may differ in each case. In other words, no leader is typical and each is unique if one studies him or her meticulously. A person may have great potential to be a formal leader but circumstances may be against such achievement.

Political environment and the state of awareness may be responsible for desolation and deprivation for a leader.

Sheer personal aggrandisement may also be a motivating factor out-weighing the philanthropic attitudes for acquiring, the position of a leader.

Philanthropism and judicious tactfulness may be responsible for putting a person in leadership position.

We found each of the leaders to be unique in his own environment although he/she may not be a-typical. That his why leadership stands as a complicated phenomenon depending on his/her geneology and circumstances.

Conclusions

On the basis of the aforesaid major findings certain broad conclusions may be drawn as follows:

(a) Distance plays a key role in development in the sense that greater the access to development centres, the better the possibility of the development of the village. Infrastructural development (metal road, bus communication, access to facilitation centres) constitute the development perspective of the village. Rate and level of literacy, occupational diversity and mobility, improvement of cultural standard are most relevant questions in case of both the development issues and the leadership issues.

(b) The socio-economic and political conditions prevalent in the rural societies influence role playing and performance of the leaders. However, the influence is not so inclusive as to be indifferent to external interventions and the internal resistance. So, there cannot be any unidirectional development of rural leaders. Rural leaders may be conventional and traditional in some respects and pro-change in some other respect. Pro-changing factors are mainly economic activities in terms of infrastructure building, agricultural development and employment guarantee. It therefore

indicates that entrusting local self-government bodies with the task of formulating need-based and priority specified village-level planning may go a long way in re-structuring the local level leadership. This would have to be done with the assured participation of all the villagers and not just the identified leaders. In other words, many potential leaders who may be able to perform cannot come forward and provide able leadership due to existing political and social discrimination. It is also felt that a systematic and need-based awareness campaign that is, both ideological training and skill improvement need be undertaken in the villages.

(c) There has been substantial change in the class basis of the leaders. But with the promotion to the post of leaders there seems to be a danger of the class-promotion of the leaders that may defeat the whole purpose of social change and strengthening the caste, class and sex dominations on the rural people. So, the possibility of replacing the old container to keep the old content cannot be possibly overlooked. Vigilance in this aspect of leadership development and the need for constant ideological rejuvenation can hardly be overemphasised.

(d) When it comes to the question of choosing between making all decisions unanimously or going by majority vote in case of socio-economic and environmental issues one should insist on unanimity. It may not however satisfy the objective specific development goal in all cases but it will certainly satisfy the felt need of the people and honour the aspirations of different groups by assimilating their interests. In essence, antagonism should be resolved by promoting non-antagonistic development issues.

The leadership is a life-process, each of the individual leaders is a unique case depending on his/her genealogy and circumstances. There cannot be any hard and fast rules about achievement of leadership positions and there may be typologies of leadership.

References

1. Beteille, A., *Caste, Class and Power*, Berkely, University of California Press, 1996.
2. Beteille, A., *Studies in Agrarian Social Structure*, Oxford University Press, Delhi, 1979.
3. Chaudhury, R., Patterns of Leadership in a West Bengal Village, *Economic Weekly*, Vol. 14, 1965.
4. Dasgupta, Biplab, Gram Banglar Sreni Binyas (Class Relations in Bengal), *Deshhitaishee*, Annual Puja Issue, 1980.
5. Gangrade, K.D., *Emerging Pattern of Leadership*, Rachna Publication, Delhi, 1974.
6. Ghosh, Bhola Nath, Social Outlook of the Aspirants for Rural Leadership: Case Study in a Gram Panchayat, in *Man and Life*, Vol. 21, Nos. 3 and 4, Calcutta, 1995, pp. 155-68.
7. Ghosh, Bhola Nath, Paschim Bangha Panchayat Mahilader Jagdan: Sak-hamatar Pathe (in Bengal), in *Arthaniti Rajniti*, Calcutta, 1999, pp. 20-25.
8. Ghosh, Bhola Nath, *SC, ST and Women's Participation in Gram Panchayat: An Evaluation Based on State-wise Distribution of Elected Panchayat Members in India*, (Mimeo of Indian Statistical Institute, Calcutta, 2000.
9. Ghosh, Bhola Nath, *Rural Leadership and Development*, Mohit Publication, New Delhi, 1996.
10. Stogdill, R.M., *Leadership, Membership and Organisation*, Psychology Bulletin, Vol. 47, No. 1, January 1950.
11. Wright Mills, C., *The Power Elite*, Oxford University Press, New York, 1956.

CHAPTER 9

Need for Transfer of Technology Through Panchayati Raj System: An Observation

Kunal Bandopadhyay & Bhola Nath Ghosh

Introduction

Since 1960 a number of scholars all over India have been carrying on researches on the process of diffusion of modern technological innovations and the factors influencing their adoption in rural areas. With the introduction of the tiered Panchayati Raj (PR) System, the researches have grown more. The reason is obvious. PR system being a thoughtfully structured extension agency is believed to streamline the flow of information from top level, (mainly the Research and Development level where technology is either upgraded or invented anew) to the grass-root level—the end users or the adopters—and *vice versa*. Moreover, democratic decentralization of power and authority at the grass-root level is believed to have enabled the panchayats to function as units of Self-Government. In other words, panchayats independently can also take the initiative to implement and diffuse technological benefits directly to the farmers with an obvious objective of developing the socio-economic and cultural environment of the villages.

R.K. Samanta (1997) had observed that "technological change and innovation occur as a result of complex sets of human interactions; information flows and transfers, individual and organisational risk-taking, and decision-making capabilities." Added to that several human factors including prior knowledge, willingness and experience influence the process of diffusion and adoption of new technologies.

In this background, panchayats being the extended arm of the Government can be regarded as the best diffusing agency at the grass-root level, since it has emerged out of that very level with a decision-making capability and an easy access to the end users. Also, many researches early have shown that village level worker of the institutional personal sources receives more attention than other extension agents. Dasgupta (1989) noted, "Although neighbours, friends and relatives received fewer top rankings than the village level worker they were ranked as the second most important sources by the farmers of a much larger number of studies. Farmer of slightly larger number of studies ranked neighbours, relatives and friends as the most important or the second most important sources of information than the village level workers. They were also ranked as the third most important sources in several studies. To put it in a different way neighbours, friends and relatives were mentioned as important sources of information more frequently than the village level worker, although the latter was ranked as the most important source of information by the farmers of a greater number of studies."

Now every member of a panchayat can be considered as a village level worker enjoying the status of credible sources of information. The term "credible" is of immense importance because it accelerates the process of adoption by the farmers in agricultural sector and by the villagers as a whole in other spheres of life.

However Ray (1998) in his study quoting Sengupta (1967) observed that "Village panchayats were unable to contribute effectively towards development programmes and could not fulfil their assigned duties due to paucity of resource, inadequate secretarial assistance and people's participation.

Ironically, even in 1998, the situation does not nullify the observations of Sengupta. The present researchers have had wide discussions with a number of personnel from different strata of PR system right from Government (state) to the end users to understand the role-performance of panchayat in transferring technology. They have felt that though the system has been operating for the last 21 years, yet the unit of Self-Government is not contributing much to the development of rural economy through diffusion of new technological innovation. Thus the objective of the present study is to enquire about whether the panchayat system has become an effective instrument of transferring technology to the farmers, specially with respect to a specific case study in Govindapur Mouza under Babla Gram Panchayat.

Area of the Study

The study has been conducted at 32 No. Govindapur Mouza under Babla Gram Panchayat in the district of Nadia, West Bengal. The area of the entire Mouza is 786.2 hectares of which irrigated land in 380.66 hectares and non-irrigated land is 321.20 hectares having 8,400 odd voters electing, 12 candidates for the Gram Panchayat consisting of 18 seats. There are number of villages like Promodnagar, Nikunjanagar, Kulia under these 12 constituencies. The entire panchayat enjoys the facility of having 3 co-operatives for agricultural development called Samavaya Krishi Unnanyan Samiti of which Govindapur Mouza enjoys the facility of having Govindapur Samavaya Krishi Unnanyan Samiti Limited with 435 local shareholders and the Government as one of the compulsory shareholders. This Unnanyan Samiti has one Agricultural Extension Officer (AEO) who in local language is known as Krishi Prayukti Sahayak (KPS) to diffuse the modern agricultural innovation in that area. It is also to be noted that 70 per cent of the population in this mouza are dependent on agricultural activities. And a considerable section of population is engaged in weaving clothes, mainly sari. Of the 12 constituencies in Govindapur Mouza under study 4 constituencies do not enjoy power at all. 4 constituencies are partly electrified mainly for shallow pump connections and the balance 4 constituencies are electrified where people get electricity for domestic consumption.

Another interesting feature of the area under study is that some of the villages like Promodnagar are as old as the Panchayati Raj System is running in the state. For instance, Promodnagar having roughly 300 households was established only 18 years back and the PR system in West Bengal has been running for last 21 years.

Methodology

The study is based on an open and wide discussion with different people associated with the PR system right from Government high officials to grass-root level workers. The area of the study was selected purposively. There were structured schedules and set questionnaires. However, among the respondents, persons holding office or enjoying some special kind of status in the area were taken as key persons irrespective of their political identity for getting better information about the real performance of the panchayat.

Observation

The discussion with the villagers (respondents) and key persons revealed that the village has been developing in terms of socio-economic condition over the years in its usual way in tandem with the developments taking place in the state as a whole and the Panchayat has played little role as a catalytic agent to this development, barring the few areas like implementation of Jawahar Rojgar Yojana (JRY) for infrastructure and environmental development involving the local mass. However, the implementation of the programmes envisaged by the Government for rural development has not been upto the mark even after so long years. The road stretching about 17 kms from the National Highway 34 is still *kuccha* except around 2 kms which have been metalled during the period. The main road becomes intransportable during the rainy season creating blockades in the link to the local market in nearby suburban area, which is about 4 kms away from the village. Majority of the villages are yet to get electricity for domestic consumption as stated earlier. Only 4 constituencies out of 12 under study are electrified. The rest are either unelectrified or partly electrified. The village Promodnagar in particular has of course a different problem of legal rehabilitation. The present villagers there, about 18 years back, set up the village forcefully grabbing the land with the help of the ruling party CPI (M) and they are yet to get the necessary legal papers regarding their possessions.

But other village like Nikunjanagar do not have such problem, nevertheless electricity is a dream to them. The ground reality is that the functional member in charge of power department at the panchayat samiti was not active in bringing electricity in the villages. The villagers have alleged that they should have got the electricity about 4 years back. They had demanded it too. And some initiatives were taken at the ground level. But the member in charge of power department at panchayat samiti did not follow up the action and the villages are still dark. It is a fact that some of the agricultural fields in the villages under Govindapur Mouza are being tilled by tractors and power tillers instead of conventional implements of cultivation. Shallow pumps are being used which have helped about 50 per cent of the total area under study being irrigated. Interestingly, the farmers understand the necessity, and efficiency of tractors and power tillers in ploughing fields, use of HYV seeds for higher yields and the use of shallow pumps for better irrigation. Some of them are also using all these but information regarding these modern technological innovations were not percolated to them by the local panchayat members. Farmers have received and adopted the higher technology through friends, kins and neighbours and mass media mainly, radio and newspapers.

The Government has policies to provide power tillers, tractors, seeds, pesticides, insecticides, fertilizers and technological knowledge through Agricultural Extension Officer in collaboration with Gram Panchayat and also has programmes to provide different term-loans in association with the banks. The monitoring agency of the policies at the local level is obviously the Gram Panchayat itself. But the information of the policies do not always percolate to the end users. Members themselves are not fully aware of the programmes. Sometimes agencies like IFCO and different pesticides and insecticides manufacturing companies hold seminars once in a blue moon to diffuse and transfer modern technological innovations in agriculture. But the farmers do not get the fertilizers regularly which they are supposed to get through AEO or KPS. The farmers sometimes want to test the soils through KPS but the report of the soil tests do not come in hand in time, only to discourage the farmers. Though the villagers have a number of ponds and some ponds were dug under JRY scheme and some are engaged in pisciculture yet neither panchayat nor the KPS has taken initiative to extend technological knowledge about the same.

The panchayat has failed to develop a market for the local produces be they handloom or agricultural commodities.

Another interesting fact is to notice the change in cropping pattern. At one point of time in Nikunjanagar — one of the villages under Govindapur Mouza—crops like sugar cane, potato and nuts were grown in abundance. Remunerative crop like jute grew well. Though some farmers still grow some jute even today but the majority have shifted to banana plantation instead of jute. The cultivation of sugar cane and nuts have been stopped. Also in Promodnagar, vegetables like brinjal and tomato had good yield although now they are not in usual practice of the farmers.

According to villagers, the farmers have changed the cropping pattern independent of the information from the panchayat and AEO or KPS with an eye to maximise profit. The panchayat also failed to successfully implementing self-employment programmes for women like Dokra. In 1997-98 in Promodnagar and adjacent areas the panchayat selected 100 women as the probable beneficiaries of the scheme. The respective member of the panchayat along with Government experts jointly held some group meetings with these women and diffused the idea involved in the scheme. But the women did not adopt the idea. Because, most of the women in this area are engaged in weaving earning Rs. 50 to 60 per day per head. And the other women selected as probable beneficiaries did not accept the programme as because they were earning more in working as agricultural labourers than they would earn from the envisaged the Dokra scheme. It is also seen that the meetings of Gram Sabha and Gram Sangsad are quite infrequent showing the communication gap between the panchayat members and the villagers. The panchayat is yet to identify the resources properly and to make plans to utilise those. The villagers, who are already paying taxes (around Rs. 5 per household) are inquisitive about the utilisation of the money. The panchayat members have alleged that they have always been facing fund crunch. Often funds earmarked for certain programmes reach panchayat at the fag-end of the financial year creating real problems to utilise the fund in the best way.

Discussion and Findings

The objective conditions for expanding democracy in rural West Bengal were created through land reforms. With the involvement of the people through the panchayats and the administrative support the names of more than 1.4 million share croppers were incorporated in the revenue records till November 1995.* Till November 1994 about 1.26 million acres of agricultural land were vested in the state and about 0.9 million acres were distributed among more than 2 million beneficiaries. On the other hand, in India 4.39 million acres of ceiling surplus agricultural land were distributed among about 4.3 million beneficiaries till 1995. A comparison of total area and percentage of cultivable land shows according to an analysis, 89,000 square kms and 66.52 per cent for West Bengal as against 3.28 million square kms and 54.43 per cent for India. To put it in different way, West Bengal having only 3.58 per cent of the country's cultivable land contributes 20.77 per cent of the total ceiling surplus land distributed in the whole country. It was an achievement of course till 1995. But the second phase of land reforms have not been successful enough because of policy planners' lack of imagination.** In addition to that the panchayats have failed to provide adequate non-land inputs to the beneficiaries of land reforms enabling them to make the best use of their lands. Naturally on one hand, the farmers have lost interest in getting land on the other hand, the panchayats too lack in taking initiatives for identifying as well as distributing the ceiling surplus land.

In Govindapur Mouza though a portion of ceiling surplus land was vested and distributed among a handful of farmers yet there is more land to be identified as ceiling surplus.

The Government of West Bengal since decades had initiated two things. One being the land reforms and the other panchayats to pursue its rural development policy in the state. A Government document says land reform received the top most priority, because the restructuring of agrarian relations was the central objective of the Government ... panchayats and peasant organisation played the most effective roles in implementing this programmes (land reform)***

---

* Panchayati Raj Update, Institute of Social Sciences, May 1998.

** *Ibid.*

*** Rural development through panchayats the West Bengal Experiences. Information and Cultural Affairs Developments, Government of West Bengal, Writers' Building, Calcutta, 1996, pp. 8-9.

There is no denying that the Government of West Bengal has a good intention to uplift the condition of the rural people through different poverty alleviation schemes involving the panchayats. There is also no denying that since all the programmes related to either agricultural or rural industries or infrastructure and environmental development are being done through panchayats in recent years, the panchayats too can claim some credits in implementing the policies at least partly. Several researchers have observed the role performance of panchayats in the state in catalysing the developmental programmes and the Government in its several documents has incorporated those favourable findings to boost up its image.

But the question is whether the Government has reached the targeted level of development in long 21 years. In fact the role of panchayats in augmenting the agricultural production is not above question. Scholar like J. Hariss (1993) has argued that the commendable performance of West Bengal is due to neither land reforms nor the panchayats. He attributed the agricultural performance to the Government policies on minor irrigation facilities.

In fact, in order to make land reforms measures effective it is essential to support the measures with a provision of non-land inputs such as irrigation, implements, fertilisers, pesticides and other facilities including infrastructure, credit and marketing. It is found that the Government has failed to provide these non-land inputs effectively.

For example, from the area under study it is found that the people are not getting enough assistance from the panchayats in acquiring loans and other non-land inputs in time, barring the irrigation. A constraint on part of the panchayat is again the financial crisis. In 1997-98 the panchayat received Rs. 1.5 lakhs in JRY programme which included development of forestry, donation to intelligent students, pond digging, road building etc. That money had to be distributed among 18 villages. Naturally, none of the villages could effectively use money to build up assets.

As for loans, the panchayat members, responsible for identifying the beneficiaries and recommending them to bank, also face some problems from the loan takers. In Gobindapur Mouza since 1996, a number of farmers have taken loans. But majority of them have not yet repaid single installment of the loans thus leading the entire system into trouble. Because without the financial assistance from bank, it is impossible for the farmers to opt for modern agricultural technology. Since the loans are not being repaid the banks have decided not to provide any loan to other farmers in concerned area. Also the panchayat members who earlier recommended the names for loans have lost their faces and now they are unable to recommend any other name. As a result, the relation between the panchayat members and the villages are becoming cold since the farmers are not getting any real assistance from them.

The farmers who have changed their cropping pattern or those who have adopted pisiculture do not also depend on the panchayat for getting better information about the practices they have adopted. They did it on their own. They do not get the inputs and information for the practices they have adopted from the AEO too. Because, the hands of AEO are tied. He is not also possessing the required inputs and technological know-how about the same. So, the adopters depend mainly on their personal sources. It clearly reveals the shortcomings of the disseminating agencies like panchayat and Agricultural Extension Office.

There is no denying that the panchayats are not getting enough funds required for all-round development. However, the utilisation of funds whatever small it be is not above question.

But what is surprising to note is the communication gap between the panchayat functionary and the end users and lack of proper planning at the grass-root levels. For instance, though the farmers have changed their cropping patterns abandoning growing jute and resorting to orchards (Banana Plantation) about four years back, the panchayat even today has not made a critical evaluation of this process and plan accordingly to provide better support to the farmers and planters.

There is also a problem of identifying the local resources as desired by the Government to make the PR system more and more self-reliant. It is found that the panchayat members do not exactly know how to identify the resources and plan with them accordingly at the local level.

There is also a problem of awareness among the panchayat members. Many of them do not know about all the programmes initiated by the Government barring a few popular once like JRY, IRDP, ICDS etc. As they lack in knowledge about both the

Government programmes and the changing scenario of the village, very often they make mistakes in selecting the beneficiaries too. The rejection of the Dokra programme by the women in Gobindapur Mouza is a vivid example of these.

The Government itself admits that due to weak financial resources the institution of panchayats have failed to live upto the expectation. As it is claimed by the Government that panchayats are playing a very useful catalyst role in raising local contribution and unleashing mass initiative for undertaking such public works as construction of small bridges, and digging small canals for extending irrigation facilities etc., it some times appears that panchayats are working more on general rural development programmes than imparting new ideas in technological innovation in agricultural sector.

In summary, it has been observed that though the PR system has been running in the state for long 21 years and the state Government has a good intention to make the system effective unit of decentralised power and planning for the upgradation of mass living on agriculture, yet the farmers in some parts of the state is bereft of the fruits of the system. It is mainly due to four reasons: communication gap between the Government officials and the panchayat members as well as between the panchayat members end users; lack of awareness among the panchayat members; lack of willingness and initiative among the panchayat members and paucity of funds.

It is felt that to make the panchayats truly units of Self-Government more training should be imparted on their members so that they cannot only identify the real needs of the villagers, farmers in particular, but also identify the resources available at local level, plan with those and implement successfully involving the end users. In this process both the institution of panchayats and the grass-root level users would find interest in innovating new ideas to develop their own socio-economic and cultural environment thus fulfilling ultimately the plans and policies of the State Government. Otherwise the enthusiasm with which the panchayats were instituted 21 years back would fade away soon and the units of the Self- Government would be engrossed simply in some routine work like JRY fixation *sans* creativity.

References

Samanta, R.K., 1997, *Socio-Cultural and Psychological Constraints in Technology Transfer for Agricultural Development in North East Asia, India*, Monograph.

Dasgupta, Satadal, 1989, *Diffusion of Agricultural Innovations in Villages of India*, Wiley Eastern Limited, New Delhi.

Ray, Debabrata, 1998, *Psychological Characteristics of the Panchayat Members and Their Role Performance in Kurukshetra*, March.

——, 1998, *Panchayati Raj Update*, Institute of Social Sciences, May.

——, 1998, *Ibid.*

——, 1996, Rural Development Through Panchayats the West Bengal Experiences, Information and Cultural Affairs Developments, Government of West Bengal, Writers' Building, Calcutta, pp. 8-9.

Hariss, John, 1993, 'What is Happening in Rural West Bengal?' Agrarian Reform, Growth and Redistribution, *EPW*, Vol. XXII, No. 27.

CHAPTER 10

Inequality Re-examined

Sumita Bajpai

Evaluation of development with the embracement of sensitive ethics is the essence of Amartya Sen's approach to economic development. Sen always wanted to establish the fact that economy centres the functional status of the society. All the realities of one's existence in respect to the society is very important to mark the developmental index. So, the principles of morality is essential to analyse economic policies. Market economy has also been framed with humanity by him. He has tried to graph the essential commodities and social stress, balanced in a democratic environment. He strongly believe that new economic policies must co-ordinate with the creation of new income generating corners for the upliftment of poor. Analysis of poverty with the reflections of social choice is an important contribution of him. He has pointed that even the important market policies cannot eradicate the hungers. The level of primary education, health, inequality of domain along with gender discrimination are the important factors behind one's capability and so also development. He has stressed on the education of women as this factor alone can improve familial health, nutritional status and educational level of children. It can also check population growth. Inequality of women's education is the reflection of the disbalanced society of India. Almost all the South Asian countries bear the pain of malnourished and illiterate women who enjoy all the disadvantages of life for male superiority. The pursuit of the interests of male persons of the family unjustly prevails over the common good and inevitably sow the seeds of instability in familial life.

Experience of Samata Vigyan Utsav

Paschim Banga Vigyan Mancha (PBVM) is one of the leading NGOs engaged in People Science Movement in India. During the celebration of its first decade (1997), the women's sub-committee conceived a 'Samata Vigyan Utsav' for the scientific motivation campaign against gender discrimination and also for self-reliance. The scheme of this Samata Vigyan Utsav concerns the way major changes have affected women's position interacting with the pre-existing social structure (women and society). It opined the science activists to find out whether traditional patriarchal structure with capitalistic development is hampering the status of women. The science activists intervened with the women of middle and lower class to reveal the basic lines of social changes that have occurred in last few decades and also the major impact that have fallen on women. The orientation camps or 'Samata melas' helped the science activists to know the experiences of the participating women on life and society. So, this programme provided approximate answers to the question of the women's liberation as a part of women's studies in various localities of the state. A specially designed open questionnaire session helped to get information in detail. Education, health, superstition, value-education, legal literacy and self-reliance were the intervening issue in the action phase of Samata. In Indian context, the dominant approach has been found to be liberal feminism, where any sort of action organised consider the existing structures for granted. Non-development of aggressive individualism might prove functional in the over all conditions of deprivation.

It is true that the largest number of poor women live in Asia with nearly 48 per cent of them in India alone. Women here live in sub-human conditions limited by malnutrition, illiteracy, disease, high infant mortality, low life expectancy, inadequate health care and access to sanitation beneath social decency. Women from all social classes, cultures and races are victims of abuse of their human rights. Women often talk among themselves including their daughters of the suffering a female child would have to undergo. An aversion for a female baby is created in the girls from young age. Here, women act as their own enemies. Economic deprivation and educational backwardness are the prime reasons. In the present status, however, slightly deviated and good picture is not at all absent but rare in some village areas. Positive land-reform and a touch of literacy movement has abled the rural ladies to become a part of human resource. Panchayati Raj with the active participation of women is now a reality. It is a good experience of the science activists that many of the rural ladies have shaded off some of their inherited superstitions whereas the women of urban slums have adopted new and modernised superstitions in their limited life style.

On the Issue of Education

Post-literacy movement expressed education of women with a focus as well as convergence of various experiences for the learner as they are given opportunities to interact. The 'Samata' activity viewed to equip women with the ability to analyse and assess their situation and gain the courage to change it. It decided equality in knowledge, power and also the abolition of gender as an oppressed cultural reality.

Prevalence of dowry system, to stay permanently in husband's house are the prime reasons that persons are generally not interested to pay more for education of daughters. It has also come out from discussions that an educated lady has to be married to a more educated person which cost more dowry. However, a few urban slum ladies have now considered education of their daughters as an important task to care about so that the girls can fight desertion. Widow or deserted ladies opined that marriage cannot fetch security but education can ensure a job. Opinions are of varied nature and it is clear that ladies have now changed from the past concepts to be just a machine to give birth to babies. Economic deprivation lies as a good factor to be gender biased but not always. Family atmosphere is also a crucial factor for education.

Health and Environment

Whether motherhood blooms a woman or not was questioned to all the participants of Samata melas and we got the answer 'yes.' Most of the ladies even disagreed on the point of 'adopted child.' It was also remarked that a 'son' is necessary for the continuity of 'Bansh' and Hindus told that only a son has the right to do necessary things in funeral ceremony of a person.

22 years old Lakshmi is a mother of two girls and rejects the advice of health workers for family planning. Rajia is 29 years old, has three daughters and still like to has a son. Sakila bibi 33 years old, a mother of two sons and two daughters explained that she

cannot accept the family planning methods for religious bars. Sobha and Sabnam, both are 22 years old, a mother of one child are using oral contraceptives and their husbands are unaware about the fact. Sudha and Rosenara are 25 years, a mother of two sons and have aborted twice with the consent of their husbands. This sort of mosaic picture is very common nowadays, in both urban slums and rural areas. So, the development of infrastructure no doubt, has changed the access to health facilities by the younger ones. Where as, a few are guided by social taboos.

The Medical Termination of Pregnancy Act allows a woman to abort but this right has not been equated to a Fundamental Right. Female foeticide has become so much dangerous feature of these days and striking fact is that the womb is actually controlled by the husband in most of the cases. Sociologists are raising the question of legal ethics of whether the right for abortion be elevated to fundamental rights or not.

The low nutritional status of female infants and children cannot be explained on the basis of poverty alone. The nutritional disparities between male and female continues even after childhood. The calorie intake of son and daughter in India is less than required but the difference is more in case of daughters than sons. Stillbirth and maternal death is associated with anaemia in most of the cases. The health of an woman is not a matter of concern unless she is pregnant or lactating. Particularly the growing girls are neglected by the Government policies as well as the society as a whole. There is a direct relation between female literacy rates and low mortality rates among the mothers. The age of marriage of a girl has been declared to be 18. But rural areas as well as urban slums still show 17-19 years old mothers. Pregnant ladies have to continue their daily duties without improvement of diet. Health personnel (CUDP/IRDP/ICDS) are engaged in improving prenatal and natal cares of the ladies of lower economic level as well as the children. Increased periphery of infrastructure has no doubt increased the basic needs of women but at the same time presence of affinity for conventional methods are the cases who lack information in detail. Recognition of own's sexual and gender sensitive preventive health information should be produced.

Facilities for toilets, drainage of water, clearing of streets and waste disposal must be created in both urban slums and villages. Active involvement of women in decision-making at all levels is essential and at the same time more data is essential to know the impact of environmental policies on women.

Legal Literacy

More and more women are participating in power, structures and decision-making, they are eager to know their rights. Non-discrimination in law and practice are the slogan of the women of both urban and rural areas. Literacy campaign has created a kind of unhappiness among the elected members of panchayat women as they disagree to implement everything by the order of male members rather they think among themselves for the real betterment of area concerned. So, power tastes bitter to atleast some panchayat women. Unfair deal to women has evoked strong reactions within the women wings of all political parties. Democracy is becoming meaningless in the traditional societies of our country without full involvement of women.

Superstition

Poverty, illiteracy and lack of information of the infrastructure are the prime reasons behind superstition. Interesting observation is that women of Panchayat areas have shown more advanced and polished mentality than urban ladies. Different types of occult science practises have been found in urban slums, whereas, the rural ladies are trying to fight against many such beliefs.

Religious biasness has evidenced the community affiliation to triumph over gender consciousness. The success of women's wings of communal parties is the result of a very critical strategy. Through agitations and campaigns they first raised the women's issues but actually motivated the ladies with the fragrance of religion for garnering support of these vital sections of the society. The political influence of some communal groups is really dangerous and extends to the very highest realms of secular power throughout the world as well as in India. Intellectual exploitations within wrong philosophical discourse is narrowing human relations more in the urban slums than the rural counterparts. Rural ladies have to work more than the women of urban slums. They have to look after their families as well as to work with their husbands in fields during sowing or harvesting. More poor ladies work in fields during cultivation on daily wage basis. These ladies pay little attention to the words of the elites.

Self-Reliance

Small scale projects of women are gradually disintegrating in the urban areas along with globalisation. Ladies here prefer to work on daily wage or even as household maids. Middle class young girls are doing tuitions to earn. But DWCRA has no doubt improved the mentality as well as economy of rural ladies. The IPP-VIII programmes of CMDA are trying to reach the access of technology for home based productions. The recent Swarno-Jayanti Rojgar Yojana is being implemented but not in a real fair way. Only 2-5 per cent of the trained ladies show knack to start something by own accord through loans. Repayment of loan was poor but now has improved somehow.

Social Choice: Present Status

It is true that advent of literacy has opened new avenues for girls and new life styles are also found in the big cities of our country. Urban slums are showing rapid changes in their daily life than the rural part of the country. Young couples are trying to overcome the poverty level by dual earning. They are sending their children to schools. Particular knack for professional courses are increasing among the teenagers. Care for overall academic life has increased. At the same time a tune of dissatisfaction can also be marked among the middle aged and aged persons. Their dolorous outlook is due to the lack of perfect upbringing of children and also for value education.

Rural girls are coming more and more in media by their remarkable ability for sports, performing art and also a few girls in academics. Middle aged ladies are highly sensitive for the establishment of their girls. Ladies engaged in DWCRA are also gradually becoming keen with social structure and its changes. They are thinking for various reforms in their life style, of course with a dressing of morality which is not a common picture of the urban slums of these days. Political interventions can be a factor of it. The urban slums are getting exploited by the simple commodities of life. So, the level of education and economy cannot bring the expected changes. So many families of the urban slums now possess a Television set at the cost of the house lady to act as house maid to extra one or two families. Those economically stable families are again interacting in the girls to enter the higher secondary level but prefer to arrange a marriage. In the same area a few widows or deserted ladies are trying hard to earn more to get her children educated at least upto the graduation level. These choice between consumerism and development of resource is really difficult to analyse for uneven information. Adequate social support will open up option and the future will tell whether these option value is positive or negative.

CHAPTER 11

Problems of Primary Education and Economic Development in India

Surendranath Banerjee

In a recent Press conference in our national capital the Nobel Laureate Prof. Amartya Sen opined that right to Primary education in India to be recognised as one of the fundamental rights of the Indian citizen for which necessary amendments to the Constitution to be made immediately. But the Indian Constitution has enunciated the following directive principle of State policy regarding the universalisation of elementary education (UEE): "The State shall endeavour to provide within a period of ten years from the commencement of the Constitution for free and compulsory education for all children irrespective of sex, caste, creed and economic status until they complete the age of 14 years" (Article 45). If all the things were gone right, universalisation was to have been achieved by 1960. But almost fifty years after the commencement of our Constitution, we are still nowhere near the goal of universalisation of Primary education even. But, since 1950 determined efforts have been made towards the achievement of this goal. Over the years there has been a considerable progress in the spread of educational institutions. According to the latest report available in 1986, 80.33 per cent of the rural population had Primary schools (Class I-V) within their habitation and 94.45 per cent of the population had such schools within a walking distance of 1 km. The number of Primary schools increased from 2. 10 lakhs in 1950-51 to 6. 10 lakhs in 1997-98, with an estimated value of 3 times increase since 1950-5 1. The gross enrolment ratio of 6-1 1 years age group increased from 42.6 per cent in 1950-51 to 89.7 per cent in 1997-98. Simultaneously, drop-out rates continue to be significant, retention of children in schools is low and wastage considerable. Though there is a decreasing trend in drop-outs since 1960-61, when such rates were 64.9 per cent for Primary (Classes I-V) and 78.3 per cent for Elementary (Classes I-VIII), which becomes 39.58 per cent for Primary and 54.14 per cent for Upper primary classes during the year 1997-98. Still the figures are alarming as enrolment by itself is of little importance if children do not continue beyond one year, many of them not seeing the school for more than a few days (Selected Educational Statistics, 1999).

In his famous article "Education and Economic Growth" published in *The Statesman* dated 26 August 1964 (republished on 19 October 1998) he referred to a study of Professors Harbison and Myers where they classified 75 countries in the world in four groups according to their 'level of human resource development' — 'Under developed,' 'Partially developed,' 'Semi advanced' and 'Advanced.' In this classification India was put flatteringly in the 'semi-advanced' group, in the company of such countries as Italy, Poland, Czechoslovakia and Norway. Though in terms of income per head India was much behind every other country in that group. It was only possible, because Harbison's and Myer's method of classification was based on weighted index of the enrolment ratios for secondary and higher education but their exercise did serve the purpose of pointing out that in the development of secondary and higher education we are considerably ahead of other poor countries. But this development of education cannot really play a very creative part in Indian economic advance because we are already ahead of other underdeveloped countries in this respect though behind them in other fields.

Prof. Sen also opined in this article "Harbison and Myers chose to construct their indices by taking secondary and higher education, but if they had taken Primary education, they would have placed in India in a lower group. Not only is our literacy rate one of the lowest in the world, our current effort towards reducing this gap is still far from satisfactory. Though the figures of the Ministry of Education, Government of India suggest that by 1960-61, the gross enrolment ratio was 62 per cent and the ratio is supposed to be somewhat higher now. These are low figures, because unless the ratio comes closer to 100 per cent, we cannot really expect to have universal literacy for many decades. Besides, the official figures seem to overstate our achievements, and other sources put the enrolment ratio much lower. Since the official figures are collected from sources that have some interest in overstating the enrolment ratio (Government grants to schools depend on enrolment), there is a systematic bias introduced in the official figures. So while the situation represented by the official figures is depressing enough, the actual position seems to be even worse. The sharp contrast between our achievements in the field of higher education and our poverty in the field of elementary education is extremely significant in the context of India's economic performance. Behind our overall economic growth of around three and a half per cent lies a rate of growth of industries of well over seven per cent. . . . (*The Statesman,* 1964)

Regarding this disparity between the achievements in higher education and primary education, Prof. Sen also criticised the report on the National Education Commission of 1967 (Kothari Commission) where more allotment of National Fund was recommended for higher education in place of Primary or Elementary education. In his famous Lal Bahadur Shastri Memorial Lecture (1970) — "Aspects of Indian Education," he told that nation should provide more fund for the sake of Primary education, which has been neglected so far. The same thing he repeated during his meeting with the Prime Minister of India after getting his Nobel Prize.

The continued failure since independence to fulfil the constitutional directive of providing education to all children upto the age of 14 years is an unrelented reality. Undoubtedly this problem qualifies for being ranked as the most fundamental problem of our educational system. More than half of all children within this age group of 6-14 years and two-thirds of the girls are outside the ambit of education. There should be a frank admission, without any hesitation, of these facts so that an honest analysis of the causes of the problem may be chosen. The focus of the various strategies adopted so far to bring all children into schools has been on the factors which lie within the educational system. This is equally true of the National Policy on Education and its Programme of Action. The socio-economic and cultural factors have played little role in educational planning. This approach to universalisation ignores the hard social realities. For instance, according to an official report, more than 4.5 crores of children, constituting one-fourth of the schoolgoing age-group are engaged in child labour, a majority of whom face brutal work conditions in both the organised and unorganised sectors. The issues of social justice with respect to educationally backward sections of society and gender bias rooted in the Patriarchal Indian Society are some of the other significant factors that have a major bearing upon participation of children in education. So, let us overview the core aspects of the major issues relating to the problem of Universalisation.

Educational Institutions

According to the latest educational statistics available from the Government of India, there has been considerable progress in the spread of educational institutions during the period 1950-51 to 1997-98. This is evident from the Table 11.1 and Figure 11.1 below:

Table 11.1
Growth of Recognised Educational Institutions Since 1951

Years	*Primary*	*Upper Primary*	*High/Hr. Sec/Inter Pre. Jr. Colleges*	*Colleges for Gen. Education*	*Colleges for Prof. Education*	*Universities*
1950-51	209671	13596	7416	370	208	27
1955-56	278135	21730	10838	466	218	31
1960-61	330399	49663	17329	967	852	45
1965-66	391064	75798	27614	1536	770	64
1970-71	408378	90621	37051	2285	992	82
1975-76	454270	106571	43054	3667	**3276	101
1980-81	494503	118555	51573	3421	**3542	110
1985-86	528872	134846	65837	4067	**1533	126
1990-91	560935	151456	79796	4862	886	184
1991-92	566744	155926	82576	5058	950	@196
1992-93	572541	153921	84076	5334	989	@207
1993-94	572923	155707	88411	5639	1125	@213
1994-95*	581305	163605	92252	6089	1230	@219
1995-96*	590421	171216	98134	6569	1354	@226
1996-97*	598354	176772	102183	6759	1770	@228
1997-98*	610763	185506	107100	7199	2075	@229

* Provisional.
** Includes Institutions for Post-Matric courses.
@ Includes Deemed Universities and Institutions of National Importance.
Source: Selected Educational Statistics, 1997-98.

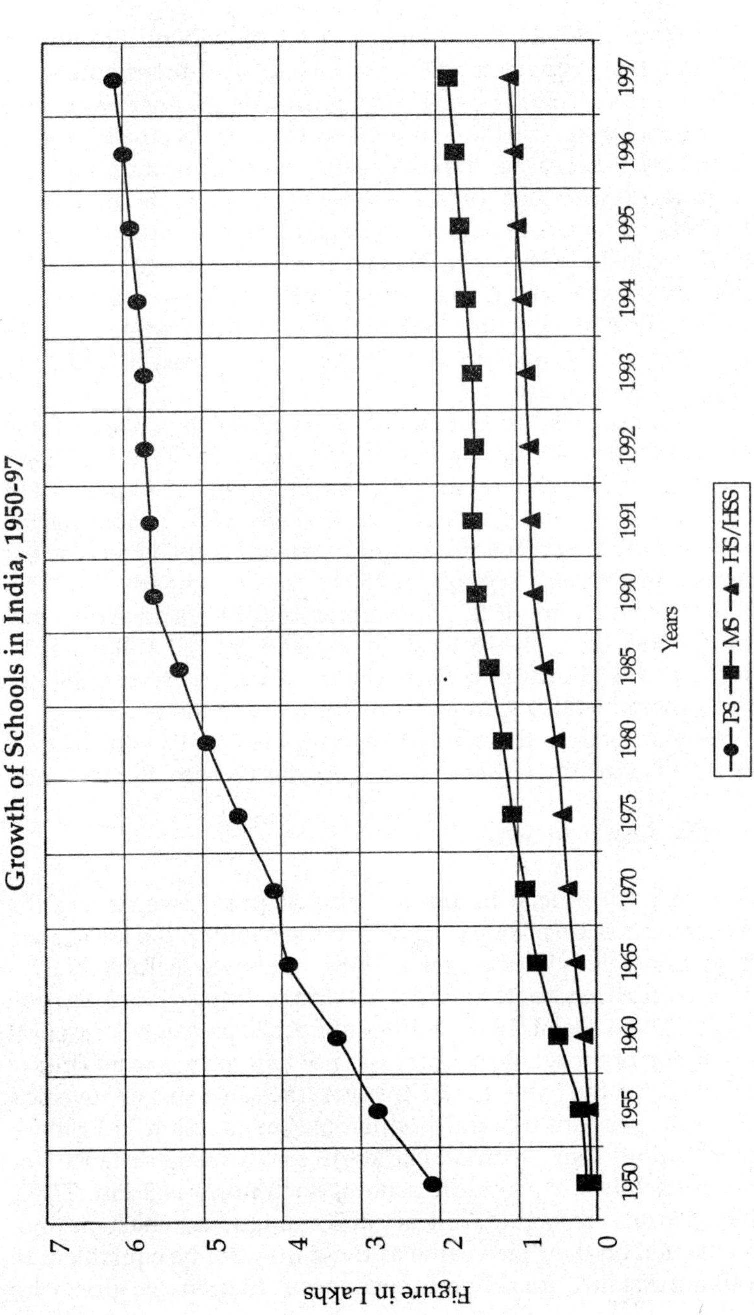
Growth of Schools in India, 1950-97
Figure in Lakhs
0
1
2
3
4
5
6
7
1950
1955
1960
1965
1970
1975
1980
1985
1990
1991
1992
1993
1994
1995
1996
1997
Years
PS
MS
HS/HSS

Figure 11.1

From Table 11.1 and Figure 11.1 it is evident that during 1997-98 while Primary schools increased by 2.91 times only since 1950-51, Upper Primary schools and Secondary/Higher Secondary schools increased by 13.65 and 14.45 times respectively during this period. Whereas for the college for general education, colleges for professional education and Universities such rate of increase are 19.45, 9.97 and 8.48 times respectively. From these figures it can be safely concluded how the Primary education has been neglected in our country during the last fifty years after independence.

Now let us consider the number of Primary schools and its percentage increase in different States of the country as shown in Table 11.2 and Figure 11.2.

As no latest official figure (upto 1997-98) available Table 11.2 and Figure 11.2 have shown the figures upto 1992-93, which reveals that in the country as a whole there is only 13.68 per cent of increase in Primary schools in 1992-93 since 1981-82. Whereas for the States and Union Territories, the highest per cent increase in the number of Primary schools is found in Chandigarh (64.71%), followed by Sikkim (46.39%), Mizoram (43.09%) and Arunachal Pradesh (33.22%) and lowest in Punjab (0.66%) followed by Meghalaya (2.86%) during this period. The most interesting feature is that there are also simultaneous decrease in the percentage of Primary schools in the states like Haryana (-0.51%) and Kerala (-0.41%). Interestingly Kerala is famous for its high literacy rate.

Physical Access to School

As no current official figure available at present regarding the physical access to primary schools in the country, the latest such figure available is for the year 1986-87, as shown in Table 11.3.

According to the Fifth All India Educational Survey (NCERT, New Delhi, 1992) in 1986, almost 20 per cent of the rural population of the whole country did not have access to a Primary school within the habitation. However, the same survey revealed that 94.45 per cent of rural population has access to a Primary school within 1 km — an official norm for 'walking distance' for Primary schools. For middle schools such norm is 3 km. These official norms are vague, arbitrary and ambiguous, which may not be accepted on their face value as these may not be equivalent to 'walking distance' for different sections of children *e.g.*, girls, who

Table 11.2
Percentage Increase in the Number of Primary Schools 1992-93 Over 1981-82

States/Union Territories	*Primary Schools*		
	1981-82	*1992-93*	*% Change*
India	503763	572541	13.68
Andhra Pradesh	40769	50201	23.14
Arunachal Pradesh	879	1171	33.22
Assam	21729	28876	32.89
Bihar	50940	53292	4.62
Goa	975	1033	5.95
Gujarat	11396	14448	26.78
Haryana	4940	4915	(-)0.51
Himachal Pradesh	6227	7548	21.21
Jammu & Kashmir	7525	9438	25.42
Karnataka	22439	23600	5.17
Kerala	6807	6779	(-)0.41
Madhya Pradesh	60874	68949	13.27
Maharashtra	36098	41759	15.68
Manipur	2860	3180	11.19
Meghalaya	4054	4170	2.86
Mizoram	745	1066	43.09
Nagaland	1184	1305	10.22
Orissa	36193	41204	13.85
Punjab	12382	12464	0.66
Rajasthan	23219	32133	38.39
Sikkim	360	527	46.39
Tamil Nadu	27767	30098	8.39
Tripura	1792	2065	15.23
Uttar Pradesh	71602	78804	10.06
West Bengal	47626	50827	6.72
Andaman & Nicobar Is.	180	188	4.44
Chandigarh	34	56	64.71
Dadra & Nagar Haveli	121	125	3.31
Daman & Diu	—	49	—
Delhi	1738	1911	9.95
Lakshadweep	18	19	5.56
Pondicherry	290	341	17.59

Daman & Diu was part of Goa, Daman & Diu Union Territory in 1981-82.

Sources: 1. Selected Educational Statistics, 1992-93, MHRD, Department of Education, New Delhi, 1993.

2. Education in India, 1981-82, MHRD, Department of Education, New Delhi.

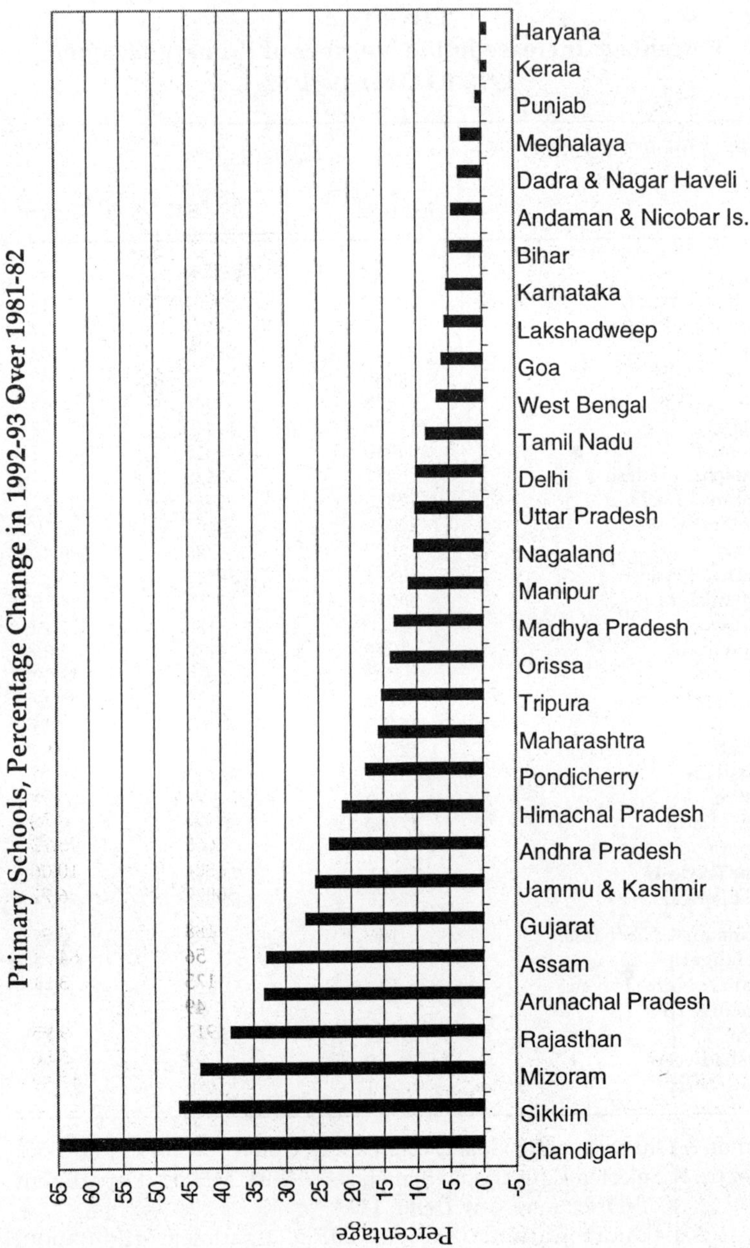
Primary Schools, Percentage Change in 1992-93 Over 1981-82
Haryana
Kerala
Punjab
Meghalaya
Dadra & Nagar Haveli
Andaman & Nicobar Is.
Bihar
Karnataka
Lakshadweep
Goa
West Bengal
Tamil Nadu
Delhi
Uttar Pradesh
Nagaland
Manipur
Madhya Pradesh
Orissa
Tripura
Maharashtra
Pondicherry
Himachal Pradesh
Andhra Pradesh
Jammu & Kashmir
Gujarat
Assam
Arunachal Pradesh
Rajasthan
Mizoram
Sikkim
Chandigarh
65 60 55 50 45 40 35 30 25 20 15 10 5 0 -5
Percentage

Figure 11.2

Table 11.3
Rural Population With and Without Primary School/Section, 1986

States/Union Territories	*% of Rural Population Served by Primary School/Section at a Distance of*							
	Within the Habitation	*Upto 0.5 km. but not within Habitation*	*0.6 to 1.0 km.*	*Upto 1.0 km.*	*1.1 to 1.5 km.*	*1.6 to 2.0 km.*	*Up to 2.0 km.*	*More than 2 km.*
INDIA	80.38	6.73	7.33	94.45	1.78	2.28	98.51	1.49
Andhra Pradesh	93.29	2.05	1.95	97.30	0.74	0.90	98.95	1.05
Arunachal Pradesh	65.85	2.47	5.03	73.35	0.93	3.42	77.70	22.30
Assam	81.74	5.40	6.43	93.57	3.59	1.83	99.06	0.94
Bihar	78.53	8.99	8.34	95.86	1.65	1.70	99.21	0.79
Goa	57.72	20.23	12.65	90.60	3.41	4.07	98.08	1.92
Gujarat	97.83	0.85	0.76	99.45	0.15	0.20	99.80	0.20
Haryana	96.68	1.62	1.07	99.37	0.15	0.35	99.88	0.12
Himachal Pradesh	46.51	11.39	18.74	76.64	4.73	10.84	92.20	7.80
Jammu & Kashmir	78.23	5.42	7.05	90.70	2.39	3.82	96.92	3.08
Karnataka	92.50	2.03	2.71	97.24	0.93	1.10	99.26	0.74
Kerala	87.67	2.59	4.13	94.39	1.51	2.06	97.96	2.04
Madhya Pradesh	81.51	5.26	6.15	92.92	1.37	3.06	97.34	2.66
Maharashtra	92.42	3.28	2.25	97.95	0.51	0.88	99.34	0.66
Manipur	89.97	3.47	3.95	97.39	0.33	0.49	98.21	1.79
Meghalaya	80.87	2.88	5.47	89.32	1.43	3.32	93.97	6.03

(Contd.)

States/Union Territories	% of Rural Population Served by Primary School/Section at a Distance of							
	Within the Habitation	Upto 0.5 km. but not within Habitation	0.6 to 1.0 km.	Upto 1.0 km.	1.1 to 1.5 km.	1.6 to 2.0 km.	Up to 2.0 km.	More than 2 km.
Mizoram	98.05	0.23	0.00	98.28	0.00	0.12	98.40	1.60
Nagaland	98.85	0.24	0.18	99.45	0.06	0.37	99.80	0.12
Orissa	77.08	8.82	6.93	92.83	1.87	2.60	97.30	2.70
Punjab	99.80	2.09	0.71	99.60	0.14	0.18	99.92	0.08
Rajasthan	86.84	1.49	4.57	92.90	0.88	2.90	96.68	3.32
Sikkim	72.13	3.80	7.17	83.10	2.26	7.19	92.55	7.45
Tamil Nadu	83.92	5.80	6.30	96.02	1.22	1.80	99.04	0.96
Tripura	57.04	12.85	14.22	84.11	5.50	5.65	95.26	4.74
Uttar Pradesh	55.69	14.05	18.82	88.56	4.45	5.00	98.01	1.99
West Bengal	79.71	11.47	6.20	97.38	1.07	1.03	99.48	0.52
Andaman & Nicobar Is.	68.41	4.35	10.26	83.02	4.27	3.78	91.07	8.93
Chandigarh	96.92	2.75	0.00	99.67	0.00	0.33	100.00	0.00
Dadra & Nagar Haveli	50.74	14.10	20.35	85.19	3.68	8.95	97.82	2.18
Daman & Diu	77.13	3.75	13.90	94.78	2.59	2.63	100.00	0.00
Delhi	98.06	1.32	0.62	100.00	0.00	0.00	100.00	0.00
Lakshadweep	100.00	0.00	0.00	100.00	0.00	0.00	100.00	0.00
Pondicherry	88.54	6.92	3.56	99.02	0.58	0.26	99.86	0.14

Source: Fifth All India Educational Survey, NCERT, New Delhi, 1992.

are involved in sibling care, domestic chores and other socio-cultural constraints make them engaged in work both within and outside the home. Parental fears at sending girls outside the village particularly with the approach of puberty cannot be dismissed. Girls belonging to SC, ST and other discriminated social groups are particularly vulnerable. In such cases, the distance of 1 km. and 3 km. to the school may be just beyond the threshold which children can cross.

There is also the issue of regional disparity involved with respect to accessibility of Primary schools. Table 11.3 provides state-wise data on this matter. It shows that there is a wide fluctuation with respect to the percentage of rural population having access to a Primary school within habitation. It fluctuates from 50.74 per cent in Dadra and Nagar Haveli to 100 per cent in Lakshadweep followed by 98.06 per cent in Delhi and 98.05 per cent in Mizoram.

Table 11.4
Availability of Primary Schools in Rural Areas

Year	*Total Rural Population (mn.)*	*Total Habitations (000's)*	*% Habitations without a Primary School*	*% of Population unserved by Primary School*	*Total Rural Population unserved (mn.)*
1965	396.6	982	62.02	28.52	113
1973	465.4	953	55.67	23.88	111
1978	509.2	965	53.20	21.47	109
1986	594.5	979	48.64	19.66	117

Source: Fifth All India Educational Survey (NCERT), New Delhi, 1992.

As per availability of Primary schools in rural areas of India as shown in Table 11.4 above, there are almost 49 per cent of the rural habitations with a total population of 11.7 crore which did not have access to a Primary school within the habitation during the year 1986-87. In view of the above facts it can be safely said that the said situation has hardly improved by the current years. So, any strategy to Universalisations of Elementary Education would have to take into account these hard realities.

Infrastructural Facilities in Primary Schools

(A) Type of School Building

Here also as no official data about the type of Primary school building is available for the recent years, the latest such data available for the year 1986-87 is given in Table 11.5.

From Table 11.5 it is revealed that during 1986-87, the primary schools lack even basic infrastructural facilities necessary for better quality of education. During this period about 14 per cent of the primary schools of India did not have any school building at all. Out of which about 8 per cent were located in open space, 5.53 per cent in thatched huts and 0.49 per cent in the tents. Only 56.26 per cent of primary schools all over the country had school buildings pucca; and 13.92 per cent had kachcha school buildings. Among the States/Union Territories only in Daman & Diu and Lakshadweep all the primary schools have pucca buildings followed by 90.91 per cent in Chandigarh, 88.21 per cent in Gujarat and 84.50 per cent in Karnataka. Surprisingly during 1986-87 there were neither any pucca primary school buildings nor any open space primary school in Mizoram. Manipur (2.21%), Tripura (3.58%), Assam (7.58%) and Meghalaya (7.80%) were the other states where there were lowest number of pucca primary school buildings. Maximum number of open space primary school buildings were in Bihar (17.83%) and Uttar Pradesh (17.22%).

(B) Instructional Rooms

The latest official data available from the Fifth All India Educational Survey (NCERT, New Delhi, 1992) the position of primary schools according to instructional rooms during the year 1986-87 is given in Table 11.6.

In India Primary Education consists of classes I-V, so there should be a minimum of five instructional rooms in any primary schools. But from the data as revealed from the Table 11.6 it is found that during 1986-87 there were only 11.25 per cent of primary schools available in the whole country where there were five or more instructional rooms. Among the States/Union Territories

Table 11.5
Primary Schools According to Type of Building, 1986

States/Union Territories	*Percentage of Primary Schools by Type of Building*					
	Pucca	*Partly Pucca*	*Kachha*	*Thatched Huts*	*Tents*	*Open Space*
INDIA	56.26	16.28	13.92	5.53	0.49	7.52
Andhra Pradesh	67.30	8.54	7.91	9.04	0.15	7.06
Arunachal Pradesh	14.92	5.36	15.13	64.60	0.00	0.00
Assam	7.58	29.29	40.59	22.53	0.00	0.00
Bihar	33.11	28.32	13.55	7.06	0.13	17.83
Goa	84.69	9.47	2.22	1.71	1.91	0.00
Gujarat	88.21	2.97	6.51	0.46	0.02	1.83
Haryana	85.85	6.72	0.43	0.02	0.00	6.97
Himachal Pradesh	24.99	17.41	55.66	0.20	0.00	1.74
Jammu & Kashmir	30.18	22.60	42.33	1.38	0.23	3.29
Karnataka	84.50	6.16	6.80	1.26	0.19	1.09
Kerala	69.82	17.22	8.66	4.30	0.00	0.00
Madhya Pradesh	54.38	22.04	12.21	4.11	0.02	7.24
Maharashtra	66.87	12.15	9.31	4.58	5.81	1.28
Manipur	2.21	17.37	49.73	30.69	0.00	0.00
Meghalaya	7.80	18.91	32.91	40.14	0.24	0.00
Mizoram	0.00	57.51	35.32	7.16	0.00	0.00
Nagaland	6.98	35.46	44.74	12.82	0.00	0.00
Orissa	48.47	23.23	17.75	2.81	0.00	7.74

(Contd.)

States/Union Territories	*Percentage of Primary Schools by Type of Building*					
	Pucca	*Partly Pucca*	*Kachha*	*Thatched Huts*	*Tents*	*Open Space*
Punjab	85.24	6.56	1.05	0.20	0.00	6.95
Rajasthan	78.18	6.76	6.56	1.05	0.00	7.56
Sikkim	29.70	31.41	28.42	10.26	0.00	0.21
Tamil Nadu	79.01	12.63	2.37	5.71	0.14	0.15
Tripura	3.58	2.23	80.59	10.07	0.00	3.53
Uttar Pradesh	74.26	5.25	2.38	0.88	0.02	17.22
West Bengal	27.97	28.02	31.85	7.14	0.11	4.91
Andaman & Nicobar Is.	57.63	7.91	7.34	27.12	0.00	0.00
Chandigarh	90.91	6.82	0.00	0.00	0.00	2.27
Dadra & Nagar Haveli	62.10	0.00	37.90	0.00	0.00	0.00
Daman & Diu	100.00	0.00	0.00	0.00	0.00	0.00
Delhi	49.67	48.31	1.69	0.05	0.27	0.00
Lakshadweep	100.00	0.00	0.00	0.00	0.00	0.00
Pondicherry	62.24	5.60	0.29	31.86	0.00	0.00

Source: Fifth All India Educational Survey, NCERT, New Delhi, 1992.

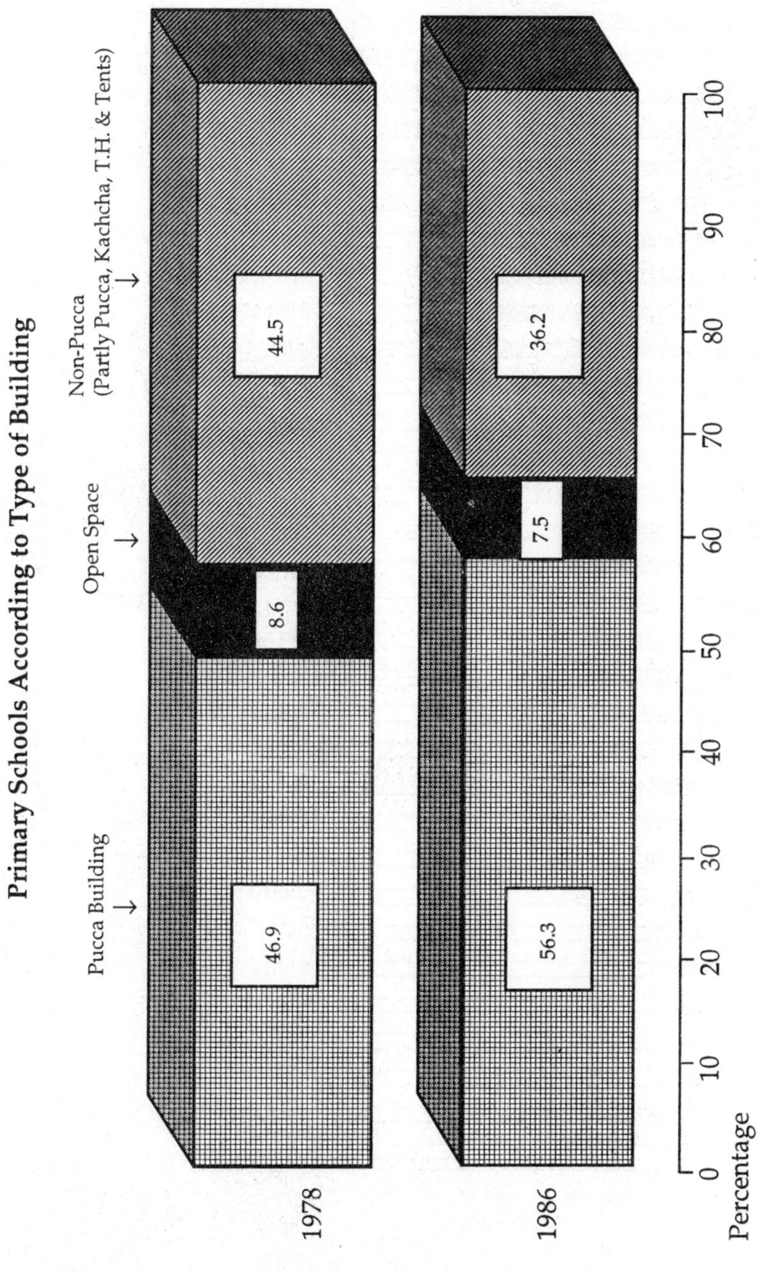
Primary Schools According to Type of Building
Pucca Building
Open Space
Non-Pucca
(Partly Pucca, Kachcha, T.H. & Tents)
1978
46.9
8.6
44.5
1986
56.3
7.5
36.2
0
10
20
30
40
50
60
70
80
90
100
Percentage

Figure 11.3

Primary Schools According to Type of Building, 1986

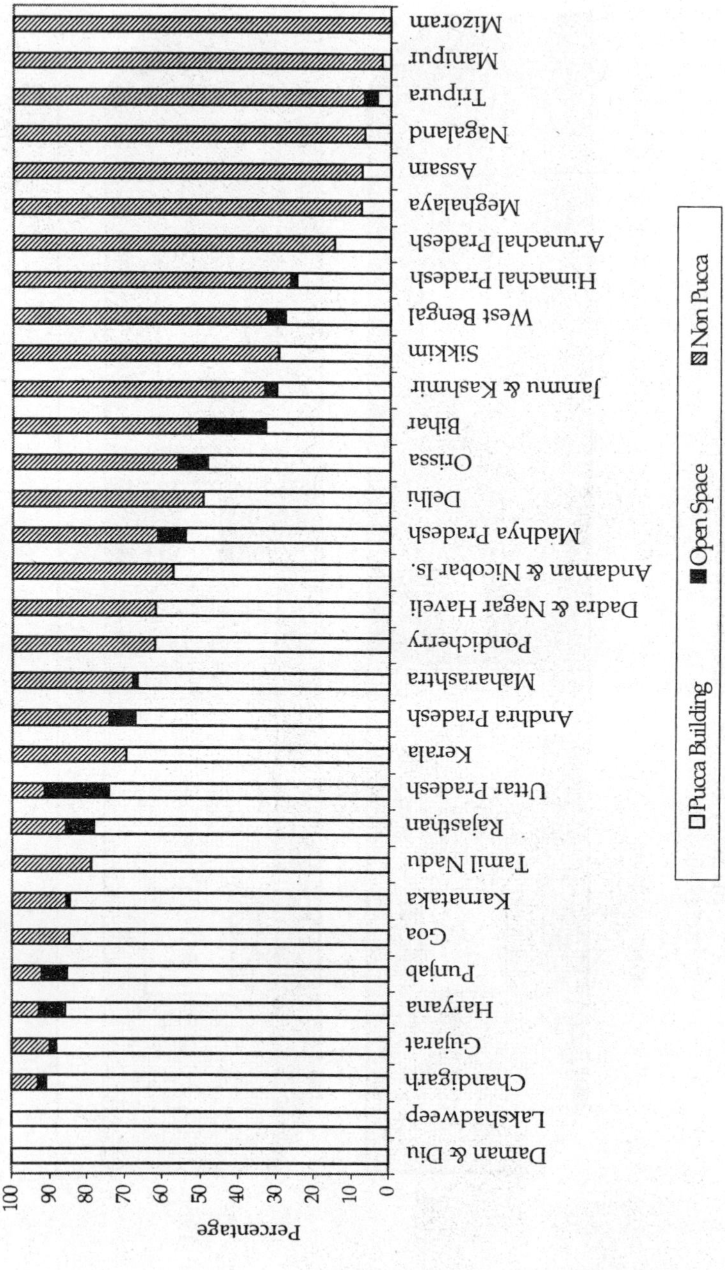

Figure 11.3A

Table 11.6
Primary Schools According to Instructional Rooms, 1986

States/Union Territories	*Percentage of Instructional Rooms*						
	Nil	*One*	*Two*	*Three*	*Four*	*Five*	*More than Five*
INDIA	7.56	34.74	23.95	14.11	8.38	4.72	6.53
Andhra Pradesh	7.18	60.92	17.18	5.95	2.92	2.16	3.68
Arunachal Pradesh	0.00	16.18	32.98	22.69	10.92	8.72	8.51
Assam	0.00	70.44	12.54	5.54	6.84	2.35	2.30
Bihar	17.97	34.89	33.46	8.23	3.66	1.30	0.50
Goa	0.00	36.46	34.34	12.69	6.45	4.03	6.04
Gujarat	2.38	59.70	21.54	5.97	3.99	1.35	5.07
Haryana	2.64	13.28	31.44	17.92	14.97	10.50	16.25
Himachal Pradesh	1.74	23.09	31.03	21.57	11.36	5.52	5.71
Jammu & Kashmir	3.29	43.12	32.19	11.77	6.27	1.51	1.85
Karnataka	2.45	71.08	16.37	3.82	2.64	0.99	2.66
Kerala	0.00	20.06	21.88	13.66	11.09	9.24	24.06
Madhya Pradesh	7.26	26.98	27.57	21.04	7.51	3.77	5.88
Maharashtra	2.70	51.47	18.75	5.38	6.29	3.50	11.89
Manipur	0.00	10.99	19.62	36.27	13.35	9.18	10.59

(Contd.)

States/Union Territories	*Percentage of Instructional Rooms*						
	Nil	*One*	*Two*	*Three*	*Four*	*Five*	*More than Five*
Meghalaya	0.00	67.80	16.06	9.67	3.93	1.54	1.00
Mizoram	0.00	15.12	11.24	14.33	25.47	22.79	11.04
Nagaland	0.00	0.27	4.33	17.77	21.49	22.99	33.16
Orissa	7.74	31.09	29.03	15.74	8.60	4.34	3.46
Punjab	1.99	14.58	34.72	18.90	13.32	8.08	8.41
Rajasthan	7.57	18.36	25.88	20.25	9.90	6.26	11.78
Sikkim	0.43	6.20	29.49	23.50	17.31	7.91	15.17
Tamil Nadu	0.00	37.20	22.65	10.59	6.54	9.80	13.22
Tripura	3.53	24.34	18.21	16.45	9.65	11.78	16.04
Uttar Pradesh	17.22	9.60	24.06	22.39	13.27	6.40	7.06
West Bengal	4.91	26.88	23.01	18.23	15.18	7.43	4.36
Andaman & Nicobar Is.	0.00	16.95	19.21	19.77	19.77	8.47	15.82
Chandigarh	0.00	2.27	6.82	2.27	11.36	13.64	63.64
Dadra & Nagar Haveli	0.00	80.65	13.71	4.03	0.00	1.61	0.00
Daman & Diu	0.00	6.25	21.88	31.25	6.25	0.00	34.38
Delhi	0.16	0.22	2.88	7.24	7.94	10.77	70.78
Lakshadweep	0.00	0.00	0.00	0.00	11.11	0.00	88.89
Pondicherry	0.00	21.24	15.04	10.32	11.50	12.68	29.20

Source: Fifth All India Educational Survey, NCERT, New Delhi, 1992.

Primary Schools According to Instruction Rooms

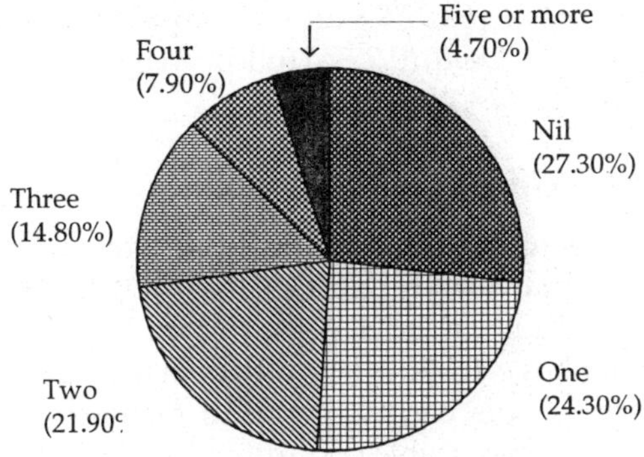

1978

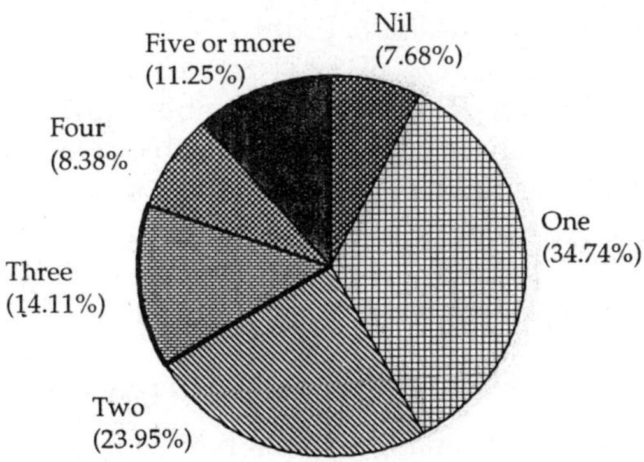

1986

Figure 11.4

highest number of five or more roomed schools were found in Lakshadweep (88.89%) followed by Delhi (81.55%) and Chandigarh (77.28%). On the other hand, lowest number of five or more roomed schools were found in Dadra & Nagar Haveli (1.61%), Bihar (1.80%), Meghalaya (2.54%) and Jammu & Kashmir (3.36%).

According to Table 11.6, during the year 1986-87 in India percentages of primary schools having one, two, three and four instructional rooms were 34.74 per cent, 23.93 per cent, 14.11 per cent and 8.38 per cent respectively. Among the states maximum number of one roomed primary schools were at Dadra & Nagar Haveli (80.65%) followed by Karnataka (71.08%), Assam (70.44%) and Andhra Pradesh (60.92%) and minimum number of such schools were found in Delhi (0.22%) followed by Nagaland (0.27%) and Chandigarh (2.27%).

(C) Playground Facility in Primary Schools

The latest available official data has been taken from the Fifth All India Educational Survey (NCERT, New Delhi, 1992) of 1986-87 and incorporated in Table 11.7 and Figure 11.5.

From the above table it is evident that in India 58.24 per cent of Primary schools had playground facilities out of which only 33 per cent were in usable condition during 1986-87. Among the States and Union Territories the highest number of playground facility available in primary schools during 1986-87 were in Tamil Nadu (86.57%, 60.88% usable), Delhi (79.76%, 61.48% usable), Arunachal Pradesh (79.31%, 60.19% usable), Chandigarh (75%, 70.45% usable), Tripura (75.92%, 48.94% usable), Mizoram (87.66%, 43.38% usable), Haryana (83.15%, 67.42% usable), Gujarat (73.28%, 45.94% usable), Uttar Pradesh (72.80%, 41.12% usable) and West Bengal (70.67%, 39.50% usable). Interestingly Lakshadweep though had 22.22 per cent primary schools with playground facilities but none of them were in usable condition.

(D) Primary Schools Having Various Ancillary Facilities

The number of primary schools having various ancillary facilities *e.g.*, drinking water, urinals, lavatory etc. in India and in different States and Union Territories during the year 1986-87 is given in Table 11.8.

As shown in Table 11.8 during the year 1986-87, among the primary schools all over the country only 47.4 per cent had drinking water facilities, 15.5 per cent with urinals out of which only 5.1 per cent had separate urinals for girls, 6.3 per cent with lavatories out of which only 2.8 per cent had separate lavatories for girl students. What a pity, after forty years of independence 52.6 per cent of the primary schools of our country could not provide the basic need *i.e.*, drinking water to the pupils. The same dismal picture was found in the primary schools of almost all the States and Union Territories excepting Chandigarh, Dadra &

Table 11.7
Availability of Playground Facility in Primary Schools, 1986

States/Union Territories	Schools Having			Percentage of Schools Having	
	Playground Facility	Usable Condition	Total Schools	Playground Facility	Usable Condition
INDIA	307982	174493	528730	58.24	33.00
Andhra Pradesh	24357	11029	44346	54.92	24.87
Arunachal Pradesh	755	573	952	79.31	60.19
Assam	6409	2122	25873	24.77	8.20
Bihar	15168	6105	51377	29.52	11.88
Goa	594	382	993	59.82	38.47
Gujarat	9313	5838	12709	73.28	45.94
Haryana	4032	3269	4849	83.15	67.42
Himachal Pradesh	4430	3313	6904	64.17	47.99
Jammu & Kashmir	3334	1673	7466	44.66	22.41
Karnataka	11712	6448	23023	50.87	28.01
Kerala	3266	2063	6096	53.58	33.84
Madhya Pradesh	36101	21936	64089	56.33	34.23
Maharashtra	27268	17205	38094	71.58	45.16
Manipur	1602	1116	2757	58.11	40.48

(Contd.)

States/Union Territories	*Schools Having*			*Percentage of Schools Having*	
	Playground Facility	*Usable Condition*	*Total Schools*	*Playground Facility*	*Usable Condition*
Meghalaya	2187	1241	3692	59.24	33.61
Mizoram	881	436	1005	87.66	43.38
Nagaland	747	495	1131	66.05	43.77
Orissa	10359	4628	34178	30.31	13.54
Punjab	8786	4544	12838	68.44	35.59
Rajasthan	18563	9447	28103	66.05	33.62
Sikkim	196	164	468	41.88	35.04
Tamil Nadu	25336	17819	29268	86.57	60.88
Tripura	1463	943	1927	75.92	48.94
Uttar Pradesh	55013	31073	75564	72.80	41.12
West Bengal	34246	19142	48456	70.67	39.50
Andaman & Nicobar Is.	77	54	177	43.50	30.51
Chandigarh	33	31	44	75.00	70.45
Dadra & Nagar Haveli	68	60	124	54.84	48.39
Daman & Diu	15	15	32	46.88	46.88
Delhi	1466	1130	1838	79.76	61.48
Lakshadweep	4	0	18	22.22	0.00
Pondicherry	201	199	339	59.29	58.70

Source: Fifth All India Educational Survey, NCERT, New Delhi, 1992.

Availability of Playground Facility in Primary Schools

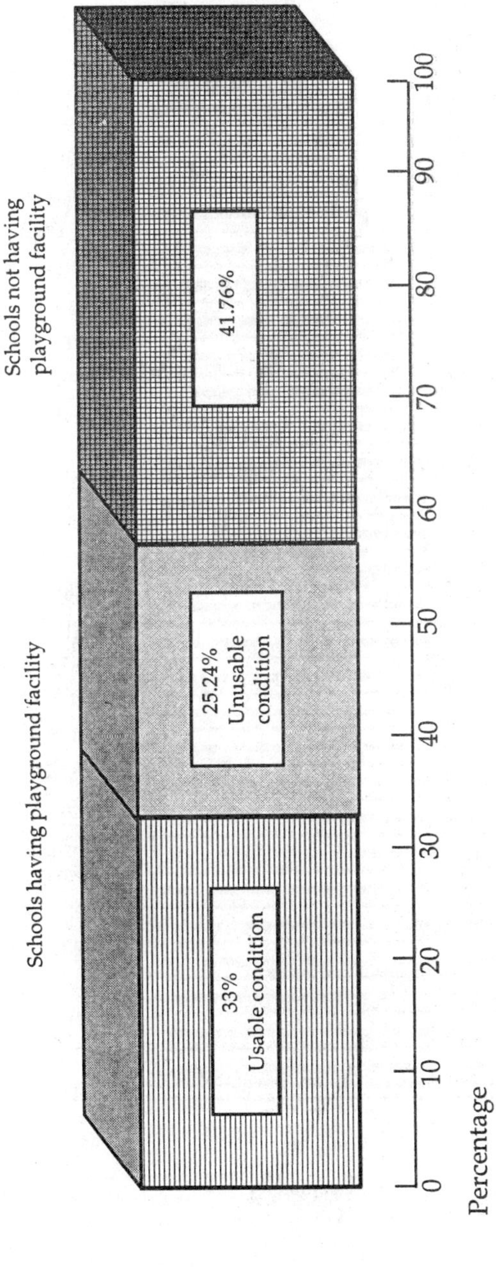

Figure 11.5

Availability of Playground Facility in Primary Schools, 1986

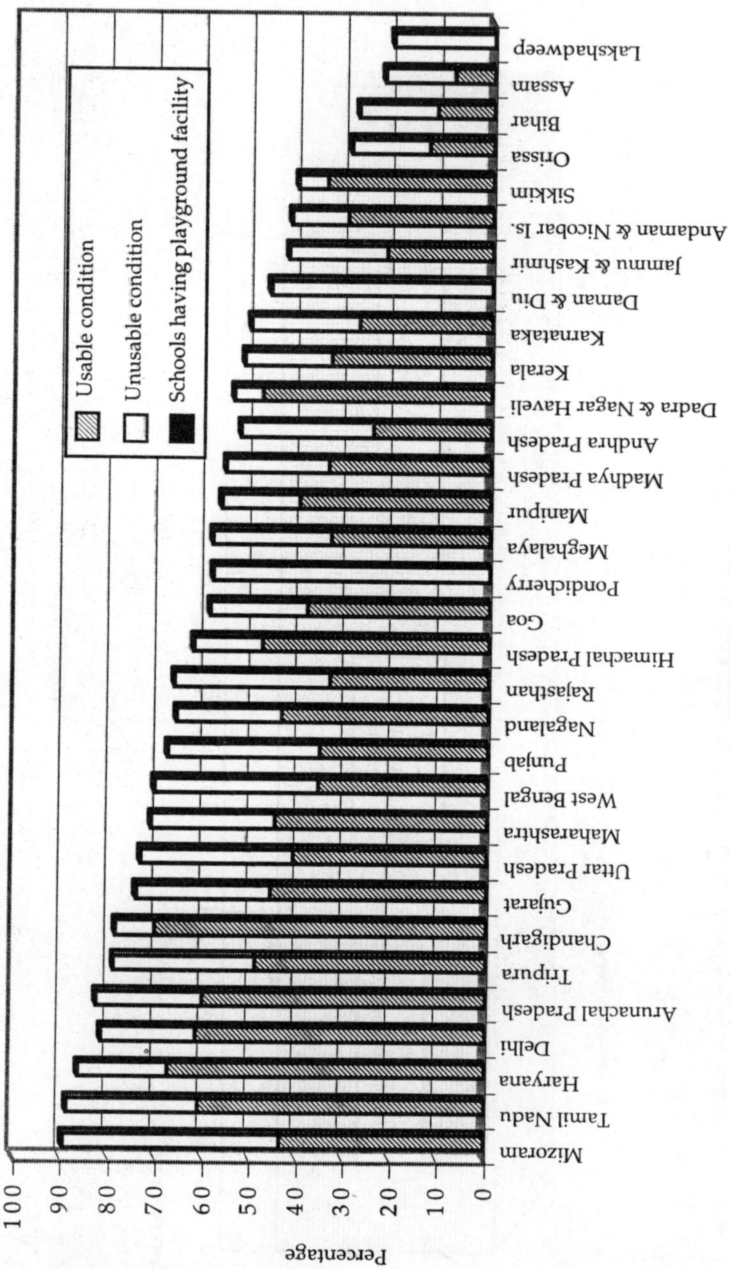

Figure 11.5A

Table 11.8
Primary Schools Having Various Ancillary Facilities, 1986

States/ Union Territories	*Percentage of Schools Having*				
	Drinking Water Facilities	*Urinals*	*Separate Urinals for Girls*	*Lavatory*	*Separate Lavatory for Girls*
INDIA	47.40	15.50	5.10	6.30	2.80
Andhra Pradesh	42.50	10.80	2.10	4.00	1.60
Arunachal Pradesh	49.20	22.90	8.40	9.20	2.40
Assam	15.40	7.20	0.00	6.70	0.00
Bihar	47.20	2.60	0.40	1.80	0.20
Goa	61.70	12.40	4.60	10.50	3.20
Gujarat	56.20	25.40	11.00	8.30	3.10
Haryana	71.30	41.50	18.10	12.60	7.00
Himachal Pradesh	50.30	8.20	5.70	5.90	4.10
Jammu & Kashmir	27.90	5.70	1.80	1.90	0.50
Karnataka	44.60	5.90	1.00	2.70	0.90
Kerala	76.40	65.00	28.70	24.90	7.20
Madhya Pradesh	32.30	10.50	4.40	4.90	2.80
Maharashtra	45.90	17.00	11.80	10.50	8.20
Manipur	25.80	16.90	4.30	5.60	1.10
Meghalaya	11.80	11.90	1.80	1.80	0.40
Mizoram	31.50	50.00	10.80	20.00	4.00
Nagaland	25.00	37.50	11.10	1.90	1.00
Orissa	24.70	6.60	2.00	1.50	0.50
Punjab	90.00	61.70	17.20	14.00	4.80
Rajasthan	52.60	13.60	6.00	6.70	3.30
Sikkim	40.80	18.40	4.70	4.70	1.10
Tamil Nadu	84.60	29.00	10.90	11.20	7.00
Tripura	37.30	13.40	3.60	5.30	1.50
Uttar Pradesh	53.10	14.70	3.20	5.60	2.00
West Bengal	58.70	22.90	4.30	6.00	1.30
Andaman & Nicobar Is.	58.80	39.00	31.10	31.60	24.90
Chandigarh	100.00	86.40	52.30	65.90	52.30
Dadra & Nagar Haveli	100.00	16.10	14.50	12.90	11.30
Daman & Diu	75.00	31.30	15.60	34.40	15.60
Delhi	93.00	92.00	46.10	87.60	45.00
Lakshadweep	50.00	50.00	33.30	44.40	33.30
Pondicherry	76.70	43.40	31.90	36.90	28.00

Source: Fifth All India Educational Survey, NCERT, New Delhi, 1992.

Nagar Haveli, Delhi and Kerala, where the pictures were somewhat better.

(E) Availability of Blackboard in Primary Schools

Percentages of Primary schools having blackboard facilities during the year 1986-87 as per Fifth All India Educational Survey, by NCERT are incorporated in Table 11.9 and Figure 11.6.

As revealed in Table 11.9, 38.50 per cent Primary schools all over the country were running without even a blackboard in the classroom. Out of remaining 61.50 per cent Primary schools of the country only 55.41 per cent schools had blackboards in usable condition. Among the States and Union Territories Bihar was in top position with 61.80 per cent of Primary schools without having any blackboard, followed by Assam (47.42%), Uttar Pradesh (47.29%), Andhra Pradesh (45.92%), Tripura (45.87%), Orissa (43.96%) and Karnataka (42.21%). Only in Lakshadweep while all the Primary schools had the blackboard facilities with usable condition, followed by Delhi (95.96%), Chandigarh (94.20%), Mizoram (92.72%), Daman & Diu (92.27%), Sikkim (92%) and Kerala (91.77%) had usable blackboards.

So, from the above facts and figures, it may be concluded that the Primary schools of the whole country lack even the basic infrastructural facilities necessary for better quality of education. Though no official data available in this connection for the current years, from the other related studies it may be safely concluded that the said situation has not improved even after fifty years of independence.

Primary Schools by Management

Here also we have to depend upon the Fifth All India Educational Survey, by NCERT, 1992, and which was the only latest available official data, which showing the Primary schools by Management of the States, Union Territories and country as a whole as shown in Table 11.10.

From Table 11.10 it is revealed that during 1986-87, only 41.31 per cent of Primary schools all over the country were managed directly by the Government, whereas 50 per cent of the States and Union Territories had either all or more than 90 per cent

Table 11.9
Availability of Blackboard in Primary Schools/Sections, 1986

States/UTs	Total No. of Primary Section	Percentage of Schools/ Working Sections		
		No Blackboard	Usable Black-board	Unusable Black-board
INDIA	2658220	38.50	55.41	6.10
Andhra Pradesh	212777	45.92	48.51	5.57
Arunachal Pradesh	4511	36.93	54.47	8.60
Assam	112037	47.42	40.03	12.54
Bihar	262791	61.80	31.50	6.70
Goa	4587	30.76	63.66	5.58
Gujarat	60990	24.05	72.58	3.37
Haryana	27434	29.79	64.56	5.65
Himachal Pradesh	35257	28.31	63.98	7.70
Jammu & Kashmir	36504	29.06	58.45	12.49
Karnataka	104948	42.21	55.41	2.38
Kerala	51199	3.45	91.77	4.78
Madhya Pradesh	332511	41.30	52.86	5.84
Maharashtra	197155	20.62	74.92	4.46
Manipur	10885	33.02	59.09	7.89
Meghalaya	18487	38.79	57.69	3.52
Mizoram	4591	3.59	92.72	3.68
Nagaland	4558	1.65	89.01	9.35
Orissa	141592	43.96	53.40	2.63
Punjab	75477	28.77	65.99	5.24
Rajasthan	146050	35.71	59.76	4.54
Sikkim	1976	4.40	92.00	3.59
Tamil Nadu	174888	16.75	77.79	5.46
Tripura	9750	45.87	48.26	5.88
Uttar Pradesh	400585	47.29	45.24	7.47
West Bengal	206475	33.01	58.78	8.21
Andaman & Nicobar Is.	893	18.92	77.04	4.03
Chandigarh	345	2.90	94.20	2.90
Dadra & Nagar Haveli	578	31.14	65.22	3.63
Daman & Diu	194	7.73	92.27	0.00
Delhi	16064	2.83	95.96	1.21
Lakshadweep	206	0.00	100.00	0.00
Pondicherry	1925	7.90	87.58	4.52

Source: Fifth All India Educational Survey, NCERT, New Delhi, 1992.

Availability of Blackboard in Primary Schools/Sections, 1986

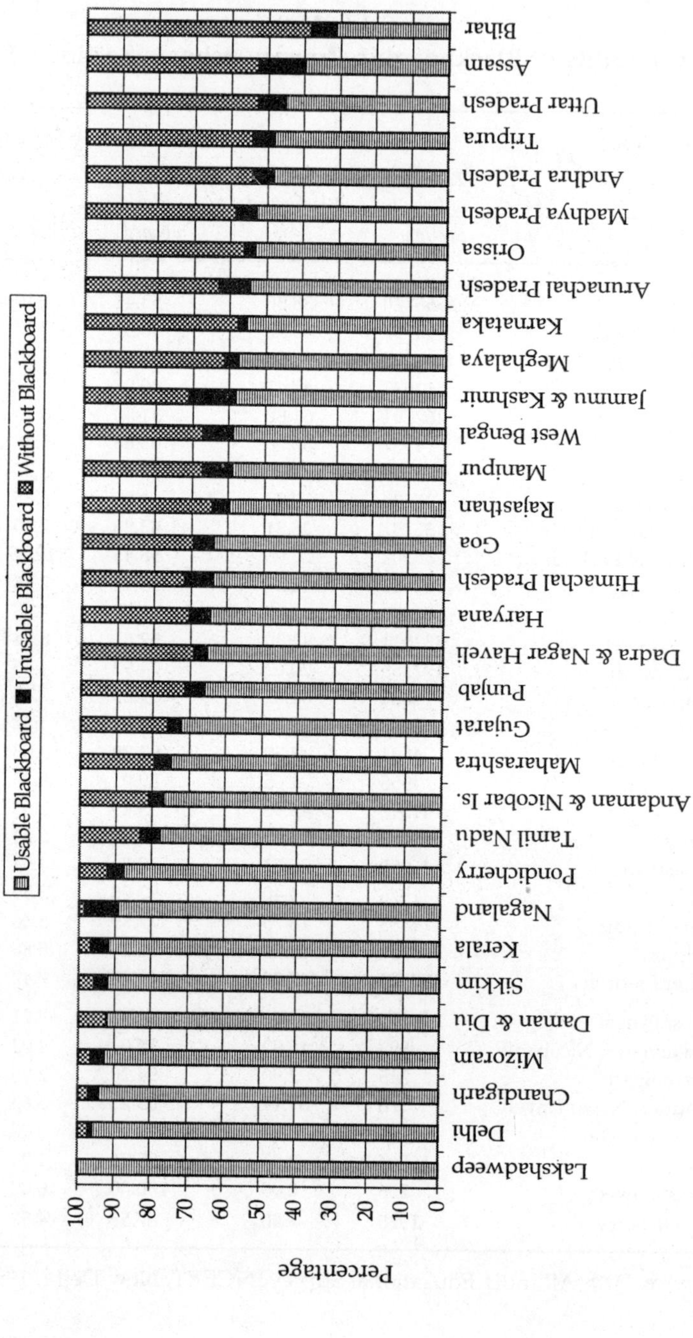

Figure 11.6

Availability of Blackboards in Primary Schools/Sections, 1986

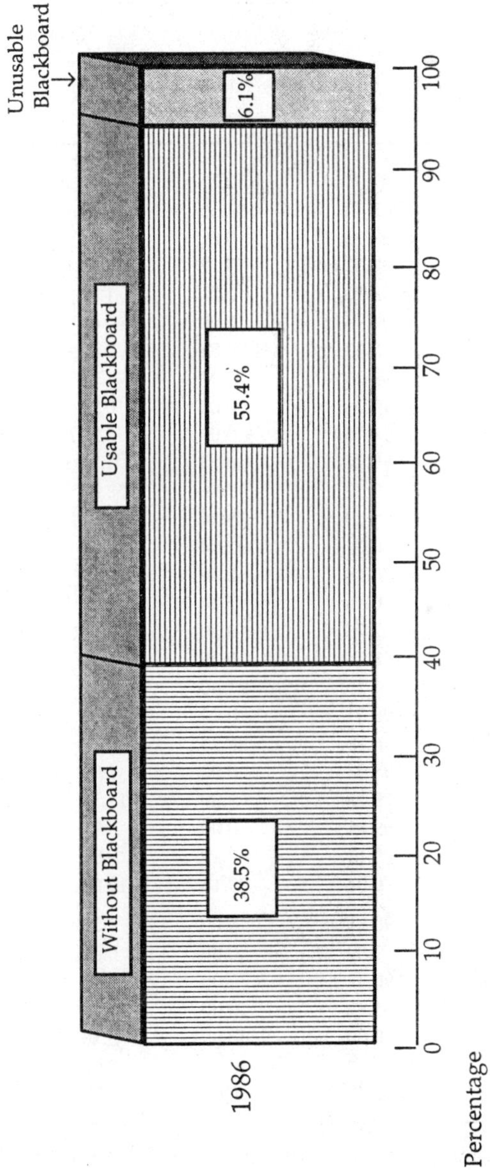

Figure 11.6A

Table 11.10
Primary Schools by Management, 1986

States/UTs	*Percentage of Primary Schools by Management*			
	Government	*Local Bodies*	*Private Aided*	*Private Unaided*
INDIA	41.38	51.71	4.34	2.57
Andhra Pradesh	2.55	91.55	4.45	1.45
Arunachal Pradesh	99.16	0.00	0.84	0.00
Assam	92.83	5.72	0.14	1.31
Bihar	98.90	0.00	1.06	0.04
Goa	94.96	0.00	0.00	5.04
Gujarat	0.33	95.55	1.43	2.68
Haryana	98.25	0.08	1.15	0.52
Himachal Pradesh	99.28	0.04	0.28	0.41
Jammu & Kashmir	98.78	0.00	0.25	0.96
Karnataka	95.54	0.02	1.22	3.22
Kerala	38.81	0.66	58.84	1.69
Madhya Pradesh	79.33	15.24	1.84	3.58
Maharashtra	0.24	92.84	3.53	3.40
Manipur	70.18	0.00	15.74	14.07
Meghalaya	0.16	67.20	17.71	14.92
Mizoram	87.76	0.50	8.76	2.99
Nagaland	98.14	0.09	1.59	0.18
Orissa	5.25	91.40	2.97	0.38
Punjab	98.91	0.09	0.51	0.50
Rajasthan	6.63	88.23	1.27	3.88
Sikkim	98.93	0.00	1.07	0.00
Tamil Nadu	79.23	3.39	17.34	0.04
Tripura	99.01	0.00	0.99	0.00
Uttar Pradesh	0.11	92.19	0.91	6.78
West Bengal	0.04	89.16	10.80	0.01
Andaman & Nicobar Is.	98.31	0.00	0.56	1.13
Chandigarh	59.09	0.00	0.00	40.91
Dadra & Nagar Haveli	90.32	0.00	9.68	0.00
Daman & Diu	96.88	0.00	0.00	3.13
Delhi	0.00	88.30	3.16	8.54
Lakshadweep	100.00	0.00	0.00	0.00
Pondicherry	79.65	0.00	1.77	18.58

Source: Fifth All India Educational Survey, NCERT, New Delhi, 1992.

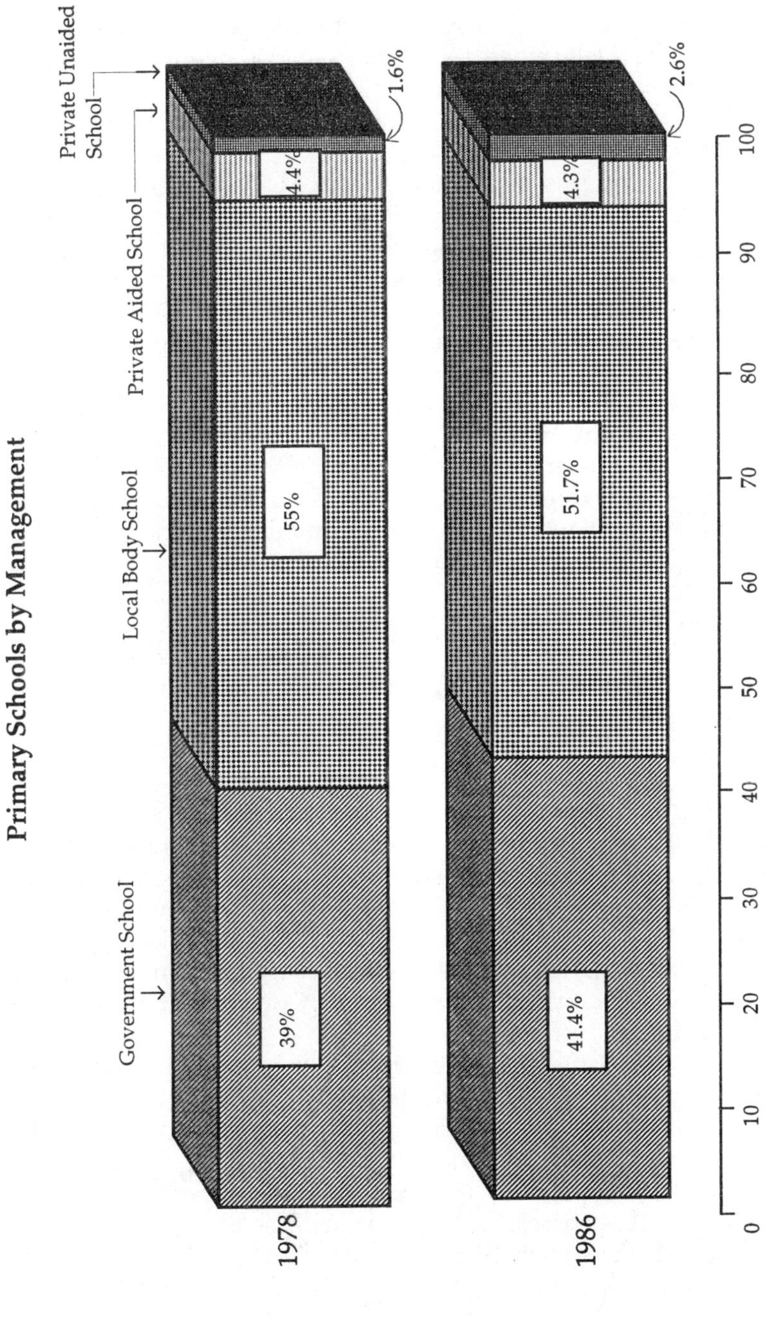
Primary Schools by Management
Government School
Local Body School
Private Aided School
Private Unaided School
1978
39%
55%
4.4%
1.6%
1986
41.4%
51.7%
4.3%
2.6%
0
10
20
30
40
50
60
70
80
90
100
Percentage

Figure 11.7

of Primary schools managed directly by the Government. Only exception is Delhi where there is not a single Government managed Primary schools, followed by West Bengal (0.04%), Uttar Pradesh (0. 11%), Meghalaya (0.16%), Maharashtra (0.24%) and Gujarat (0.33%).

During this period there were 51.71 per cent of Primary schools of the whole country had management of the 'local bodies' like Primary education councils or School boards. Among the states where more that 88 per cent of Primary schools were running under these local bodies were, Gujarat, Maharashtra, Andhra Pradesh, Uttar Pradesh, Orissa, West Bengal, Delhi and Rajasthan.

Besides these there were also 4.34 per cent of Private aided Primary schools and 2.57 per cent of Private unaided primary schools in all over the country. Among the states only in Kerala there were maximum number of Private aided primary schools—58.84 per cent whereas maximum number of Private unaided primary schools were found in Chandigarh (40.91%) during this period.

From the experience it can be said that direct Government managed Primary schools enjoyed the best infrastructural and other facilities in comparison to Primary schools managed by other management.

Enrolment

Students when enrolled in any educational institution for undergoing systematic instructions in a course of study are classified as enrolment. Table 11.11 presents the growth of gender-wise school enrolment for different stages of school education since 1950-51. The said data has been compiled from the Selected Educational Statistics 1997-98 (MHRD, Government of India, New Delhi, 1999).

From Table 11.11 it is revealed that the total enrolment at Primary stage during the period 1950-51 to 1997-98 increased by 5.66 times while the corresponding increase for the boys is 4.43 times and for the girls 8.79 times. Whereas at the upper primary stages (classes VI-VIII) the corresponding increase during this period is 12.74 times, for boys the increase is 9.11 times and for girls such increase is 31.6 times. At the Secondary and Higher secondary stage the total increase is more than 18 times, for boys

Table 11.11
Sex-wise Enrolment by Stages/Classes Since 1951 — Second Level (In Million)

Year	Primary			Middle/Upper Primary			High/Hr. Secondary		
	Boys	Girls	Total	Boys	Girls	Total	Boys	Girls	Total
1950-51	13.80	5.40	19.20	2.60	0.50	3.10	1.30	0.20	1.50
1955-56	17.10	7.50	24.60	3.80	1.00	4.80	2.20	0.40	2.60
1960-61	23.60	11.40	35.00	5.10	1.60	6.70	2.70	0.70	3.40
1965-66	32.20	18.30	50.50	7.70	2.80	10.50	4.40	1.30	5.70
1970-71	35.70	21.30	57.00	9.40	3.90	13.30	5.70	1.90	7.60
1975-76	40.60	25.00	65.60	11.00	5.00	16.00	6.50	2.40	8.90
1980-81	45.30	28.50	73.80	13.90	6.80	20.70	7.60	3.40	11.00
1985-86	52.20	35.20	87.40	17.70	9.60	27.10	11.50	5.00	16.50
1990-91	57.00	40.40	97.40	21.50	12.50	34.00	12.80	6.30	19.10
1991-92	58.60	42.30	100.90	22.00	13.60	35.60	13.50	6.90	20.40
1992-93	57.90	41.70	99.60	21.20	12.90	34.10	13.60	6.90	20.50
1993-94	55.10	41.90	97.00	20.60	13.50	34.10	13.20	7.50	20.70
1994-95*	62.30	46.80	109.10	24.50	15.80	40.30	16.00	8.40	24.40
1995-96*	62.40	47.40	109.80	25.00	16.00	41.00	16.10	8.80	24.90
1996-97*	62.50	47.90	110.40	24.70	16.30	41.00	17.20	9.80	27.00
1997-98*	61.20	47.50	108.70	23.70	15.80	39.50	17.08	10.16	27.24

* Provisional.

(Contd.)

Percentage of Girls Enrolment to the Total Enrolment by Stages

Year	*Primary I-V*	*Middle VI-VIII*	*Sec/Hr.Sec 10+2/Inter*	*Hr. Education (degree and above)*
1950-51	28.10	16.10	13.30	10.00
1955-56	30.50	20.80	15.40	14.60
1960-61	32.60	23.90	20.50	16.00
1965-66	36.20	26.70	22.00	20.40
1970-71	37.40	29.30	25.00	20.00
1975-76	38.10	31.30	26.90	23.20
1980-81	38.60	32.90	29.60	26.70
1985-86	40.30	35.60	30.30	33.00
1990-91	41.50	36.70	32.90	33.30
1991-92	41.90	38.20	33.80	32.30
1992-93	42.60	38.80	33.90	33.20
1993-94	42.70	39.10	34.30	33.50
1994-95*	42.80	38.90	34.40	34.00
1995-96*	43.20	39.00	35.30	37.20
1996-97*	43.40	39.80	36.20	38.20
1997-98*	43.60	40.10	37.10	34.80

* Provisional

Source: Selected Educational Statistics, 1997-98.

Growth of School Enrolment in India, 1950-97

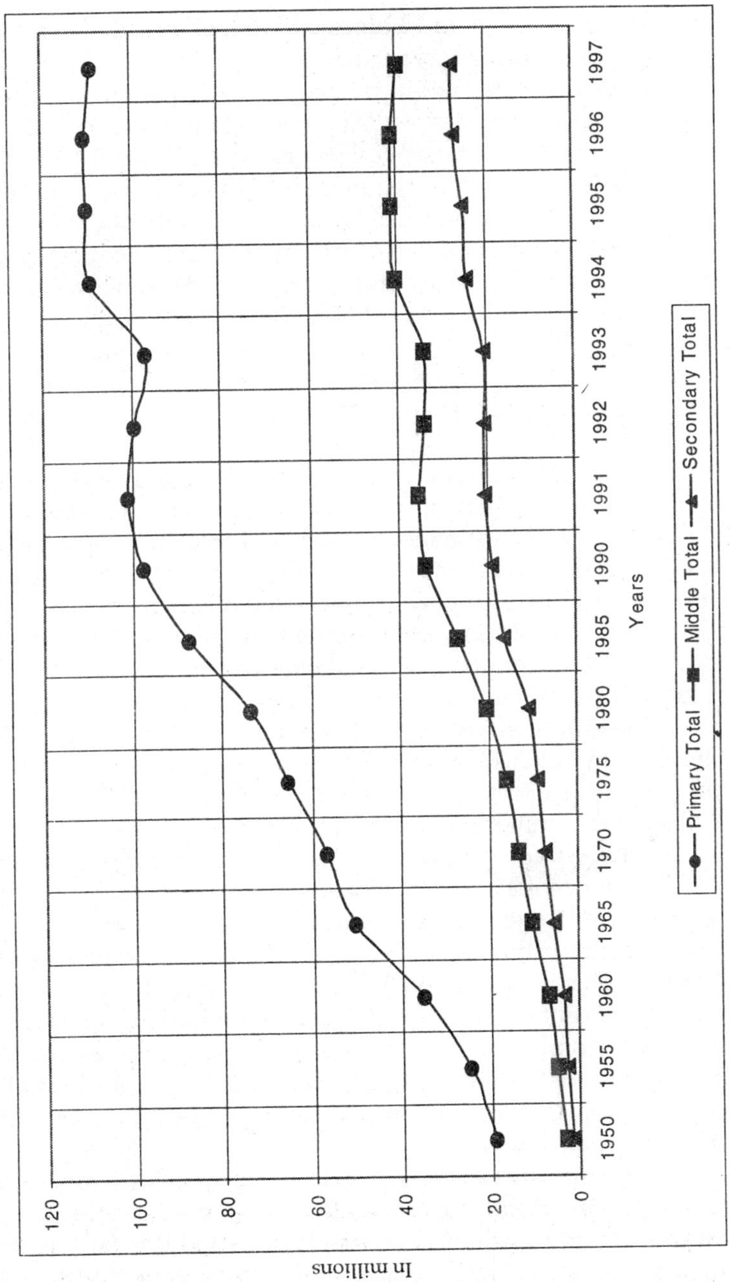

Figure 11.8

the increase is more than 13 times and that of girls the increase is about 51 times during this period.

From the above findings it may be said that during the last 47 years rate of enrolment is Primary education has been always lower than that of middle school, Secondary and Higher secondary stages of education, which requires immediate intervention. Now if we consider the percentage of girls enrolment to total enrolment we find that the participation of girls at all stages of education has been increasing steadily over the time since 1950-51. However, the percentages are still much below fifty per cent at all stages of education.

Gross Enrolment Ratios

Gross enrolment ratio is defined as the percentage of the enrolment in classes I-V (primary), VI-VIII (upper primary) and I-VIII (elementary) to the estimated child population in the age groups 6-11 years, 11-14 years and 6-14 years respectively. Gross enrolment ratios at primary, upper primary and elementary level are presented in Table 11.12. Enrolment in these stages includes under age and over-age children, hence the total percentage may be more than 100 per cent in some cases.

The official statistics on percentage of children enrolled in schools as found in Table 11.12 and Figures 11.9 and 11.10 show a phenomenal rise from 42.6 per cent in, 1950-51 to 89.7 per cent in 1997-98 at the primary level, from 12.7 per cent in 1950-51 to 58.5 per cent at the upper primary level and from 32.1 per cent in 1950-51 to 78.6 per cent in the total elementary level. From the data it is also revealed that gross enrolment ratio for girls are always much lower than that of boys in each year, which clearly shows the gender disparity. This is true not only for primary education but also for the Upper Primary, High and Higher Secondary Education. It is also clear from the above data that a wide gap between the development of Primary education and that of Secondary/Higher secondary education in the country always exists, as pointed out by Prof. Amartya Sen.

These statistics are not normally accepted on their face value. A number of studies have revealed that the actual number of children attending schools even in classes I and II is far less than what is claimed officially. For instance, in a recent study by the

Table 11.12
Gross Enrolment Ratios

Year	*Boys*		
	I-V Primary	*VI-VIII Upper Primary*	*I-VIII Elementary*
1950-51	60.60	20.60	46.40
1960-61	82.60	33.20	65.20
1970-71	95.50	46.50	75.50
1980-81	95.80	54.30	82.20
1990-91	114.00	76.60	100.00
1991-92	112.80	75.10	101.20
1992-93	95.00	72.50	87.70
1993-94	90.04	62.10	80.23
1994-95*	114.80	79.00	101.80
1995-96*	114.50	79.50	101.80
1996-97*	98.70	70.90	88.85
1997-98*	97.70	66.50	86.40

Year	*Girls*		
	I-V Primary	*VI-VIII Upper Primary*	*I-VIII Elementary*
1950-51	24.80	4.60	17.70
1960-61	41.40	11.30	30.90
1970-71	60.50	20.80	44.40
1980-81	64.10	28.60	52.10
1990-91	85.50	47.00	70.80
1991-92	86.90	49.60	73.20
1992-93	73.46	48.94	65.70
1993-94	73.10	45.40	63.70
1994-95*	92.60	55.00	78.80
1995-96*	93.30	55.00	79.30
1996-97*	81.90	52.80	71.80
1997-98*	81.20	49.50	70.00

(Contd.)

Year	*Totals*		
	I-V *Primary*	*VI-VIII* *Upper Primary*	*I-VIII* *Elementary*
1950-51	42.60	12.70	32.10
1960-61	62.40	22.50	48.70
1970-71	78.60	33.40	61.90
1980-81	80.50	41.90	67.50
1990-91	100.10	62.10	86.00
1991-92	100.20	61.35	87.70
1992-93	84.50	67.50	77.15
1993-94	81.90	54.20	72.30
1994-95*	104.30	67.20	90.70
1995-96*	104.00	67.60	90.90
1996-97*	90.60	62.40	80.70
1997-98*	89.70	58.50	78.60

* Provisional

Source: Selected Educational Statistics, 1997-98.

present author in a few districts of West Bengal, has shown that many children whose names were enrolled in the school register had in fact not attended school for more than a few days. It was pointed out that since teachers are under pressure to show better enrolment targets they keep the names of these children alive in their registers. In this connection it is very relevant to quote Prof. Amartya Sen here, ". . . . Besides, the official figures are collected from sources that have some interest in overstating the enrolment ratio (Government grants to school depend on enrolment), there is a systematic bias introduced in the official figures. So while the situation is depressing enough, the actual position seems to be even worse. The sharp contrast between our achievements in the field of higher education and our poverty in the field of elementary education is extremely significant in the context of India's economic performance. . . . . (*The Statesman*, 19 October, 1998)

Statewise enrolment ratios for the year 1995-96 in classes I-V and VI-VIII, as shown in Table 11.13, clearly indicates the regional disparity.

Gross Enrolment Ratio at Primary Stage, 1950-97

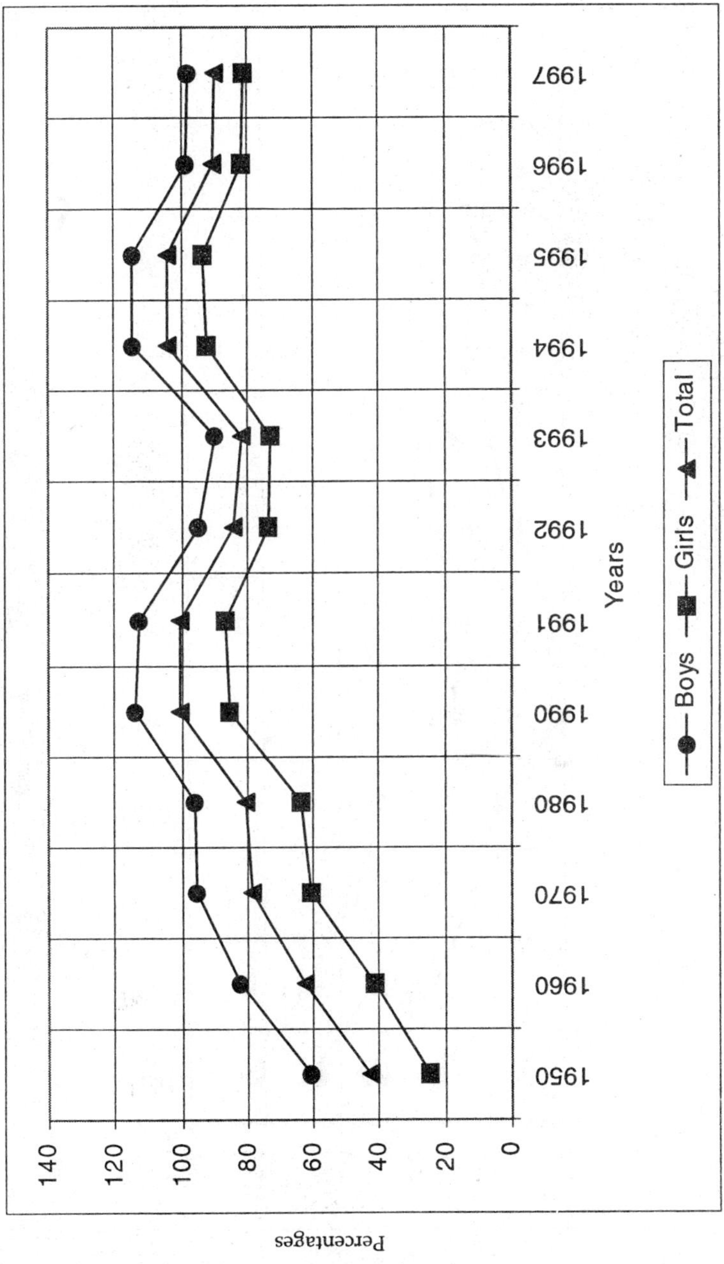

Figure 11.9

Gross Enrolment Ratio at Elementary Stage, 1950-97

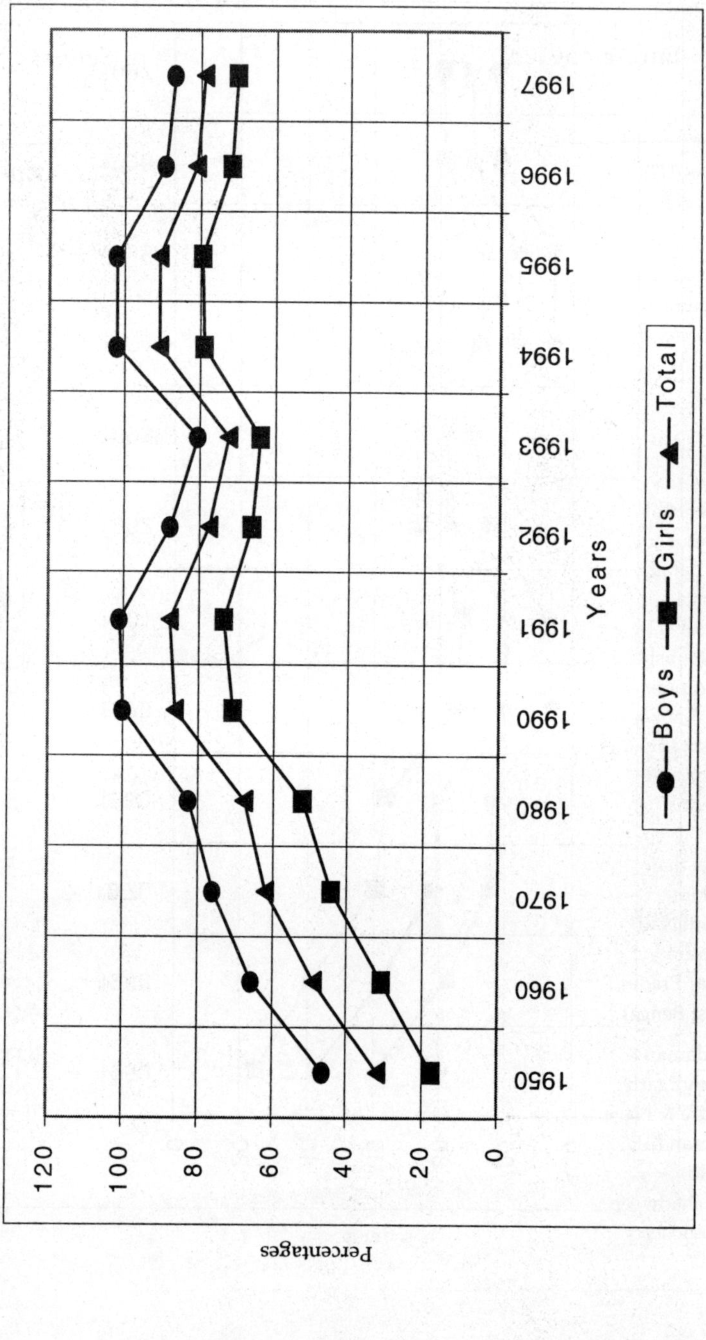

Figure 11.10

Table 11.13
Enrolment Ratio in Classes I-V and VI-VIII of Schools for General Education (1995-96)

States/UTs	*Classes (I-V) (6-11 age group)*			*Classes (VI-VIII) (11-14 age group)*		
	Boys	*Girls*	*Total*	*Boys*	*Girls*	*Total*
Andhra Pradesh	99.60	89.90	94.90	57.30	41.80	49.70
Arunachal Pradesh	115.50	103.90	110.00	61.30	45.20	53.30
Assam	133.40	124.00	128.80	91.60	65.90	79.10
Bihar	93.00	55.40	75.10	47.50	21.90	35.30
Goa	90.60	100.50	95.10	95.10	84.10	89.60
Gujarat	158.30	106.80	131.40	81.10	61.50	71.60
Haryana	86.40	84.80	85.60	70.90	56.70	64.20
Himachal Pradesh	108.40	113.70	110.80	112.70	90.50	101.80
Jammu & Kashmir	88.60	72.20	81.20	73.30	46.80	60.50
Karnataka	131.10	123.50	127.40	78.10	66.80	72.60
Kerala	98.40	95.40	96.90	105.10	101.50	103.30
Madhya Pradesh	112.90	88.90	101.40	91.60	43.30	68.40
Maharashtra	125.50	120.20	122.90	92.40	77.20	85.00
Manipur	93.10	100.30	96.40	69.40	63.20	66.40
Meghalaya	105.30	125.40	114.40	51.60	45.50	48.60
Mizoram	112.60	124.80	118.10	67.30	67.70	67.50
Nagaland	120.60	135.50	127.30	52.50	51.20	51.90
Orissa	113.40	78.20	95.60	73.00	39.80	56.20
Punjab	92.40	90.70	91.50	74.00	65.00	69.70
Rajasthan	129.30	75.30	103.40	79.90	32.00	56.90
Sikkim	104.20	118.40	110.60	50.50	50.80	50.70
Tamil Nadu	159.30	145.60	152.60	118.20	99.50	109.10
Tripura	122.70	124.40	123.50	66.80	57.00	62.00
Uttar Pradesh	104.30	72.00	89.10	72.30	34.90	54.70
West Bengal	128.60	122.30	125.50	102.80	91.50	97.20
Andaman & Nicobar Is.	76.60	69.20	72.90	73.50	68.60	71.10
Chandigarh	36.40	40.40	38.20	36.40	34.90	35.60
Dadra & Nagar Haveli	121.00	102.70	112.70	59.20	40.80	50.60
Daman & Diu	93.00	88.60	90.80	92.50	84.70	83.70
Delhi	67.70	77.80	72.10	71.10	67.30	69.30
Lakshadweep	125.30	125.30	125.30	112.00	81.20	96.60
Pondicherry	117.20	133.30	124.50	113.00	109.60	111.30
India	114.50	93.30	104.30	79.50	54.90	67.60

From a study of Y.P. Aggarwal, the proportion of children in different age-groups attending schools during the year 1986 is presented in Table 11.14.

Table 11.14
Proportion of Children Attending School During 1986

Population	*6-11 years*	*11-14 years*	*6-14 years*
All	47.15	51.96	48.72
Male	54.88	63.81	58.11
Female	38.45	38.67	38.52
Rural			
All	41.27	45.69	42.69
Male	50.57	59.52	53.50
Female	31.28	30.12	30.93
Urban			
All	68.83	72.93	70.26
Male	72.70	78.32	74.66
Female	64.71	66.98	65.52

Source: Aggarwal, Y.P. Towards Education for All, 1988.

From the above findings it is revealed that during 1986 almost 53 per cent of children in 6-11 years of age group did not attend school and this proportion raises to 62 per cent in case of girls. The simultaneous figures in the rural areas were even more disappointing where about 60 per cent of children of this age group and about 70 per cent of the girls did not attend school during this period. This percentages do not correspond to enrolments in this age group. With the official claim of gross enrolment ratio in this age group touching the level of 98 per cent in 1986-87, the gulf between this claim and ground realities widens even further. While, according to estimates based upon Census of India figures, the number of children out of school in the age group of 6-11 years were about 5 crores, the Ministry's Statistics on enrolment placed this number to 20 lakh only. So there exists a gross disparity in the enrolment data. Notwithstanding the serious doubts raised above about the validity of the enrolment data, a close examination of the Tables 11.11 and 11.12 draws attention to some interesting problems. As Table 11.13 shows that during 1997-98, 81.2 per cent of girls and 49.5 per cent girls, enrolled in classes I-V and VI-VIII respectively, which does not tally with the corresponding figures of girls enrolment to total enrolment during this period shown in Table 11.11, which are 43.6 per cent and 40.1 per cent respectively.

Enrolment ratios of students belonging to Scheduled Castes (SC) and Scheduled Tribes (ST) in Class I-V and VI-VIII are given in Tables 11.15 and Table 11.16.

From Tables 11.15 and 11.16 it is evident that the official figures show that 127.56 per cent of SC and 129.96 per cent of ST students were enrolled in classes I-V during the year 1995-96 in all over the country, out of which 95.12 per cent and 94.87 per cent respectively were females. Although the enrolment figures at the Primary stage, particularly in rural and tribal areas do not necessarily reflect the reality and are often inflated, these can be taken as some kind of rough indicators. In spite of the tendency to inflate enrolment figures, it is noteworthy that there are wide gaps in enrolment ratios in different States and Union Territories, with the levels falling down to 27.50 per cent for SC and 11.66 per cent for ST in the case of girls in some states.

Now, if we consider the percentage of SC and ST students enrolled to total children enrolled during the year 1995-96 at Primary and Middle (elementary) school level it is found that the percentage are only 15.9 per cent for SC and 7.9 per cent for STs at the Primary level and 12.4 per cent for SC and 4.9 per cent for STs in the middle/elementary school level of the total enrolment for the SC and ST children.

Retention

Retention of students has been calculated from the rate of drop-out which means the percentage of the number of children to total enrolment dropping out of the school educational system in a particular year. Latest official figures of drop-out rates obtained

Table 11.15
Enrolment Ratio of Students Belonging to Scheduled Castes (1995-96)

States/UTs	*Classes (I-V) 6-11 years*			*Classes (VI-VIII) 11-14 years*		
	Boys	*Girls*	*Total*	*Boys*	*Girls*	*Total*
Andhra Pradesh	140.68	121.73	131.40	67.03	42.63	55.08
Arunachal Pradesh	25.33	27.50	26.20	21.00	13.00	17.00
Assam	257.62	239.07	248.50	190.13	161.51	176.16
Bihar	102.04	51.39	77.80	38.20	14.03	26.62
Goa	105.31	116.77	110.40	69.50	55.33	62.79
Gujarat	213.43	155.06	182.90	117.32	76.00	97.32
Haryana	108.12	105.84	107.00	65.81	47.85	57.36
Himachal Pradesh	115.15	115.75	115.40	90.14	63.06	76.80
Jammu & Kashmir	96.14	83.93	90.60	80.24	59.68	70.34
Karnataka	158.59	137.96	148.50	81.78	57.60	70.04
Kerala	107.64	102.45	105.00	118.31	114.56	116.46
Madhya Pradesh	129.68	93.48	112.20	80.98	35.62	59.19
Maharashtra	268.31	257.96	263.30	180.15	137.47	159.53
Manipur	153.65	179.19	165.00	93.64	92.00	92.86
Meghalaya	—	—	—	—	—	—
Mizoram	—	—	—	—	—	—
Nagaland	—	—	—	—	—	—
Orissa	152.85	95.29	123.70	71.82	43.17	57.29
Punjab	134.77	129.98	132.40	79.75	64.83	72.65
Rajasthan	121.53	48.62	86.50	78.13	21.44	50.93
Sikkim	103.75	114.00	108.40	50.83	43.17	47.00
Tamil Nadu	176.76	154.02	165.60	111.26	84.74	98.34
Tripura	147.05	144.14	145.70	63.43	66.69	65.01
Uttar Pradesh	88.94	42.05	68.80	53.34	15.82	35.70
West Bengal	129.79	116.93	123.50	72.03	69.00	70.59
Andaman & Nicobar Is.	—	—	—	—	—	—
Chandigarh	82.85	92.93	87.30	68.33	59.02	68.83
Dadra & Nagar Haveli	74.67	87.00	79.60	99.00	93.00	96.00
Daman & Diu	—	—	—	—	—	—
Delhi	83.49	91.76	87.00	72.66	68.66	70.83
Lakshadweep	—	—	—	—	—	—
Pondicherry	141.29	170.18	154.40	147.36	154.87	151.03
India	127.56	95.12	111.91	74.88	46.77	61.33

Table 11.16
Enrolment Ratio of Students Belonging to Scheduled Tribes (1995-96)

States/UTs	*Classes (I-V) 6-11 years*			*Classes (VI-VIII) 11-14 years*		
	Boys	*Girls*	*Total*	*Boys*	*Girls*	*Total*
Andhra Pradesh	144.09	100.82	122.96	48.35	20.30	34.60
Arunachal Pradesh	121.15	98.62	116.26	56.60	41.30	48.90
Assam	196.62	171.11	184.18	116.30	92.61	104.70
Bihar	90.73	62.82	77.40	35.53	20.81	28.34
Goa	13.00	11.66	12.38	18.50	13.75	16.10
Gujarat	122.04	112.37	140.91	67.60	42.25	55.30
Haryana	—	—	—	—	—	—
Himachal Pradesh	105.36	96.01	101.09	84.67	47.64	66.40
Jammu & Kashmir	—	—	—	—	—	—
Karnataka	162.39	135.85	149.52	76.42	53.04	65.00
Kerala	124.51	118.04	121.32	101.84	99.04	100.40
Madhya Pradesh	93.95	59.07	77.18	41.01	21.04	31.40
Maharashtra	137.79	121.08	129.71	67.05	45.30	56.50
Manipur	123.51	127.64	125.38	72.81	62.74	67.90
Meghalaya	102.47	123.14	111.86	49.46	45.03	47.20
Mizoram	118.98	132.47	125.02	71.56	72.05	71.00
Nagaland	143.64	161.39	151.62	62.60	60.93	61.70
Orissa	121.86	58.15	89.64	46.96	19.32	32.90
Punjab	—	—	—	—	—	—
Rajasthan	121.66	49.21	86.84	80.87	20.21	51.70
Sikkim	96.28	105.19	100.35	43.80	43.13	43.40
Tamil Nadu	147.24	73.15	132.15	78.32	54.10	66.00
Tripura	151.11	135.31	143.95	55.69	46.00	50.90
Uttar Pradesh	99.12	63.94	82.54	56.94	23.08	41.00
West Bengal	123.53	122.64	123.09	82.50	71.06	76.80
Andaman & Nicobar Is.	51.44	45.50	48.47	41.53	43.17	42.30
Chandigarh	—	—	—	—	—	—
Dadra & Nagar Haveli	127.04	102.61	116.02	55.67	32.95	44.90
Daman & Diu	—	—	—	—	—	—
Delhi	—	—	—	—	—	—
Lakshadweep	137.21	134.90	136.14	121.41	86.59	104.00
Pondicherry	—	—	—	—	—	—
India	129.96	94.87	113.03	61.59	37.63	50.04

from the Selected Educational Statistics 1997-98 (MHRD, Government of India, 1999) has been indicated in Table 11.17.

Table 11.17
Year-wise Drop-out Rates at Primary and Middle School Stages

Classes I-V	*1960-61*	*1970-71*	*1980-81*	*1986-87*	*1990-91*	*1992-93*	*1995-96*	*1997-98*
Boys	61.7	64.5	56.2	45.84	40.1	43.83	37.92	38.23
Girls	70.9	70.9	62.5	50.27	46.0	46.67	41.31	41.34
Total	64.9	67.0	58.7	48.90	42.6	45.01	39.37	39.58
Classes I-VIII								
Boys	75.0	74.6	68.0	58.29	59.1	58.23	54.99	50.72
Girls	85.0	83.4	79.4	69.72	65.1	65.21	61.70	58.61
Total	78.3	77.9	72.7	60.7	60.9	61.1	57.77	54.14

Source: Selected Educational Statistics 1997-98, MHRD, Government of India, 1999.

So, it is observed from the Table 11.17 above though the rate of dropouts has been decreasing year after year with only exception in the 1992-93, where the rate was found increased considerably in both the stages of education, a large percentage of children about 40 per cent still drop-out in the early stages of primary education before reaching class V. Similarly at the middle school level, about 55 per cent of children who began education at class I still drop-out before reaching class VIII. This percentage can be as high as 42 per cent and 59 per cent in the case of girls at the primary and middle school levels respectively. Though the retention rate at both the stages of education has been found to be considerably improved since 1960-61, still a large population of children remain out of the ambit of Primary education.

In Table 11.18 the dimension of regional disparity is reflected in state-wise analysis of drop-out rates at both the primary and middle school levels.

Table 11.18
Drop-out Rates in Classes I-V and Classes I-VIII for the Year 1995-96 (Provisional)

States/UTs	*Classes (I-V)*			*Classes (I-VIII)*		
	Boys	*Girls*	*Total*	*Boys*	*Girls*	*Total*
Andhra Pradesh	56.27	54.36	55.44	71.11	74.86	72.73
Arunachal Pradesh	55.49	52.46	54.19	70.16	69.83	70.02
Assam	39.83	41.75	40.69	68.58	73.21	70.66
Bihar	61.46	64.03	62.37	75.96	81.76	77.95
Goa	1.56	9.45	5.39	10.44	19.21	14.73
Gujarat	35.49	41.15	38.02	53.76	62.76	57.78
Haryana	5.78	7.32	6.48	26.44	36.55	30.99
Himachal Pradesh	20.18	27.00	23.43	9.63	27.00	17.84
Jammu & Kashmir	53.13	41.48	48.36	50.13	72.40	59.24
Karnataka	34.88	35.72	35.28	54.02	66.69	60.15
Kerala	-4.93	-1.99	-3.49	0.32	0.52	0.42
Madhya Pradesh	28.06	33.23	30.25	45.96	64.82	54.04
Maharashtra	21.79	27.36	24.40	42.30	52.77	47.24
Manipur*	35.04	36.30	35.64	70.66	70.89	70.77
Meghalaya**	59.61	62.53	61.07	48.76	48.13	48.46
Mizoram	57.71	72.28	57.20	69.71	67.45	68.65
Nagaland	39.93	31.40	35.98	42.99	45.20	44.08
Orissa	52.88	53.79	53.24	60.90	72.84	65.67
Punjab	22.86	22.52	22.70	39.07	42.78	40.78
Rajasthan	50.57	56.00	52.38	76.20	82.15	78.10
Sikkim	61.97	53.74	58.17	69.28	64.98	67.33
Tamil Nadu	14.88	16.97	15.85	28.60	37.11	32.54
Tripura	53.49	57.27	55.24	73.39	74.46	73.88
Uttar Pradesh	22.31	22.94	22.53	32.28	48.86	38.11
West Bengal	49.93	66.84	58.72	67.47	74.19	69.08
Andaman & Nicobar Is.	7.84	13.43	10.56	23.42	24.90	24.13
Chandigarh	30.68	30.98	30.82	18.46	17.18	17.86
Dadra & Nagar Haveli	31.21	50.80	39.57	59.33	66.55	62.29
Daman & Diu	-10.24	-11.76	-10.96	10.49	15.70	12.88
Delhi	18.15	30.53	24.37	30.35	15.26	23.03
Lakshadweep	-0.42	7.37	3.16	26.87	33.18	29.88
Pondicherry	-4.07	-7.06	-5.49	5.25	-0.29	2.69
India	37.92	41.31	39.37	54.99	61.70	57.77

* Decrease is due to exclusion of enrolment of Class I-A from Class I and considered against pre-primary in 1991-92.

** Increase is due to students in classes A and B (age 6 and above) promoted in class I as per new Education Structure w.e.f. 1991-92.

The official figures of drop-out rates of SC and ST school children are available only for the year 1986-87 and 1987-88. The corresponding figures for the subsequent years are not yet available. The drop-out rates of the SC and ST students for the year 1986-87 and 1987-88 are given in Table 11.19.

Table 11.19
Drop-out Rates of SC and ST School Children for the Years 1986-87 and 1987-88

Years	*Classes I-V*		*Classes I-VIII*	
	SC	*ST*	*SC*	*ST*
1986-87	50.80	66.10	69.20	80.20
1987-88	51.60	65.21	68.81	80.01

Source: POA, MHRD, 1992.

From the figures as shown in Table 11.19 it is evident that the drop-out rates of SC and ST school children are very high at both the level of education and much higher than those of the rest of the communities at all the stages. An idea of retention rate at primary and middle school level can be obtained from Table 11.20 and Figure 11.11.

The National Policy on Education (NPE, 1986) sought to adopt an array of meticulously formulated strategies based on micro-planning and applied at the grass-root level all over the country, to ensure children's retention at school. Programme of Action (POA, 1986) also sought to replace enrolment drives by participative planning in which the teachers and the villagers would formulate family-wise and child-wise design of action to ensure that every child regularly attended school or non-formal education centre and completed at last five years of schooling or its non-formal equivalent. In spite of all these measures drop-out rates nearly 40 per cent in the primary level and 55 per cent in the upper primary level during the year 1997-98, indicate that all those measures were only in paper and pencil without any vigilance or proper inspection of schools.

Table 11.20

Retention Rate: Class V and Class VIII, 1964-65 to 1989-90

Year	*Class V*		*Class VIII*	
	Total	*Girls*	*Total*	*Girls*
1964-65	37.10	32.00	—	—
1965-66	34.20	29.50	—	—
1966-67	34.80	30.30	—	—
1967-68	35.00	31.00	24.20	18.40
1968-69	33.10	28.90	22.00	16.40
1969-70	33.10	28.70	22.00	16.40
1970-71	33.00	29.10	22.10	16.60
1971-72	33.50	29.70	21.00	15.70
1972-73	35.00	31.30	20.90	15.80
1973-74	36.00	32.80	20.70	15.70
1974-75	36.80	33.30	21.30	16.30
1975-76	37.20	33.80	22.40	17.20
1976-77	36.90	33.20	22.80	17.80
1977-78	38.90	34.70	23.10	18.30
1978-79	38.60	34.70	23.70	19.30
1979-80	40.40	36.50	24.20	19.10
1980-81	42.60	38.30	27.10	21.50
1981-82	48.10	43.70	28.30	22.50
1982-83	49.21	44.50	28.80	25.00
1983-84	51.16	47.10	31.20	25.20
1984-85	50.38	47.54	35.65	29.60
1985-86	54.52	51.01	36.43	30.30
1986-87	49.65	47.67	36.72	30.79
1987-88	51.04	49.22	36.72	31.96
1988-89	54.83	52.03	38.76	32.60
1989-90	51.91	49.65	35.90	31.24

Note: Retention Rate for Class V for a given year is calculated as a percentage of students enrolled in Class V to the enrolment in Class I four years earlier.
Retention Rate for Class VIII for a given year is calculated as a percentage of students enrolled in Class VIII to the enrolment in Class I seven years earlier.

Sources: 1. A Handbook of Educational and Allied Statistics, MHRD, Department of Education, Government of India, New Delhi, 1987.
2. Computed by the author based on the information given in Education in India (Vol. I), different years.

Retention Rate (Class V and VIII)

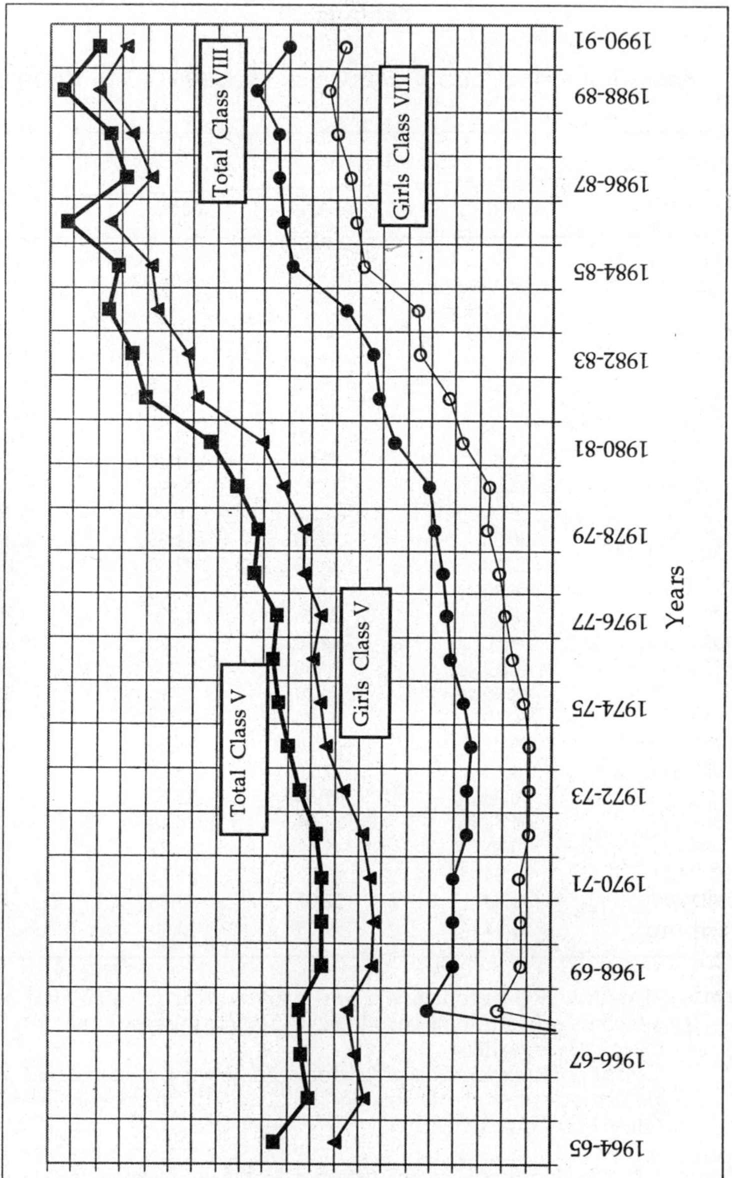

Figure 11.11

Availability of Teachers

The distribution of Teachers by the type of schools since 1950-51, has been presented in Table 11.21.

From Table 11.21 it is revealed that in absolute terms, a substantial increase in the number of teachers since 1950-51 to 1997-98 which are more than three times in primary level and about fourteen times in the upper primary level, while the rate of increase of female teachers during these periods is about eight times in the primary level and about 32 times in the upper primary level. Still the percentage of female teachers to total teachers is below 30 per cent in both primary and upper primary level during 1997-98 in the country. On the basis of the school enrolment and the number of teachers, the teacher-pupil ratio since 1950-51 is presented in Table 11.22.

From Table 11.22 it is evident that during the year 1950-51 the Teacher-pupil Ratio in Primary schools was 1:24 and in upper-primary schools it was 1:20. But in 1997-98 this ratio has now increased to 1:42 in Primary schools and 1:37 in Upper primary schools, which shows that in spite of rise in the total number of schools and teachers since 1950-51, population (enrolment) rise sharper than the number of both the schools and teachers and as a result the availability of the schools and teachers in population is declining continuously during this period. So, measures on war-footing should be adopted to reverse this trend.

A state-wise study of Teacher-pupil Ratio in Primary schools as in Table 11.23 shows that it has in fact increased in most states between 1981-82 and 1992-93, with the exception of Sikkim, Tripura, Lakshadweep, Pondicherry, Delhi, Himachal Pradesh, Goa, Nagaland etc. where a decreasing trend in the teacher-pupil ratio is evident during this period. All India figure also shows that the teacher-pupil ratio during this period increased from 39 to 45 in Primary level and from 34 to 43 in Upper primary level. If this trend continues, all expectations of moving towards better quality of elementary education would be belied. Indeed a higher teacher-pupil ratio adversely affects quality of education. This also results in problems of class-room discipline for maintenance of which teacher may feel to take recourse to undesirable practices including corporal punishment.

Table 11.21
Distribution of Teachers by Type of Schools Since 1951 (in '000)

Year	*Primary*			*Upper Primary*			*High/Hr. Secondary*		
	Male	*Female*	*Total*	*Male*	*Female*	*Total*	*Male*	*Female*	*Total*
1950-51	456	82	538	73	13	86	107	20	127
1955-56	574	117	691	132	19	151	155	35	190
1960-61	615	127	742	262	83	345	234	62	296
1965-66	764	180	944	389	139	528	368	111	479
1970-71	835	225	1060	463	175	638	474	155	629
1975-76	955	283	1248	554	224	778	-559	200	759
1980-81	1021	342	1363	598	253	851	669	257	926
1985-86	1094	402	1496	663	305	968	793	339	1132
1990-91	1143	473	1616	717	356	1073	917	417	1334
1991-92	1152	492	1644	714	365	1079	931	450	1381
1992-93	1137	514	1651	709	376	1085	941	454	1395
1993-94	1110	513	1623	723	406	1124	953	492	1445
1994-95*	1181	533	1714	732	390	1122	956	490	1446
1995-96*	1187	553	1740	756	409	1165	982	511	1493
1996-97*	1205	585	1790	768	428	1196	1003	539	1542
1997-98*	1229	643	1872	775	437	1212	985	536	1521

* Provisional

Growth of School Teachers, 1950-97

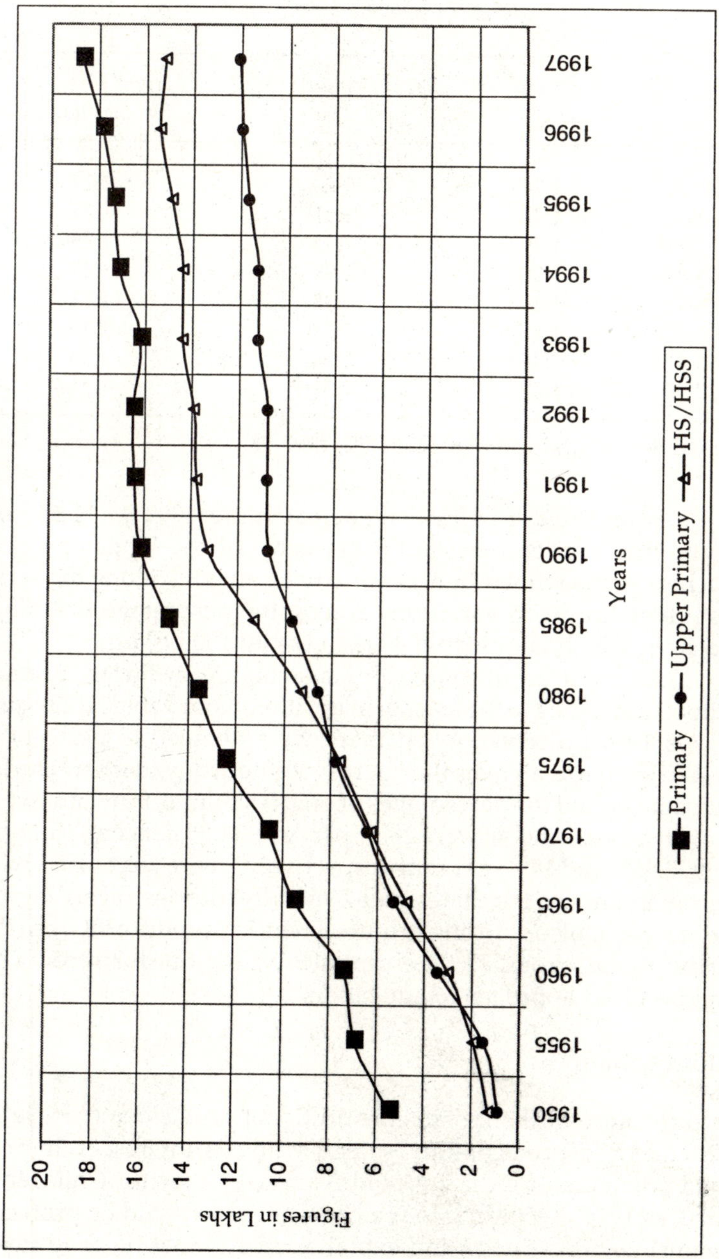

Figure 11.12

Table 11.22

Year	*Primary*	*Upper Primary*	*High/ Hr. Secondary*
1950-51	1:24	1:20	1:21
1960-61	1:36	1:31	1:25
1970-71	1:39	1:32	1:25
1980-81	1:38	1:33	1:27
1990-91	1:43	1:37	1:31
1995-96	1:47	1:38	1:33
1996-97	1:45	1:38	1:33
1997-98	1:42	1:37	1:31

Source: Selected Educational Statistics, 1997-98.

From Table 11.24 it is evident that during 1992-93, 11 per cent of the Primary teachers and 9 per cent of the Upper primary teachers of the whole country were not trained. Among the states also there are wide variations among the percentage of trained teachers, which varies from 40 per cent to 100 per cent .

As no current official figure is available regarding the Primary schools according to the teacher in position, from Table 11.25 which shows 1986 positions, when there were about 0.43 per cent of Primary schools all over the country without any teacher. During the same period the percentages of one, two, three, four and five or more teachers schools were 28.91 per cent, 31.85 per cent, 15.11 per cent, 8.88% and 14.83 per cent respectively. There were also a wide variation among the States and Union Territories regarding the Primary schools according to the teachers in proportion. Given this situation, the school lack the essential Pre-condition for introducing child centred approach to education.

Child Labour

In pursuance of the Indian constitutional provisions (Article 24, 39e and 39f) of protecting and safeguarding the interest of children, the Parliament of India adopted National Policy for Children as early as 1974. According to which "Children should be protected against neglect, cruelty and exploitation and that no child under

Table 11.23
Pupils Per Teacher, 1981-82 and 1992-93

States/UTs	1981-82		1992-93	
	Primary Schools	Upper Primary Schools	Primary Schools	Upper Primary Schools
INDIA	39	34	45	43
Andhra Pradesh	51	39	53	50
Arunachal Pradesh	30	21	@30	23
Assam	36	24	39	31
Bihar	41	35	52	43
Goa	29	29	21	19
Gujarat	41	39	44	42
Haryana	42	36	44	42
Himachal Pradesh	37	16	33	23
Jammu & Kashmir	27	21	26	24
Karnataka	45	44	41	58
Kerala	33	33	32	31
Madhya Pradesh	37	27	45	33
Maharashtra	40	37	37	40
Manipur	17	16	18	11
Meghalaya	30	17	36	19
Mizoram	30	15	30	12
Nagaland	21	15	19	21
Orissa	35	26	36	32
Punjab	39	16	40	24
Rajasthan	42	28	46	34
Sikkim	20	19	14	15
Tamil Nadu	40	38	47	47
Tripura	42	29	23	25
Uttar Pradesh	39	26	58	39
West Bengal	38	29	55	@42
Andaman & Nicobar Is.	19	19	21	21
Chandigarh	9	30	24	21
Dadra & Nagar Haveli	45	34	40	30
Daman & Diu	*	*	35	63
Delhi	36	24	31	20
Lakshadweep	31	27	26	25
Pondicherry	30	34	27	28

* Daman and Diu was part of Union Territory of Goa, Daman and Diu in 1981.
— Data not available.
@ Figures related to 1991-92.

Sources: 1. Education in India, Vol (I), 1981-82, MHRD, Department of Education, New Delhi.
2. Selected Educational Statistics, 1992-93, MHRD, Department of Education, New Delhi, 1993.

Table 11.24
Percentage of Trained Teachers, 1992-93

States/UTs	*Percentage of Trained Teachers*			
	Primary Schools	*Upper Primary Schools*	*High Schools*	*Higher Secondary Schools*
INDIA	89	91	90	92
Andhra Pradesh	99	99	100	100
Arunachal Pradesh	40	40	39	63
Assam	66	28	33	26
Bihar	89	91	94	94
Goa	95	97	92	68
Gujarat	97	98	100	100
Haryana	99	100	100	99
Himachal Pradesh	86	99	97	98
Jammu & Kashmir	68	69	72	80
Karnataka	95	96	97	100
Kerala	95	91	99	92
Madhya Pradesh	*	*	*	*
Maharashtra	94	95	97	96
Manipur	56	29	32	48
Meghalaya	42	35	32	98
Mizoram	84	80	48	*
Nagaland	48	29	30	@50
Orissa	100	97	97	50
Punjab	99	98	99	99
Rajasthan	98	99	98	97
Sikkim	48	41	42	50
Tamil Nadu	100	100	100	99
Tripura	33	34	37	61
Uttar Pradesh	98	95	97	97
West Bengal	68	71	73	70
Andaman & Nicobar Is.	97	97	99	98
Chandigarh	100	100	100	100
Dadra & Nagar Haveli	93	94	98	99
Daman & Diu	100	100	100	100
Delhi	100	99	99	99
Lakshadweep	100	100	97	*
Pondicherry	91	97	98	100

* Data not available.

@ Figures relate to 1991-92.

Source: Selected Educational Statistics, 1992-93, MHRD, Department of Education, Government of India, New Delhi, 1993.

Table 11.25
Primary Schools According to Teachers in Position, 1986

States/UTs	*Primary Schools According to Number of Teachers in Position*					
	Zero	*One*	*Two*	*Three*	*Four*	*Five or more*
INDIA	0.43	28.91	31.85	15.11	8.88	14.83
Andhra Pradesh	0.53	40.66	36.26	8.98	4.83	8.72
Arunachal Pradesh	0.42	55.25	26.89	8.51	2.00	6.93
Assam	0.00	34.41	41.15	12.24	6.00	6.20
Bihar	1.47	25.89	45.56	16.07	6.81	4.20
Goa	0.00	16.82	42.20	16.21	11.58	13.19
Gujarat	1.97	37.64	36.11	9.25	5.01	10.02
Haryana	0.87	7.88	38.98	21.20	12.29	18.79
Himachal Pradesh	0.45	28.26	45.97	9.07	5.53	10.72
Jammu & Kashmir	0.47	58.67	31.36	5.68	1.66	2.17
Karnataka	0.00	62.33	27.95	4.27	2.32	3.13
Kerala	0.00	0.31	1.00	5.17	16.39	77.13
Madhya Pradesh	0.20	34.58	33.55	14.50	6.67	10.50
Maharashtra	0.51	43.73	24.04	7.10	6.73	17.89
Manipur	0.00	18.50	29.74	20.75	11.93	19.08
Meghalaya	0.00	53.33	28.33	9.62	3.87	4.85
Mizoram	0.00	11.84	27.16	23.18	17.61	20.20
Nagaland	0.00	3.71	11.67	14.85	19.10	50.66
Orissa	0.59	41.29	25.59	18.94	6.59	7.00
Punjab	1.31	11.35	31.68	17.26	14.41	23.99
Rajasthan	0.19	54.63	21.85	7.26	3.98	12.09
Sikkim	0.00	4.49	14.32	18.80	16.67	45.73
Tamil Nadu	0.00	9.31	35.59	17.56	10.66	26.89
Tripura	0.05	7.52	26.57	26.41	15.83	23.61
Uttar Pradesh	0.19	11.77	29.18	20.93	13.73	24.20
West Bengal	0.00	3.46	29.03	28.88	19.42	19.21
Andaman & Nicobar Is.	0.00	23.16	24.29	17.51	10.73	24.29
Chandigarh	0.00	2.27	6.82	4.55	4.55	81.82
Dadra & Nagar Haveli	1.61	66.94	22.58	6.45	2.42	0.00
Daman & Diu	0.00	9.38	9.38	12.50	25.00	43.75
Delhi	0.00	0.16	0.49	0.98	2.94	95.43
Lakshadweep	0.00	5.56	0.00	0.00	0.00	94.44
Pondicherry	0.00	22.12	14.75	5.90	10.62	46.61

Source: Fifth All India Educational Survey, NCERT, New Delhi, 1992.

Primary Schools According to Teachers in Position

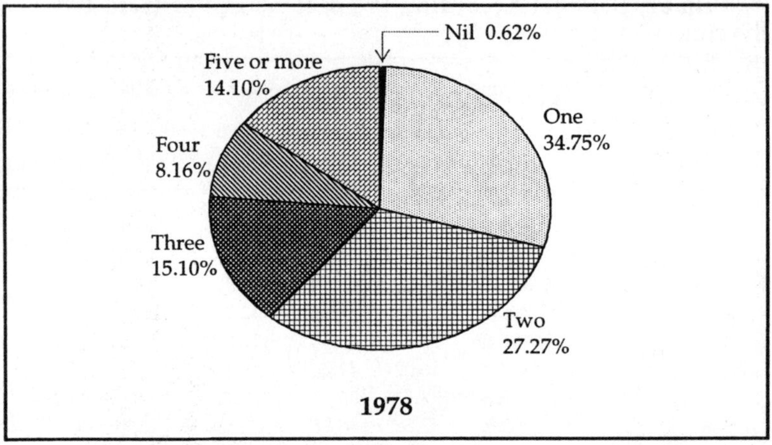

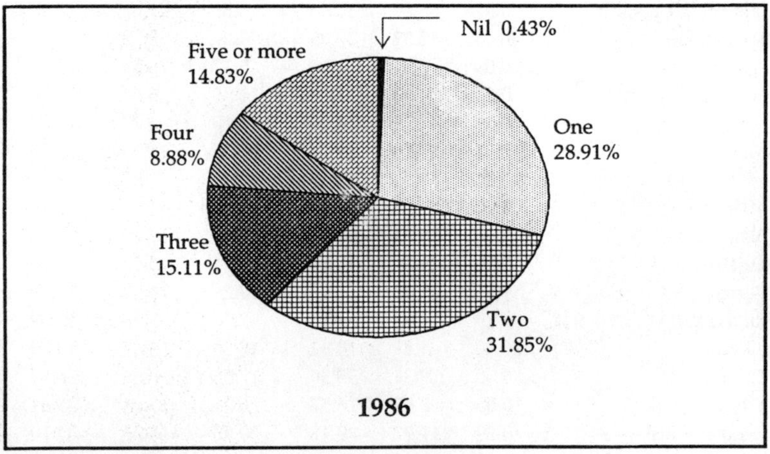

Figur 11.13

14 years shall be permitted to be engaged in any hazardous occupation or be made to undertake heavy work." Conventions of the International Labour Organisation are even more explicit as well as emphatic in this respect when they stipulate that children below 14 years of age must not be put to work. But in reality all these are mere writing in the books yet to be implemented.

The problem of child labour is inextricably link to the low participation rate of children in elementary education. According to the 1991 census, there were about 5 crores of child workers in the country out of which 40 per cent were girls and about 7 per cent of the child workers were found to live in urban areas. 83 per cent of the child workers are engaged in activities related to agriculture. It is seen that the work force participation rate rises sharply as the child attains the age of 10 years. This is presumably due to the child becoming useful at this age for certain types of manual work. There are altogether three categories of out of school child workers *e.g.*,

(i) Children between the age group of 6-10 years, most of whom are not working on wages.
(ii) Children in the age group of 6-14 years who are in labour market, and
(iii) Children in the age group of 10-14 years, who are not in labour market.

The policy of Universalisation of elementary education should be viewed separately for these three categories. The children of the first group can be brought into the school system with improvement in the quality of education. For the second group of children the strategy would have to be based on the principle that the children cannot be dissociated from their employment. There should be special schools for these groups according to their need and time, or they should be enrolled in the non-formal education system. For the third group of children strategy would promote vocational training, skill formation and also aim at equipping the child with minimum level of knowledge.

Proportion of such out of school children in different states can be obtained from Tables 11.26 and 11.27.

Though no current official figure is available in this connection Table 11.26 is based on the figure of 1987-88 (NSSO, Report, 1992) and Table 11.27 is for the projected population in 1995 on the basis of 1991 census report. From the figure as shown in Tables 11.26 and 11.27, there are wide inter-state variations in the proportion of children attending school in different states in the age groups, 5-9, 10-14 and 5-14. On the one extreme we have Kerala with universal coverage, on the other extreme, there are states such as, Bihar, Haryana, Himachal Pradesh, Orissa, Punjab, Jammu & Kashmir, Madhya Pradesh, Uttar Pradesh and Rajasthan with about only one-tenth or less of their children in the rural area in the

Table 11.26
Proportion of Children Attending School,
Aged 5-14 Years, 1987-88

States	*Rural*			*Urban*			*Rural + Urban*
	Male	*Female*	*Total*	*Male*	*Female*	*Total*	
Andhra Pradesh	60.36	38.73	49.66	79.51	69.63	74.57	58.54
Assam	62.38	58.97	60.84	82.36	75.69	79.45	64.27
Bihar	34.90	19.77	34.90	63.66	54.25	59.42	42.60
Delhi	69.70	39.14	56.57	87.12	82.69	85.01	81.99
Gujarat	69.63	52.31	61.44	77.21	75.51	76.42	67.53
Haryana	43.19	26.43	35.54	83.45	74.77	79.72	47.15
Himachal Pradesh	47.51	37.28	42.55	91.99	89.79	91.06	49.01
Jammu & Kashmir	37.93	22.84	30.38	77.30	70.69	74.16	41.28
Karnataka	60.92	48.10	54.55	74.22	71.23	72.72	61.58
Kerala	90.43	87.09	88.80	93.40	93.43	93.41	89.96
Madhya Pradesh	32.33	22.60	27.82	79.94	70.29	75.39	41.00
Maharashtra	71.65	55.02	63.87	84.92	80.00	82.54	72.06
Orissa	29.90	20.01	25.02	78.99	68.76	74.12	35.98
Punjab	38.35	31.25	35.08	83.20	80.99	82.14	52.52
Rajasthan	35.50	10.20	24.04	75.28	54.94	65.84	35.95
Tamil Nadu	55.27	41.43	48.47	84.48	77.71	81.16	63.81
Uttar Pradesh	32.92	15.87	25.30	65.02	54.80	60.24	34.81
West Bengal	48.12	42.15	45.27	72.22	68.01	70.20	52.59
All India	46.47	32.25	39.80	76.96	70.00	73.64	50.14

(Contd.)

Note: Attendance rates in the NSS survey results (for Source see Tables 1 and 2) have been reported for age groups 5-9 and 10-14. Attendance rates for age groups 5-14 are weighted average of the attendance rates for age groups 5-9 and 10-14.

Aged 5-9 Years, 1987-88

States	*Rural*			*Urban*			*Rural + Urban*
	Male	*Female*	*Total*	*Male*	*Female*	*Total*	
Andhra Pradesh	63.30	45.20	54.23	79.70	72.80	76.31	61.98
Assam	48.60	47.80	48.23	72.60	66.10	69.70	51.90
Bihar	18.80	10.60	18.80	53.70	45.80	50.13	28.43
Delhi	36.00	0.00	18.58	84.40	81.10	82.84	76.11
Gujarat	63.10	52.40	57.89	72.00	74.90	73.35	63.88
Haryana	3.60	2.40	3.04	81.80	71.00	77.11	22.60
Himachal Pradesh	0.00	0.00	0.00	90.30	82.40	87.04	10.36
Jammu & Kashmir	0.90	1.10	1.00	73.50	67.00	70.27	17.67
Karnataka	57.00	50.60	53.82	70.20	69.50	69.84	59.91
Kerala	86.90	82.80	84.81	93.40	92.50	92.95	86.87
Madhya Pradesh	33.00	17.00	25.28	71.30	64.50	67.97	36.56
Maharashtra	64.00	54.40	59.42	79.70	76.60	78.18	67.53
Orissa	2.70	2.10	2.41	75.80	66.60	71.13	17.14
Punjab	4.00	3.40	3.72	83.30	80.70	82.04	33.51
Rajasthan	6.00	2.70	4.49	68.30	54.70	62.08	20.57
Tamil Nadu	39.70	34.30	37.03	90.40	86.00	88.26	60.90
Uttar Pradesh	5.70	3.50	4.70	58.90	49.40	54.37	17.83
West Bengal	34.30	33.10	33.73	64.40	61.60	63.03	41.81
All India	27.60	23.50	25.65	72.60	67.70	70.24	38.85
Proportion of Children Attending School, Aged 10-14 Years, 1987-88							
Andhra Pradesh	57.00	30.90	44.29	79.30	66.20	72.62	54.55
Assam	76.10	70.90	73.79	90.50	84.30	87.85	76.56
Bihar	54.60	28.70	54.60	75.00	64.00	70.06	59.57
Delhi	96.00	86.10	92.25	89.80	84.20	87.11	87.67
Gujarat	76.50	52.20	65.39	82.10	76.10	79.32	71.32
Haryana	81.80	51.60	68.28	85.10	78.70	82.38	71.96
Himachal Pradesh	92.50	73.00	83.07	93.30	95.10	94.08	84.68
Jammu & Kashmir	77.50	45.80	61.58	80.70	74.60	77.93	65.80
Karnataka	65.00	45.50	55.31	78.00	73.00	75.55	63.27
Kerala	99.30	91.20	92.31	93.40	94.30	93.83	92.69
Madhya Pradesh	31.60	29.90	30.85	88.30	76.80	83.10	46.07
Maharashtra	79.40	55.70	68.55	90.00	83.50	86.91	76.72
Orissa	61.20	38.90	49.94	81.80	71.20	77.07	56.26
Punjab	72.10	59.30	66.25	83.10	81.30	82.24	72.02
Rajasthan	69.60	19.20	47.01	83.20	55.20	70.00	53.71
Tamil Nadu	70.70	48.70	59.97	78.60	69.70	74.21	66.70
Uttar Pradesh	63.80	30.70	49.24	71.30	60.80	66.50	54.10
West Bengal	64.30	52.80	58.81	79.60	74.50	77.20	64.58
All India	67.00	42.30	56.59	81.30	72.40	77.11	62.38

Source: National Sample Survey Organisation, 1992.

Table 11.27
Number of Children, Aged 6-11, Not Attending Schools, 1995

States	*Rural*		*Urban*		*Total*
	Male	*Female*	*Male*	*Female*	
Andhra Pradesh	1,734,359	2,636,282	333,100	494,612	5,198,352
Assam	764,482	802,621	41,478	56,232	1,664,814
Bihar	5,033,684	5,297,293	397,705	457,400	11,186,083
Delhi	34,522	58,512	92,831	115,171	301,036
Gujarat	752,844	1,072,258	278,563	275,535	2,379,200
Haryana	721,782	798,670	60,092	85,104	1,665,649
Himachal Pradesh	218,051	252,733	2,651	3,323	476,759
Jammu & Kashmir	344,345	397,700	36,088	44,332	822,465
Karnataka	1,085,882	1,471,507	308,680	346,145	3,212,214
Kerala	143,621	191,309	40,015	39,378	414,322
Madhya Pradesh	3,278,272	3,549,820	281,731	404,268	7,514,091
Maharashtra	1,264,279	1,935,309	387,208	511,451	4,098,247
Orissa	1,713,962	1,947,212	79,980	116,994	3,858,149
Punjab	746,031	728,877	82,573	84,540	1,642,021
Rajasthan	2,239,368	2,793,818	238,677	408,194	5,680,057
Tamil Nadu	1,261,996	1,603,218	226,549	319,838	3,411,601
Uttar Pradesh	7,812,295	8,129,294	936,955	1,111,159	17,989,702
West Bengal	2,441,236	2,636,151	393,384	440,141	5,910,913
Total (18 States)	31,591,011	36,302,584	4,218,260	5,313,817	77,425,675
All India	31,640,908	36,779,818	4,339,682	5,431,004	78,191,413

Note: To estimate the population of children aged 6-11 in 1995, state-wise population growth rates (based on Census of India) for the period 1981-91 have been used. For Jammu & Kashmir, all India population growth rates have been used. For Assam, base year population was from 1971 and this was projected to 1995 using all-India population growth rates. Attendance rates used are as in Table 11.3.

Source: Census of India, 1981 (1988), Part IV-A, Social and Cultural Tables, Tables C-1 to C-6, by P. Padmanabha, Registrar General and Census Commissioner, India.

5-9 years age group attending schools. The situation in these states is much worse for female child in the age group of 5-10 years. The position in the urban areas is better as compared to the rural areas. Here the male-female disparity is also low, whereas in rural areas suffer in pronounced male-female disparity. The situation has improved very little in the year 1995 as revealed from the Table 11.27. So there is need for area-based model of educational planning.

Curriculum and Its Application

The prevailing curriculum of primary education suffer from several lacunae, some of which are enumerated below:

(i) There is no standard curriculum for the whole country. There are different curriculum for different states.

(ii) In some states there is only one language, *i.e.*, mother tongue to be taught at the primary level, whereas in some other states there is a second language, English by the side of the mother tongue, which creates language burden to the children.

(iii) Viewing the curriculum mostly in the cognitive domain and there too, by and large in recalling facts at the time of examinations. Old and faulty examination system.

(iv) Inflexible and unresponsive to the local needs and environment, not at all child centred. No scientific approach to keep pace with modern world.

(v) Devoid of the component of skill formation.

(vi) Lacking in social and cultural inputs from the community.

(vii) Unrelated to the 'world of work' which exercises a strong pull on the life of large number of children after the age of 10 years.

(viii) Transaction mostly through lectures in a non-participative mode.

(ix) Near absence of activity based learning.

(x) Discouraging exploration, inquiry, creativity and initiative on the part of the students.

(xi) No change in curriculum for years together.

Unless and until the above deficiencies of the curriculum and its application are removed the universalisation of Primary education would remain a dream.

Teacher and Administration

The school teacher is at the bottom of a vast bureaucratic machinery where there is hardly any scope for charting any fresh course of action. Supposed to be burdened with the inspectorate system and suffering from a low social status, the teacher has, more or less, lost the interest in his/her own profession. Since the teacher himself/herself is a victim of a poor school system and unfair examinations, he/she suffers from severe limitations, in terms of knowledge, aptitude for learning and understanding of children. These limitations in turn constrain the development of the next generation of teachers. Training of teachers also are not adequate. The curriculum and method of such training are also obsolete no connection with the modern methods and techniques of training. There is neither any motivation to teach nor any dedication among most of the teachers. It should be kept in mind that at the time of recruitment, many among the teachers often have to resort to all sorts of unfair and unethical means. He/she has learnt to return this experience in the same coin at the time of examining his/her students. From the experience it may be said that in a large number of Primary schools of our country particularly in rural areas a majority of teachers do not attend schools regularly, doing some other business. In some cases, they appoint some of their close relatives (under educated) with some pocket money to take classes on his/her behalf. They do not even bother to know about the curriculum and syllabus of Primary education. They mostly encourage for private tuition and draw as much amount as they can with this practice. Moreover the fate of teachers postings, transfers and applications for facilities under the service conditions is determined through political and high level bureaucratic interventions. So there is little reflection of 'ideal school teachers' in the average teacher.

All these are only possible because of the lack of school inspection. In the present set up of Primary School Council or Board there are inspectors at various levels, *e.g.*, circle inspector directly concerned with the primary schools, sub-inspectors, Assistant

Inspector of schools and above all District Inspector of schools. All of them are so preoccupied with some other kind of jobs *e.g.*, to deal with monthly pay bill of teachers and sub-staffs, their leave, transfer, pension, gratuity etc., they can hardly afford time to visit the school once in a month even. Though their designations are "School Inspectors" they are doing the jobs of an UD or LD clerk. With this state of affairs, one faces an up-hill task in empowering the school system for the purpose of universalisation of elementary education.

Expenditure on Education

There are some notable general features of education expenditure in India. First, since education is on the concurrent list, both Central and State Governments are responsible for education. However, the Centre accounts for only a small proportion of total expenditure. This can be evident from the following tables showing the budgeted expenditure on education.

From Tables 11.28-11.31, it is evident that the percentage of budgeted expenditure on education to total budget expenditure for India remain unchanged since 1981-82, on the country though it decreases slightly from 20 per cent to 19.60 per cent during 1996-97. But during 1995-96, this was all time low in the Central budget, *i.e.*, 1.28 per cent only. There are also wide variations among the states regarding this percentage, which is as low as 4.94 per cent in Sikkim and as high as 27.23 per cent in Delhi followed by Manipur (25.17%), Kerala (25.04%) and West Bengal (23.02%). In almost all the states excepting a few the percentage of budgeted expenditure to total expenditure have been decreased considerably since 1992-93. Since the education expenditure is predominantly on the revenue accounts, that is main component is recurrent expenditure, in 1992-93, only 1 per cent of expenditure was from the capital account for States and Centre combined. Moreover, the bulk of education expenditure is on the non-plan account, *i.e.*, towards the payments of salaries for the teachers. In 1995-96, around 13 per cent of the total expenditure in education was plan expenditure.

Public expenditure on education has grown at a positive rate over the last 50 years, expenditure per pupil grew at 1.9 per cent per annum in real terms, however, expenditure on education (excepting teachers' salary) remains grossly inadequate and is also

Table 11.28
Budgeted Expenditure on Education, 1981-82 and 1992-93

States/UTs	*Per Capita Budgeted Expenditure**		*% of Budgeted Expenditure on Education Deptt to Total Budgeted Expenditure of State*	
	1981-82	*1991-92*	*1981-82*	*1992-93*
INDIA	57.7	229.9	20.0	20.0
Andhra Pradesh	62.6	225.0	19.7	19.6
Arunachal Pradesh	129.3	512.5	8.2	11.2
Assam	50.4	217.4	23.7	24.7
Bihar	40.4	163.3	14.0	21.2
Goa	128.9	617.7	18.4	19.4
Gujarat	70.7	256.4	18.9	19.1
Haryana	72.5	254.9	16.8	15.9
Himachal Pradesh	112.4	457.2	16.3	19.1
Jammu & Kashmir	86.3	213.0	16.8	11.3
Karnataka	60.9	236.2	19.5	20.8
Kerala	101.8	288.3	31.8	26.2
Madhya Pradesh	42.6	196.2	17.5	17.8
Maharashtra	72.3	245.9	18.9	17.7
Manipur	128.3	433.9	21.2	20.5
Meghalaya	83.7	436.8	13.0	17.7
Mizoram	162.9	670.7	11.6	14.9
Nagaland	180.4	605.5	12.4	11.1
Orissa	48.5	194.6	19.8	19.4
Punjab	82.7	315.0	23.2	17.8
Rajasthan	51.1	221.5	22.2	21.5
Sikkim	155.0	649.7	10.1	17.4
Tamil Nadu	61.9	252.3	19.4	20.1
Tripura	83.8	453.8	20.2	20.1
Uttar Pradesh	35.4	147.8	20.5	18.1
West Bengal	56.2	252.7	24.2	27.5
Andaman & Nicobar Is.	209.8	705.3	10.7	12.7
Chandigarh	172.0	660.1	24.2	20.9
Dadra & Nagar Haveli	104.4	335.6	29.6	11.1
Daman & Diu	**	561.3	**	15.6
Delhi	111.7	367.1	29.9	29.5
Lakshadweep	399.4	949.2	18.2	11.0
Pondicherry	120.9	601.9	17.6	15.6

* At current prices.

** Included in Goa.

Sources: Selected Educational Statistics, 1992-93, MHRD, Department of Education, Government of India, New Delhi, 1993.

Analysis of Budgeted Expenditure on Education, 1990-91 to 1992-93, MHRD, Department of Education, Government of India, New Delhi, 1993.

A Handbook of Educational and Allied Statistics, MHRD, Department of Education, Government of India, New Delhi, 1983.

Table 11.29

Budgeted Expenditure (Revenue Account) on Education, 1996-97

States/UTs	*Budgeted Expenditure (Revenue Accounts)*			*Population as on 01-03-97 (in '000')*	*Per capita Budgeted Expenditure (in Rs.)*	*% of Budgeted Expenditure on Education to Total Budget (Revenue Account)*
	Plan	*Non-plan (Rs. in Crores)*	*Total*			
Andhra Pradesh	351.43	2286.54	2637.97	72960	361.56	16.16
Arunachal Pradesh	56.33	45.92	102.25	1018	1004.42	15.14
Assam	458.17	794.31	1252.48	25149	498.03	27.14
Bihar	181.72	2277.71	2459.43	94669	259.79	24.82
Goa	35.24	108.30	143.54	1367	1050.05	14.52
Gujarat	191.67	2029.11	2220.78	46199	480.70	20.87
Haryana	207.65	583.67	791.32	18911	418.45	12.95
Himachal Pradesh	152.28	299.82	452.10	5847	773.20	18.52
Jammu & Kashmir	81.63	380.20	461.83	8692	531.34	15.93
Karnataka	512.58	1634.46	2147.04	50060	428.89	18.00
Kerala	150.22	1822.51	1972.73	31344	629.38	25.04
Madhya Pradesh	520.02	1952.31	2472.33	75546	327.26	16.29
Maharashtra	500.22	3593.17	4093.39	87883	465.78	17.29
Manipur	33.52	149.93	183.45	2154	851.68	25.17
Meghalaya	67.11	79.18	146.29	2081	702.97	19.88

(Contd.)

States/UTs	Budgeted Expenditure (Revenue Accounts) (Rs. in Crores)			Population as on 01-03-97 (in '000')	Per capita Budgeted Expenditure (in Rs.)	% of Budgeted Expenditure on Education to Total Budget (Revenue Account)
	Plan	Non-plan	Total			
Mizoram	18.08	72.59	90.67	812	1116.62	14.81
Nagaland	19.39	97.14	116.53	1433	813.19	13.05
Orissa	533.73	782.81	1316.54	34825	378.04	20.12
Punjab	224.34	913.95	1138.29	22705	501.34	16.81
Rajasthan	489.34	1524.04	2013.38	50722	396.95	23.90
Sikkim	30.61	31.59	62.20	478	1301.38	4.94
Tamil Nadu	280.61	2541.43	2822.04	60095	469.60	20.40
Tripura	81.22	163.02	244.24	3234	755.20	21.97
Uttar Pradesh	574.18	3722.01	4296.19	159613	269.16	19.98
West Bengal	196.22	2321.16	2517.38	75768	332.25	23.02
Andaman & Nicobar Is.	9.10	32.12	41.22	330	1248.96	11.12
Chandigarh	17.54	71.72	89.26	758	1177.59	20.15
Dadra & Nagar Haveli	3.12	5.71	8.83	163	541.67	8.94
Daman & Diu	2.46	6.52	8.98	119	754.34	11.27
Delhi	212.08	449.83	661.91	11645	568.40	27.23
Lakshadweep	1.93	9.82	11.75	61	1928.10	8.50
Pondicherry	27.66	48.07	75.73	949	798.09	13.55
India	6221.40	30830.67	37052.07	949894	390.07	19.60

Share of Budgeted Expenditure on Education to Total Budget (Revenue Account), 1992-93

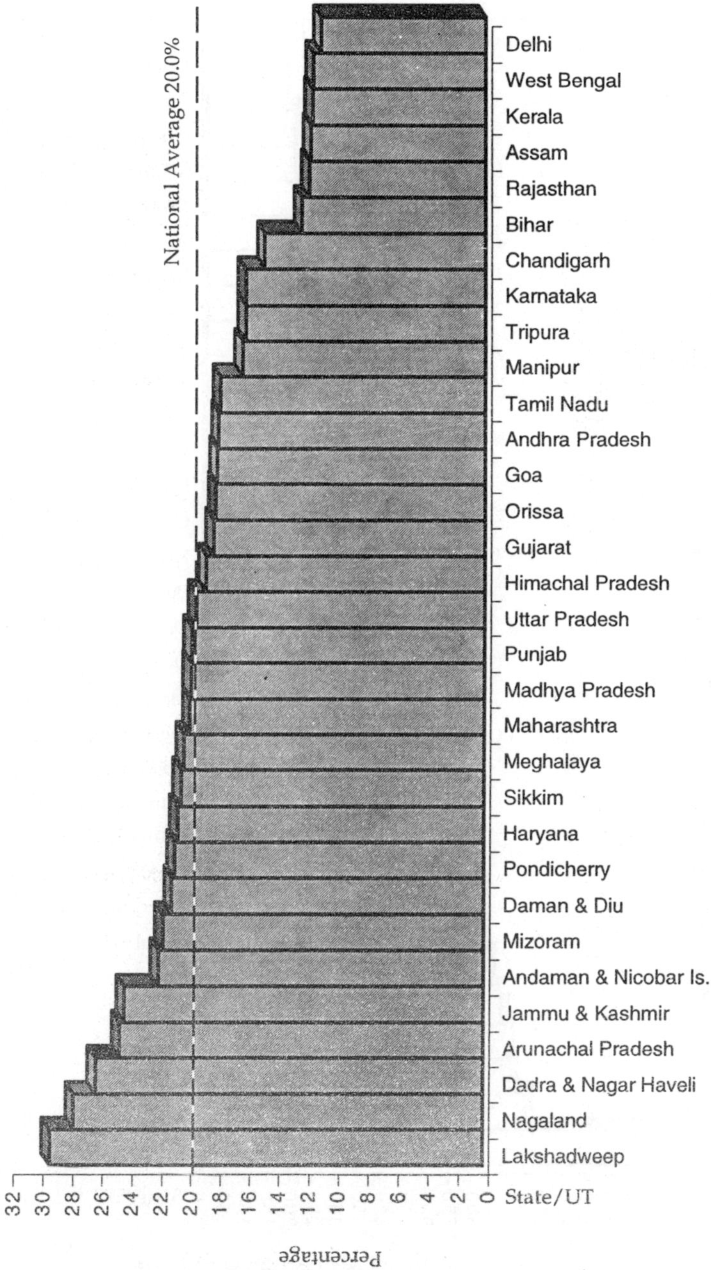

Figure 11.14

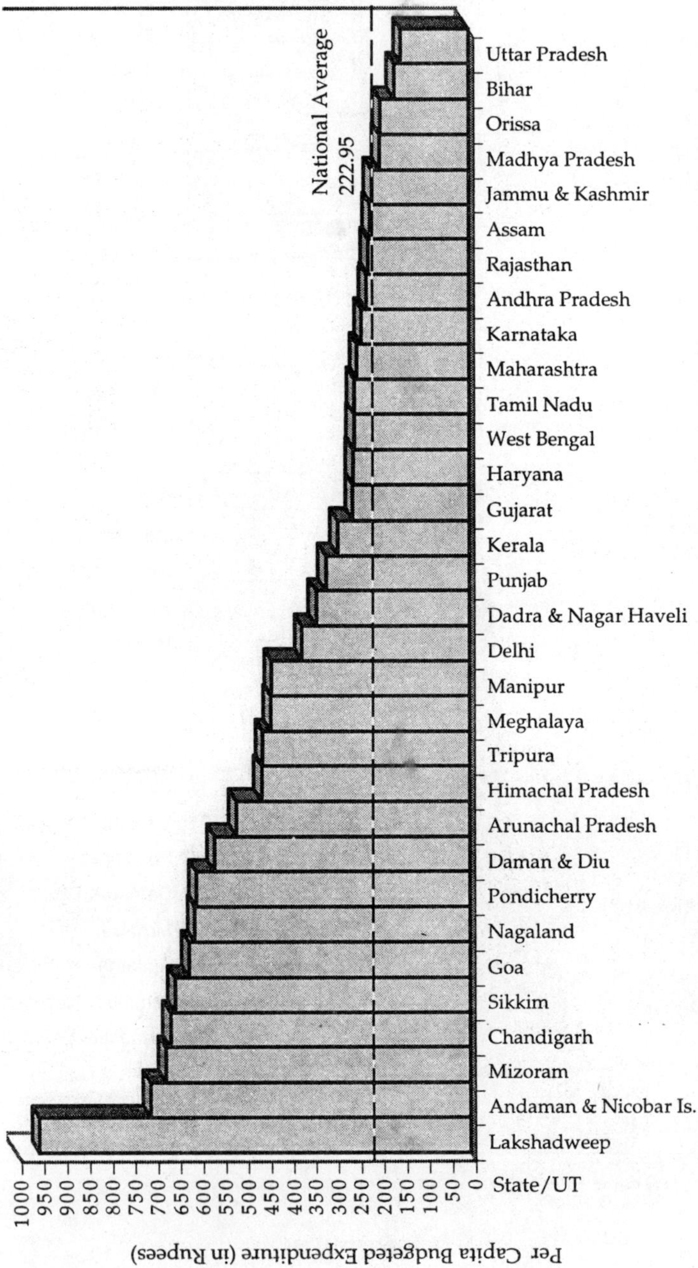

Figure 11.15

Per Capita Expenditure on Education (Revenue Account), 1991-92

Table 11.30
Percentage of Sector-wise Approved Outlays to Total Outlays on Education During Eighth Five Year Plan (1992-97)

States/UTs	*Elementary*	*Adult*	*General*	*Technical*	*Total*
Andhra Pradesh	63.03	6.13	79.78	20.22	100
Arunachal Pradesh	75.00	1.84	100.00	0.00	100
Assam	61.80	2.00	95.07	4.93	100
Bihar	64.55	6.61	79.69	20.31	100
Goa	35.00	1.42	83.33	16.67	100
Gujarat	47.26	7.09	71.61	28.39	100
Haryana	39.44	1.25	79.29	20.71	100
Himachal Pradesh	36.36	0.65	84.56	15.44	100
Jammu & Kashmir	47.16	2.14	94.32	5.68	100
Karnataka	42.85	1.96	94.77	5.23	100
Kerala	12.60	0.44	46.67	53.33	100
Madhya Pradesh	61.50	2.82	87.86	12.14	100
Maharashtra	36.64	2.30	76.43	23.57	100
Manipur	55.51	2.79	92.52	7.48	100
Meghalaya	69.95	3.66	98.51	1.49	100
Mizoram	50.76	2.76	92.28	7.72	100
Nagaland	38.93	1.52	90.52	9.48	100
Orissa	39.76	7.36	86.42	13.58	100
Punjab	11.42	2.62	52.52	47.48	100
Rajasthan	59.12	3.18	89.57	10.43	100
Sikkim	62.98	1.18	95.16	4.84	100
Tamil Nadu	52.91	8.38	92.22	7.78	100
Tripura	57.28	1.93	98.77	1.23	100
Uttar Pradesh	49.33	1.80	80.86	19.14	100
West Bengal	58.33	4.45	83.33	16.67	100
Andaman & Nicobar Is.	37.42	0.61	76.18	23.82	100
Chandigarh	24.01	1.20	79.11	20.89	100
Dadra & Nagar Haveli	54.77	0.47	84.35	15.65	100
Daman & Diu	31.26	1.76	59.02	40.98	100
Delhi	57.46	1.14	80.36	19.64	100
Lakshadweep	23.93	2.28	100.00	0.00	100
Pondicherry	31.72	0.70	65.23	34.77	100
All States/UTs	49.82	3.24	83.86	16.14	100
Centre	38.69	18.81	88.93	11.07	100
Total (Centre+States/UTs)	45.59	9.16	85.78	14.22	100

Table 11.31
Relationship Between Budgeted Expenditure on Education and Net Domestic Product of States/UTs

States/UTs	*Year*	*Expenditure on Education by Education Deptt.*	*Estimates of NSDP at Current Prices*	*% of Budget of Education Deptt. (Rev.) to Net Domestic Product*
Andhra Pradesh	1993-94	1427.82	46318	3.08
Arunachal Pradesh	1993-94	56.64	728	7.51
Assam	1992-93	777.08	14034	5.54
Bihar	1992-93	1390.29	33382	4.16
Goa	1993-94	87.18	1434	6.08
Gujarat	1992-93	1356.11	32896	4.12
Haryana	1993-94	448.74	18057	2.49
Himachal Pradesh	1991-92	254.04	3539	7.18
Jammu & Kashmir	1992-93	325.85	3471	9.39
Karnataka	1993-94	1241.97	32927	3.77
Kerala	1994-95	1126.23	18837	5.98
Madhya Pradesh	1993-94	1216.20	38261	3.18
Maharashtra	1993-94	2622.37	91208	2.88
Manipur	1991-92	107.91	1046	10.32
Meghalaya	1993-94	92.24	1054	8.75
Mizoram	1992-93	55.71	478	11.65
Nagaland	1991-92	49.46	681	7.26
Orissa	1993-94	678.08	15694	4.32
Punjab	1993-94	666.08	26002	2.56
Rajasthan	1993-94	1211.95	24285	4.99
Sikkim	1991-92	26.71	224	11.92
Tamil Nadu	1993-94	1710.02	42147	4.06
Tripura	1992-93	122.87	1081	11.37
Uttar Pradesh	1993-94	2318.67	69120	3.35
West Bengal	1993-94	1609.23	43562	3.69
Andaman & Nicobar Is	1992-93	23.19	208	11.15
Delhi	1993-94	131.58	15398	0.85
Pondicherry	1992-93	41.12	793	5.19
All India	1994-95	@27593.98	* 839504	3.29

@ Total Expenditure on Education by All States and Centre
* GNP.

very low, both in absolute terms and as a proportion of GNP, which is only 3.29 per cent during 1994-95, as compared to other developed and developing countries. Data in the Human Development Report, 1994 show that India ranked 82nd position out of 116 countries in terms of proportion of public expenditure on education to GNP. And in terms of the share of education in public expenditure, India ranked 68th out of 89 countries. In 1995-96, public expenditure on elementary education was less than 1 per cent of GDP. The National Policy on Education (NPE, 1986) and its Programme of Action (POA, 1992) state the need for "an unqualified priority to universalisation of elementary education, universal enrolment and universal retention of children upto 14 years of age." They also state that "Neither normal linear expansion nor the existing pace and nature of improvement can meet the needs of the situation." The NPE called for an investment of 6 per cent of the GDP in education during the Eighth Five Year Plan. But in reality we find at the end of Eighth Plan such expenditure is less than 1 per cent of GDP (Table 11.32).

While reviewing the Education Commission's Report of 1967 (Kothari) Prof. Amartya Sen opined, "cost figures are obviously relevant if the pattern of education in India has to be determined. According to the Education Commission Report, if we look at the relative expenses of education at different categories, the average annual cost per pupil is estimated to be Rs. 328 for undergraduate studies in arts and commerce, Rs. 1,167 for that in science and vocation training, Rs. 3,000 for postgraduate studies in arts and commerce and Rs. 5,000 for that in science and vocation. This has to be compared with Rs. 30 per pupil per year in lower primary education. That is, when we decide to give undergraduate education to one more person in arts and commerce we sacrifice resources equivalent roughly to that needed 11 persons' primary education, a person in science and vocation training absorbs each year resources equal to 39 persons lower primary education. Similarly for a person in postgraduation in arts, commerce and science sacrifices of resources equivalent to 100 and 170 persons lower primary education. We must bear in mind in this context, the fact that the people receiving primary education come by and large from much poorer sections of the community than those receiving graduate or postgraduate education. . . . My conclusion is that the Education Commission vastly over estimates the requirement of

Table 11.32
Budgeted Expenditure on Education by Education Department for 1995-96 in Order of % age of Education Budget to Total Budget (Revenue Account)

(Rs. in crores)

States/UTs	*Budget of Education Deptt.*			*Total State Budget*	*% of Education Budget to Total State Budget*
	Plan	*Non-plan*	*Total*		
Andhra Pradesh	195.36	1670.00	1865.35	10888.16	17.13
Arunachal Pradesh	28.24	37.09	65.33	482.15	13.55
Assam	356.78	543.86	900.64	3717.16	24.23
Bihar	173.70	1684.28	1857.98	8410.12	22.09
Goa	21.16	81.65	102.81	617.67	16.64
Gujarat	33.27	1663.14	1696.41	8195.35	20.70
Haryana	101.13	428.78	529.91	5048.50	10.50
Himachal Pradesh	88.67	254.41	343.08	1852.32	18.52
Jammu & Kashmir	69.89	288.05	357.94	2295.56	15.59
Karnataka	384.71	1336.42	1721.14	9093.63	18.93
Kerala	79.06	1492.65	1571.71	5861.19	26.82
Madhya Pradesh	224.87	1365.65	1590.52	9677.03	16.44
Maharashtra	239.31	2651.90	2891.21	16765.70	17.24
Manipur	17.28	116.36	133.64	508.94	26.26
Meghalaya	49.77	68.51	118.28	600.35	19.70
Mizoram	10.81	52.75	63.56	430.05	14.78
Nagaland	10.56	87.78	98.34	767.41	12.81
Orissa	162.52	717.71	880.23	5115.26	17.21
Punjab	126.75	702.11	828.85	7507.64	11.04
Rajasthan	344.01	1259.78	1603.79	7988.20	20.08
Sikkim	16.94	26.00	42.94	565.43	7.59
Tamil Nadu	111.17	1994.56	2105.73	10060.61	20.93
Tripura	43.15	127.08	170.23	897.11	18.98
Uttar Pradesh	324.01	2716.22	3040.23	18041.00	16.85
West Bengal	155.32	2125.20	2280.52	9633.90	23.67
Andaman & Nicobar Is.	7.47	26.86	34.33	296.59	11.57
Chandigarh	10.08	61.49	71.57	348.69	20.53
Dadra & Nagar Haveli	2.41	4.04	6.45	64.53	9.99
Daman & Diu	2.11	5.06	7.17	56.72	12.63
Delhi	140.23	363.02	503.26	1884.70	26.70
Lakshadweep	1.40	8.25	9.65	115.04	8.39
Pondicherry	15.58	38.30	53.88	391.26	13.77
All States/UTs	3547.72	23998.96	27546.68	148177.95	18.59
Centre	1823.34	880.23	2703.57	138328.00	1.28
Total (Centre+ States/UTs)	5371.06	24879.19	30250.25	284505.95	10.67

university educated manpower and vastly underestimates the necessary speed of the expansion of primary education to fulfil the stated objectives. And as a consequence, it indicates a manpower policy which is neither economically efficient nor oriented towards creating a just society in this country" (*The Statesman*, 19 April 1967).

Educational Management

Soon after adoption of NPE (1986) its POA (1992), the Central Advisory Board of Education (CABE, 1992) recommended following measures for toning up educational management.

(i) Decentralisation of planning and management of education at all levels, involving elected representatives of people in decision-making at the district, sub-district and panchayat levels (as per Seventy-second Constitution Amendment Bill, 1991 on Panchayati Raj institutions). These bodies are to be entrusted to education including Primary, Secondary, Technical, Vocational, adult, non-formal, libraries and Cultural activities and also responsible for the preparation of plans for the economic development and social justice.

(ii) Local level committees, *e.g.*, district level bodies, village education committee, urban local bodies, voluntary organisations, and non-Governmental agencies with due representation, to women, teachers, educationists, representatives of guardians and minorities to assist in the working of Primary education and to oversee its functioning, such as, effective and regular functioning of the schools and centres, ensuring participation, enrolment, retention of all the local children in the age group of 6-14 years.

(iii) Provision of Primary school for all children within one km of walking distance and facilities of non-formal education centres for school drop-outs, working children and girls who cannot attend schools.

(iv) Improvement of ratio of Primary schools to Upper-primary schools from the existing 1:4 to 1:2, for widening girls' participation at Upper-primary stage.

(v) Reduction of drop-out rates between classes I-V and I-VIII.

(vi) Improvement of school facilities by revamped Operation Blackboard, to be extended to upper-primary level also.

(vii) Achievement of minimum levels of learning by approximately all children at the Primary and Upper primary levels.

(viii) Regular inspection to be conducted by the district/block level inspecting authorities to schools in order to evoke a culture of participation and providing correctives rather than the existing practice of fault finding.

(ix) To set up State Advisory Board of Education (SABE) in the lines of CABE, to function as an apex body to co-ordinate all human resource development programmes.

(x) Improvement of the monitoring system by undertaking periodic evaluation of high priority programmes such as Universalisation of elementary education, non-formal education, women's education, education of SC/ST and minorities by reputed social science research organisations, Universities departments, etc., and findings of these evaluation exercises may be placed before CABE and SABE.

(xi) All these recommendations towards the goal of universalisation of elementary education are to be implemented on a state-wise basis during the Eighth Plan.

But in reality, at the end of Eighth Plan there is no noticeable improvement to the elusive goal of universalisation of elementary education as most of the above recommendations still remain in a stage of paper and pencil. Because education in India has been largely a budget based system where efficiency is rated by ability to consume budget and to demand more. Performance at delivery point has not been an important criterion. The on-going economic reforms and structural adjustment would therefore, demand a shift from inputs to performance and outcomes — consideration of cost effectiveness should inform all levels of educational administration and planning. Absence of effective decentralisation failure to evolve priorities and pursue objective-oriented programmes, weak personnel management system and ineffective intra-departmental and inter-departmental co-ordinating mechanisms have adversely affected the performance of the education system. Even routine tasks, like the supply of textbooks, teaching in the class-room, conduct of periodic evaluation/ examinations and operation of academic calendar are not being properly attended to.

Now if we consider the views of Prof. Amartya Sen regarding education and economic growth, where he emphasised the need for rural education, particularly the primary education. In his famous book jointly with Jean Dreze *India: Economic Development and Social Opportunity* he wrote, "A peculiar thing is happening in India, here, on one side there is a large number of higher educated persons and on the other side there is a long procession of illiterate people — who do not recognise even A, B, C, D. World market has been flourished with the commodities made in China and South Korea. But those who are manufacturing these, do not possess any higher university degree, but all of them have primary education, which helps them to maintain the quality of their products. In a country where majority of the people remain illiterate, where the people can't read the written direction, concept of modern industry is impossible there. There is a direct link between primary education and skill. The gender discrimination which has been in vogue for long years is also due to lack of primary education. In developed countries gender discrimination is not so acute only because, females are not deprived of education there, and as a result a large number of females are associated with the economic growth of these countries" (Sen and Dreze, 1995).

The National Policy on Education (1986) has stated its 'Resolve' for UEE in the following words: "The new education policy will give the highest priority to solving the problem of children dropping out of school and will adopt an array of meticulously formulated strategies based on micro-planning, and applied at the grass-root level all over the country, to ensure children's retention at school. This effort will be fully co-ordinated with the network of non-formal education. It shall be ensured that all children who attain the age of about 11 years by 1990 will have had five years of schooling, or its equivalent through the non-formal stream. Likewise by 1995 all children will be provided free and compulsory education upto 14 years of age. But what we see during the middle of 1999 — the position remains almost same as in 1986. It may be noted that no strategy, how so ever 'meticulously formulated' it may be, can be effective as long as enrolment is not similarly stressed. Under today's condition, if all of the children attending class I are retained upto class VIII, it may still amount to provision of schooling to merely 50 per cent of the children and one-thirds of the girls in the relevant age-group. Obviously this was not intended by the National Policy. But one thing is significant that a National Policy admits that the school may not be able to reach all children, therefore it envisages a major role for the non-formal stream in moving towards Universalisation of Elementary Education.

Regarding non-formal education (NFE) the following features has been envisaged by NPE (1986).

(i) NFE should strive to reach school drop-outs, for children for habitations without schools, working children and girls who cannot attend whole day-schools.

(ii) The curriculum framework of NFE would be on the lines of the National core curriculum, based on the needs of the learners and related to the local environment.

(iii) NFE should promote a 'learner-centred approach' emphasis On 'learning rather than teaching,' continuous learner evaluation, creation of participatory learning environment and joyful extracurricular activities.

(iv) NFE should organise activities to enable 'learners to progress at their own pace' and to 'learn from each other.'

(v) All measures would be taken to ensure that the quality of non-formal education is comparable with formal education (NPE, 1986).

But, the views of the Programme of Action (POA, 1992) of NPE (1986) was also significant, "For their healthy development and to ensure that they enjoy conditions of freedom and dignity, the education system will strike to have all children in whole time schools of good quality, and till that becomes possible they will be provided opportunities of part-time non-formal education" (POA, 1992). But, in reality, the functioning of the NFE centres during the last ten years were only superficial and not at par with the recommendations of NPE (1986) and its POA (1992). Even the POA (1992) itself places NFE at a level lower than the formal education (school). A feeling widely persists, legitimately or not, that NFE is some kind of a second-grade education for the poor, while the formal school is meant for those who are relatively better off. This feeling has grown in the public mind only because that due to the poor infrastructure, teachers and management, NFE centres never becomes at par with the formal schools, notwithstanding the fact that formal schools themselves are in poor shape and provide, by and large, what can be fairly described as second grade education. In order to justify this reality the following excerpts from a very recent report of the West Bengal Assembly's Committee on Education would be relevant.

To commemorate Prof. Amartya Sen's winning the Nobel Prize, the State Government has announced that by 2002 it would ensure 100 per cent enrolment in Primary schools. The State Government has pledged to immediately open 3,000 new Primary schools with a target of 2,000 during 1998-99. From a State Government document that notes "it won't be possible to meet the target of setting up 2,000 Primary schools cleared by the State Education Department during the past two years," the Assembly's Committee regrets the fact and cites lack of teachers as its primary reason. The report says, "A primary school has at least, four classes, one or two teachers cannot run it in a proper manner. The problem with the sanctioned 2,000 schools is that the Government is unable to employ teachers in adequate numbers. Primary education in the state is suffering for want of teachers. At present nearly 29 per cent of the state's 51,000 odd schools are run by two teachers and 8 per cent by one teacher. The problem is compounded by a delay in filling up vacancies after teachers' retirement or death. Some teachers do not reach school on time, or they leave before the school is over. Teachers, who are elected panchayat/municipal functionaries, divide their time between teaching and doing panchayat/municipal work. The volume of non-educational work-like conducting census, economic review and the preparation of voter's list—often forces many of the one teacher or two teachers schools to temporarily suspend classes for days on end. The state of the existing schools are as follows:

(i) till now, the states' 2,485 primary schools have no class-room of their own;

(ii) 11,204 schools have just one class-room each;

(iii) at least 20 per cent schools cannot be reached by foot;
(iv) many thatched and *pucca* schools are not fit for use as repairs haven't been done for ages;
(v) roofs of many schools are such that rain seeps into classroom forcing school authorities to often call it a day; and
(vi) some concrete roofs are so precarious that there could be disasters any time. (*The Statesman*, 7 August 1999).

Now, if we consider Prof. Amartya Sen's view in his article on "Education and Economic Growth," he writes, " . . . our industrial productivity is still low, . . . but in agriculture we are still far behind even the first stage of learning. Agricultural productivity per acre remains dismally low, much lower than even in other Asian countries, not to mention countries further away from us. . . under-utilisation of irrigational opportunities, need for fertilisers and pesticides are the main problems. What is more difficult to see, though no less true, is the link between all these and the peasants, education, motivation and skill. . . . In both these fields education has a crucial role to play and in both these fields our lack of emphasis on elementary education has cost us much.

While it is often pointed out, correctly that literature is only a small part of education, it does not seem to be adequately recognised that it opens up other possibilities of education in a way nothing else does. The complaint is often heard that the Indian rural youth who is lucky enough to learn his letters forgets them rapidly once he leaves school. This is not surprising, for there is very little literature today in India that a rural youth can easily get hold of and that he can read with interest and profit. It is not sufficient to leave the rural boy with some knowledge of letters and a couple of boring textbooks indicating the position of the 'cat on the mat.' In all the countries where the rapid spread of rural education has been achieved, *e.g.*, all the communist countries, UAR, etc., discussions on vital political, economic and social questions have played an important part. A more purposive educational policy can bridge a vital gap in the Indian rural community. If the peasant does not use much fertiliser because he is suspicious of it, and does not make full use of irrigational facilities because he does not have permanency in the land he cultivates, expansion of rural education can play a vital part in solving these problems. If the expansion of rural education is accepted as an integral part of India's economic development and not as a luxury to be indulged in as circumstances permit, a generous allocation of resources for this should not be grudged. For the resources we don't have to depend on foreign aids, and if well-planned it may not even make a great demand on domestic resources such as steel and cement. The main requirement for this activity is secondary and higher educated men and women, one of the few resources we have in plenty. . . . What we need in the next Five Year Plan is a bold plan of rural educational expansion to bring life into rural society. We have luckily, the resources to do it, thanks to our developed base of secondary and higher education . . . . if we still hesitate, we shall prove to the world that we richly deserve the trouble in which we find ourselves today" (*The Statesman*, 19 October 1998).

To conclude it may be said that the dismal picture that has emerged shows that at the one end of the continuum an insignificant proportion of highly selective and motivated high achieving students, largely from the high socio-economic classes of English medium schools and selected Government managed schools of urban areas enjoying the best of schooling facilities and at the other end, an overwhelming number (about 85 per cent of the total) of under achieving children of rural and urban slum areas suffering from a chronic want of basic facilities. An elitist bias in primary education is rather apparent here, and the picture surely, is farthest from our cherished goal of universalisation of elementary education and total literacy. In order to achieve the universalisation the following points deserve urgent attention of the authorities concerned to improve the planning and administration of Primary education in the country:

(i) To set up common school system to provide all children, irrespective of caste, creed, locations and sex, opportunities upto certain level to have access to education of comparable quality, as recommended by Kothari Commission, NPE (1986), POA (1992), must be implemented immediately.

(ii) To increase significantly, in the outlay for elementary education and provision of special allocations for improvement of school system in backward areas, urban slums, tribal areas, hilly tracts, desert and marshy areas, drought and flood-prone zones, coastal belts and islands.

(iii) All the disparities, between the English-medium and other regional language medium schools and between schools of different management must have to be removed without delay, to protect children from the beginning of formal education, for not becoming the victim of class and caste prejudice. Elementary school children must not be made aware of 'disadvantaged class.'

(iv) There should be sufficient school buildings with at least four rooms each within the walking distance. All the existing dilapidated primary school buildings are to be reconstructed or upgraded.

(v) Emphasis has to be shifted from mere enrolment in the primary schools to classified enrolment of the learners, who deserve special attention for mainstreaming and who does not require any such special attention. This should be strictly done periodically. Considering education as one of the minimum/basic needs in democratic republic society the cause of children requiring special attention must not be left unturned or treated as casual issue.

(vi) Introducing objective screening procedure at the admission stage to identify normal children and children who need special education or special attention for keeping pace with the mainstream.

(vii) Provision for sufficient trained teachers at least four for each primary school be there, who would be able to make the primary education truly attractive to the pupils for acquiring true social competency as per age-norm.

(viii) Integrated Child Development Schemes (ICDS) to be an important vehicle for early childhood care and education. Both these approaches must share the feelings and responsibilities for preparing children and their families to utilise the benefit of Universalisation of Elementary Education drive of the Government. Otherwise, the social accountability of the ICDS will remain open to question. Their implementation modalities must develop and strengthen linkages with primary education without delay. ICDS workers get the best opportunity to build motivational infrastructure for acceptance of the primary schools as an essential element of modern

social life by the local people. Quality of primary education of the population concerned badly needs encouraging social environment and strong community support. All types of non-formal education agencies must work jointly for the said quality of education.

(ix) There should be extensive revision of the present curriculum and syllabus for the primary education, based on the needs of the learners and related to local environment and free from unnecessary burden to the children. There should be a common syllabus for formal and non-formal education.

(x) All non-formal education centres should be in functional mode with proper infrastructure and should enrolled with school drop-outs, children for habitations without a primary school, working children and girls who cannot attend whole day schools. Teachers of the NFE should be equivalent to the primary school teachers.

(xi) Strengthening the network of Inspecting officers of District Primary Education Councils to conduct frequent inspection of all the primary schools to ensure the proper implementation of the Government directives and removing irregularities in order to achieve the goal of universalisation.

(xii) The environment of primary schools, its class-rooms transactions and evaluation procedure have to be made scientific, attractive and meaningful to the beneficiaries, and remedial measures should be taken for all the deficiencies.

(xiii) Introducing the concept of Minimum Level of Learning (MLL) in terms of competencies in the subjects to be taught in the classes I-V.

(xiv) Strict adherence to implement Juvenile justice measures to abolish child-labour and prevent misuse of the abilities of growing children by the ignorant or negligent guardians, violating the constitutional rights of children.

(xv) The lack of awareness of parents and teachers concerned with primary education of the locality to review primary education as an important element in the composite education programme of the country has to be removed

by intensive parents counselling and in-service orientation of the teachers and supervisors without delay.

(xvi) Strict community vigilance to maintain hygienic environment of school, suggest local administrative authorities to demarcate the below-norm schools in a locality in order to provide facilities for their upgradation to safeguard the best interest of the children and protect local schools from false enrolment in the registers for receiving Government grant-in-aids.

(xvii) Strict community vigilance to ensure the regular running of the school, in the locality, against the absence of teachers without any valid reasons, regular attendance of all the children, timely evaluation, remedial teaching for the weaker children, so that the spirit of "Minimum Level of Learning" efficiency or gains is to be maintained. Strict community vigilance to ensure that all primary school children should get all the benefit meant for them by the Government, which includes books, dress and foods/food grains for midday meal and those are not sold in the local market.

At a Press conference, on 19 August 1999, the Nobel Laureate Prof. Amartya Sen said, after formally launching the 'Pratichi Trust,' set up with his Nobel Prize money, that the trust would conduct research on the political, social and economic effects of the lack of attention to Primary education in the country. The problems of poor management of Primary schools, the reasons why many parents don't send their children to school, the high drop-out rate from primary schools and the relationship between teachers and students and guardians would also be looked into. The trust would also look the public health problems, particularly child undernourishment and gender inequality. With the help of this trust the West Bengal Government took the programme of setting up 3,000 Primary schools in the Ninth Plan period (*The Statesman*, 20 August 1999). With all these initiatives, we may hope, that such grave condition of Primary education in our country would not last long — a better future ahead.

References

Banerjee, Surendranath (1993), "A Study on the Impact of Minimum Learning Programme on the Performance Measures of Bangalee Children in the Primary School Leaving Class," *Unpublished Ph.D. thesis*.

Banerjee, Surendranath (1996), "Impact of Certain Socio-economic Factors on Primary Education," *Socio-economic Transformation in India*, Kanishka Publishers, Distributors, New Delhi.

Government of India, Ministry of Human Resource Development (1992), "*National Policy on Education—1986, (with modification in 1992)*," Department of Education, New Delhi.

Government of India, Ministry of Human Resource Development (1992), "*Programme of Action—1992*," Department of Education, New Delhi.

Government of India, Ministry of Human Resource Development (1997), "*Annual Report 1996-97*," Department of Education, New Delhi.

Government of India, Ministry of Human Resource Development (1999), "*Selected Educational Statistics—1997-98*," Department of Education, Planning, Monitoring and Statistics Division, New Delhi.

NIEPA (1994), *Education for All*, NIEPA, New Delhi.

Sen, Amartya (1964), "Education and Economic Growth," *The Statesman*, Calcutta, 26 August 1964, Republished on 19 October 1998.

Sen, Amartya (1967), "Undue Sacrifice of Primary Education," *The Statesman*, Calcutta, 19 April 1967, republished on 21 October 1998.

Sen, Amartya and Dreze, Jean (1995), *India: Economic Development and Social Opportunity*, Clarendon Press, Oxford.

Sen, Amartya (1998), "Excerpts from His Lecture in the Netaji Indoor Stadium, Calcutta on 27 December 1998," *West Bengal*, No. 27, January 1999.

CHAPTER 12

Demographic Indicators of Economic Development

Pranati Datta

Until recently development is identified with economic development. Economic development is a long-term process of fundamental structural change so that a low income country is transformed into high income country by proper utilisation of natural resource, capital resource and human resource. In a much wider sense it incorporates aspects of social development including social justice, egalitarian distribution, removal of poverty; demographic aspects relating to fertility and mortality decline, improvement in education and environmental aspects etc.

Demographic process may act as determinant and consequence of economic development. There are five demographic processes. They are, fertility, mortality, migration, nuptiality and social mobility. We would like to concentrate on process of demographic transition in terms of some demographic indicators. We will highlight mainly on some fertility and mortality indicators of development. Couple protection rate, Government expenditure on health and family planning will also be taken into account.

The main sources of data are census reports and sample registration system.

Process of fertility and mortality transition is determined and determining factor of economic development. Regarding fertility aspects of development we use child-woman ratio, crude, birth rate, general fertility rate, general marital fertility rate, total fertility rate, gross reproduction rate, age specific fertility rate and mean age at effective marriage over decades as per availability of data.

Mortality aspects of development deal with infant mortality rate, expectation of life at birth, crude death rate, age specific death rate, neonatal and postnatal mortality rate. Apart from these indicators, couple protection rate, Government expenditure on health have been used to trace the process of development.

Fertility Indicators

In a developing country like India rapid population growth is the main reason for sluggish economic growth. The Government is paying much attention and taking great deal of effort to control fertility. Hence, assessment of levels and trends of fertility is of great importance. Fertility is actual birth performance. Although fertility is biological phenomenon it depends to a great extent on economic, social, religious, political and legal factors. Fertility regulation is subject to several moral, religious and socio-economic consideration. Fertility regulation involves ethical choice. There are various measures of fertility *e.g.* child-woman ratio, crude birth rate, total fertility rate, general fertility rate, age specific fertility, rate. Trends of these measures may help to trace the role of development to bring about declining fertility.

Child-woman ratio is often used as an indicator of fertility. This index is often referred to as general fertility ratio or index of effective fertility. This is shown in Table 12.1. This follows a declining trend over the decade 1971-81 and 1981-91.

Table 12.1
Child-Woman Ratio for India, 1971-1981

Child-woman ratio	*1971*	*1981*	*1991*
c (0-4)/w (15-49) *	655	545	540
c (5-9)/w (20-54) *	755	696	637

Sources : *(a)* Registrar General, Census of India 1981 (based an 20 per cent sample data).
(b) Technical Group on Population Projection, R.G. India 1996.

India being the second most populous country of the world, the demographers and economists are interested in demographic transition in India. The fertility transition can be viewed rom Table 12.2a and 12.2b since 1901 to 1994. India had a very high fertility

Table 12.2a
Birth Rates and Death Rates in India, 1901-1981

Decades	*Birth rate*	*Death rate*
1901-1911	49.2	42.6
1911-1921	48.1	47.6
1921-1931	46.4	36.3
1931-1941	45.2	31.2
1941-1951	39.9	32.4
1951-1961	41.7	22.8
1961-1971	41.2	19.0
1971-1981	37.2	15.0

Table 12.b
Crude Birth Rate and Death Rate in Rural and Urban India, 1980-95

Year	*Crude birth rate*			*Crude death rate*		
	Rural	*Urban*	*Combined*	*Rural*	*Urban*	*Combined*
1980-82*	35.4	27.6	33.8	13.6	7.7	12.3
1981-83	35.4	27.8	33.8	13.3	7.7	12.1
1982-84	35.3	28.6	33.8	13.3	8.0	12.1
1983-85	35.0	28.6	33.6	13.3	8.1	12.1
1984-86	34.6	28.2	33.2	13.0	8.0	11.8
1985-87	34.1	27.5	32.6	12.4	7.6	11.3
1986-88	33.6	26.9	32.1	12.0	7.6	11.0
1987-89	33.0	26.3	31.5	11.7	7.4	10.7
1988-90	32.3	25.4	30.8	11.2	7.2	10.3
1989-91	31.6	24.7	30.1	10.7	7.1	9.9
1992	30.9	23.1	29.2	10.9	7.0	10.1
1993	30.4	23.7	28.7	10.6	5.8	9.3
1994	30.5	23.1	28.7	10.1	6.7	9.3
1995	30.0	22.7	28.3	9.8	6.6	9.0

Source: R.G. India.
SRS 1980-95.
* = 1980 to 1991 three year moving average.

in the beginning of the twentieth century. It was as high as 49.2 per thousand population during 1901-1911. Birth rates have been erratic during 1901-1971 though it declined very slowly over the decades. Latest SRS estimate shows birth rate 28.3 in 1995. Hence crude birth rate, CBR 41.2 for 1961-1971 to 28.3 in 1995 is a reflection of the process of fertility transition. CBR in rural India is quite higher compared to urban areas probably due to lack of knowledge of family planning and improved health facilities in rural areas. CBR is very crude measure of fertility indicator. It is not sensitive to small fertility changes. In fact it tends to minimise them.

Fertility indicators showing general fertility rate GFR, general marital fertility rate GMFR, total fertility rate TFR, total marital fertility rate TMFR and gross reproduction rate GRR are shown in Table 12.3 to highlight fertility transition in India.

Table 12.3
Fertility Indicators of India, 1981, 1990, 1993

Indicator	*Rural*			*Urban*			*Combined*		
	1981	*1990*	*1993*	*1981*	*1990*	*1993*	*1981*	*1990*	*1993*
GFR	149.4	132.6	125.2	107.7	96.1	93.5	140.9	123.9	116.6
GMFR	—	170.0	162.4	—	135.7	128.9	—	162.4	153.7
TFR	4.8	4.1	3.8	3.3	2.8	2.8	4.5	3.8	3.5
TMFR	—	5.4	5.1	—	4.6	4.3	—	5.2	4.9
GRR	2.3	2.0	1.8	1.6	1.3	1.3	2.2	1.8	1.7

— Not available

Sources: RG, India
SRS.

General fertility has fallen from 140.9 in 1981 to 116.6 per 1,000 women in 1993. General marital fertility rate is 153.7 per 1,000 married women in 1993. Total marital fertility rate for 1993 is 4.9 child per married woman. Gross reproduction has fallen from 2.2 in 1981 to 1.1 in 1993. All the indices of fertility provide a declining trend which substantiate the fact that India is passing through transitional fertility.

Fertility varies by age of mother. Within the reproductive span fertility is not constant. In the beginning of reproductive span it rises with rise in age, reaches a peak around 25 years and then starts falling after that. Sets of age specific fertility rates, ASFR and age specific marital fertility rate, ASMFR, representing age pattern of fertility has been shown in Tables 12.4a and 12.4b for rural and urban India. ASFR in rural areas of India follows a declining trend. ASMFR also follows the same pattern. For urban areas of India these rates are much smaller compared to rural areas. Fertility reaches its peak in age group 20-24 both in rural and urban areas.

Table 12.4a
Age Specific Fertility Rates and Age Specific Marital Fertility Rates for Rural India, 1984, 1991, 1993

Age Group	*Rural*					
	1984		*1991*		*1993*	
	ASFR	*ASMFR*	*ASFR*	*ASMFR*	*ASFR*	*ASMFR*
15-19	93	225	85	235	81	240
20-24	267	318	245	309	248	312
25-29	246	263	202	220	196	213
30-34	175	185	129	137	124	132
35-39	107	115	76	82	71	76
40-44	53	60	35	40	34	37
45-49	25	30	14	17	11	13

Table 12.4b
Age Specific Fertility Rates and Age Specific Marital Fertility Rates for Urban India, 1984, 1991, 1993

Age Group	*Urban*					
	1984		*1991*		*1993*	
	ASFR	*ASMFR*	*ASFR*	*ASMFR*	*ASFR*	*ASMFR*
15-19	58	289	46	284	37	213
20-24	195	323	201	316	196	293
25-29	187	228	159	183	174	194
30-34	118	124	82	88	89	95
35-39	60	65	37	41	38	41
40-44	25	26	15	17	14	16
45-49	9	11	5	6	7	9

Source: SRS Publications.

ASFR have been presented graphically to identify level and trends of fertility behaviour of India over time. Fertility is gradually diminishing over time. The age curve of fertility, Fig. 12.1 and Fig. 12.2 look like a unimodal positively skewed normal curve. Age specific marital fertility is very high in the age group 15-19 for both rural and urban areas of India.

ASFR follows three types pattern, (1) pre-transitional, (2) transitional, and (3) post-transitional. India's fertility transition reflects that India is passing through second stage *i.e.*, transitional fertility.

No significant change is observed for ASMFR in 15-19 age group for 1984, 1991 and 1993 in rural areas of India. But in urban India ASMFR for 15-19 age group is falling from 284 in 1984 to 213 in 1993 (Figure 12.4). The downward shift of ASMFR curve over the years highlights that India is in the process of declining fertility under the impact of development.

Mean age at effective marriage of female in India (Table 12.5) also has increased over time. It is 19.6 for 1993. The legal age at marriage for woman is 18 years. Higher age at marriage is fertility inhibiting factor.

Table 12.5
Mean Age at Effective Marriage (Female) India: 1991, 1993

	Rural		*Urban*		*Combined*	
	1991	*1993*	*1991*	*1993*	*1991*	*1993*
Mean age at effective marriage (female)	19.2	19.4	20.6	20.5	19.5	19.6

Mortality Indicators

The study of infant mortality deserves special mention as it is sensitive indicator of general health condition and child health in particular. The infant mortality rate for developing countries is less reliable than crude death rate since infant deaths are more likely to be unregistered than adult deaths. Table 12.6 shows levels and trend of infant mortality rate by sex.

Age Specific Fertility Rates in Rural India, 1984, 1991, 1993

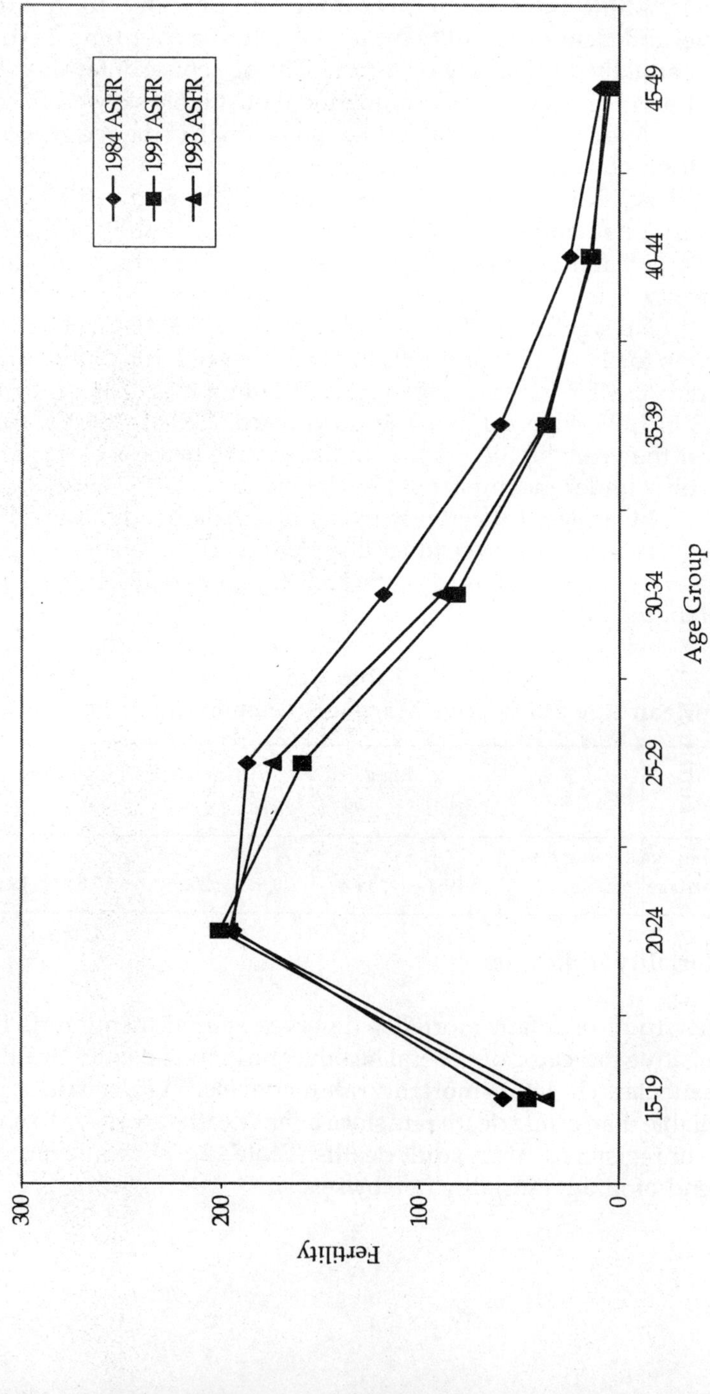

Figure 12.1

Age Specific Fertility Rates in Urban India, 1984, 1991, 1993

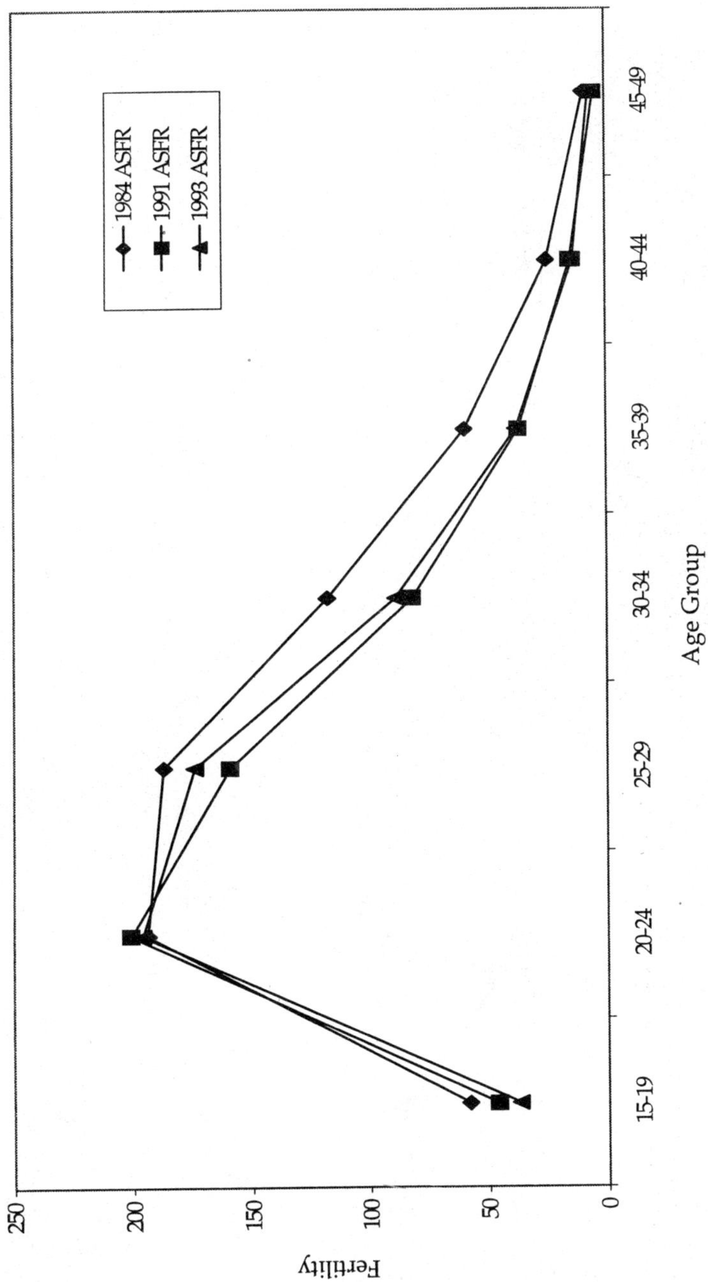

Figure 12.2

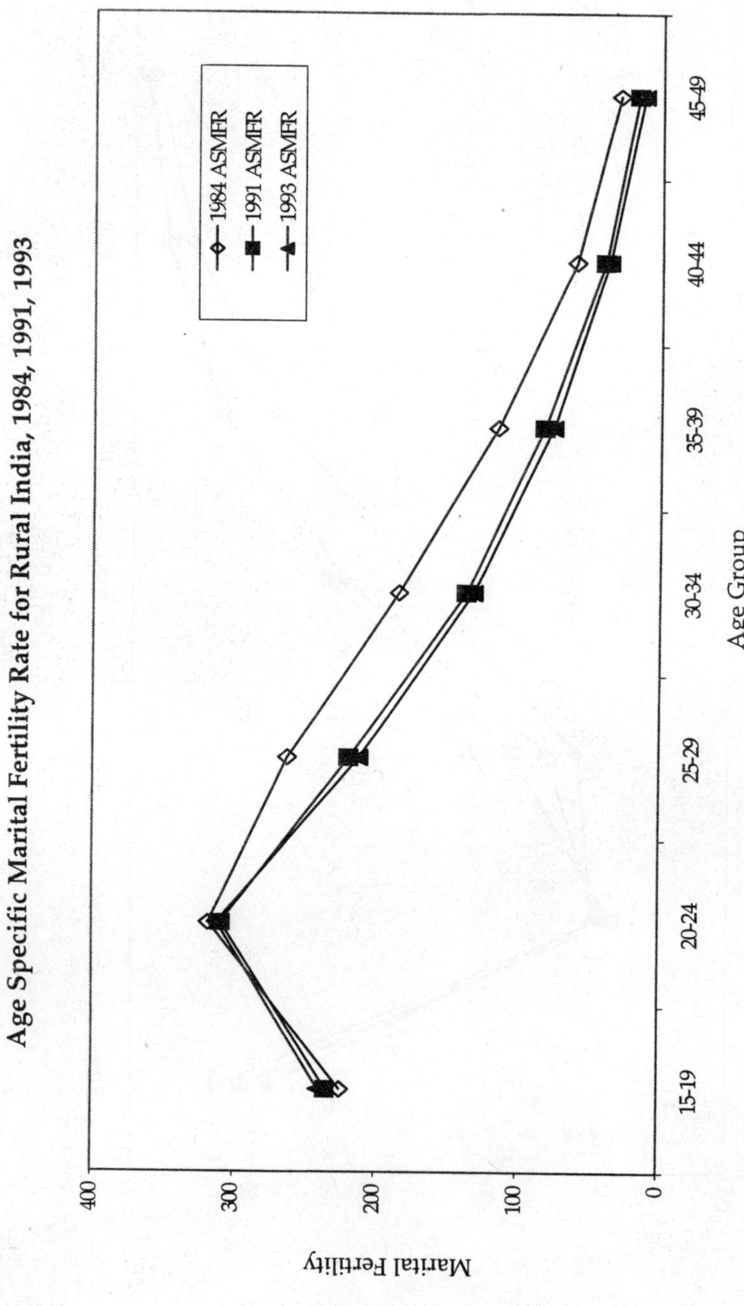
Age Specific Marital Fertility Rate for Rural India, 1984, 1991, 1993
1984 ASMFR
1991 ASMFR
1993 ASMFR
Marital Fertility
400
300
200
100
0
15-19
20-24
25-29
30-34
35-39
40-44
45-49
Age Group

Figure 12.3

Age Specific Marital Fertility Rate for Urban India, 1984, 1991, 1993

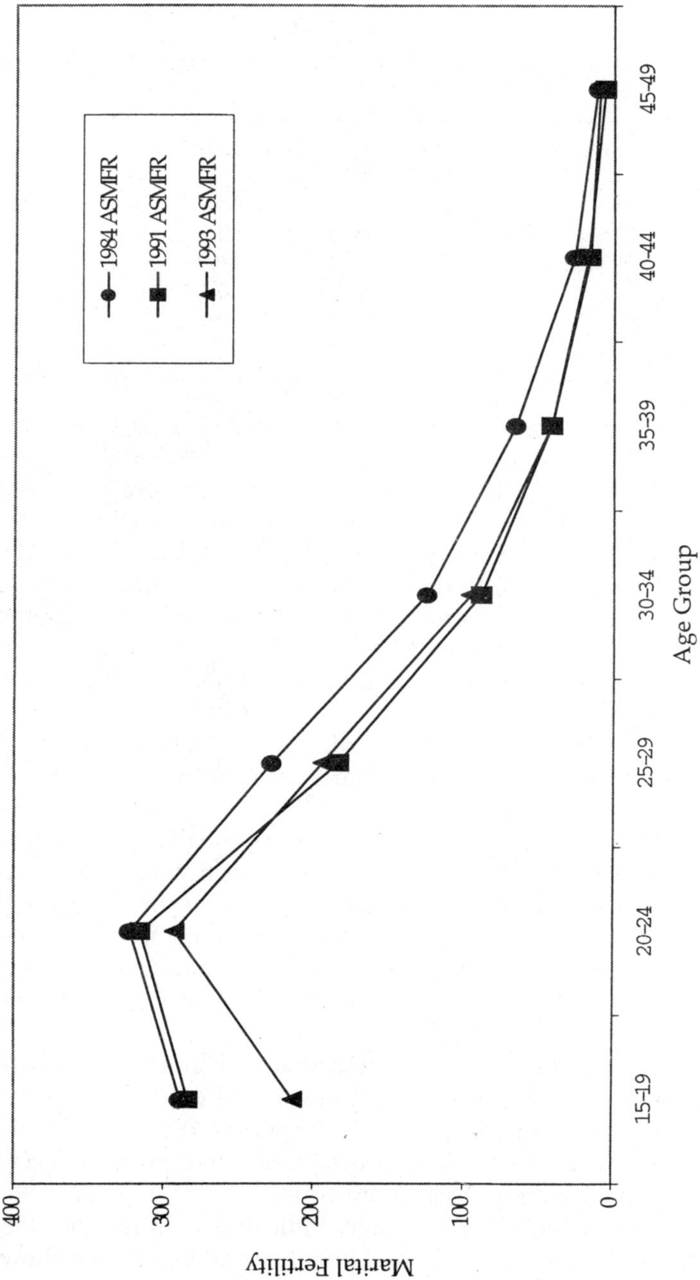

Figure 12.4

Table 12.6
Infant Mortality Rate by Sex in India: 1980, 1985, 1990-93

Year	*Male*	*Female*	*Total*
1980	113	115	114
1985	96	98	97
1990	78	81	80
1991	81	80	80
1992	79	80	79
1993	73	75	74

There is gradual decline in mortality in the past. Infant mortality rate is 74 per 1,000 population in 1993. There is not much variation of this IMR by sex. Achievement of this gradual low IMR can be attributed to improvement in sanitation, personal hygiene, health, education, health public measures, immunisation, neonatal and postnatal care. Various public health measures and disease control measures imported from developed countries have contributed to decline in IMR. The measures *e.g.*, DDT spraying, use of antibiotics like penicillin, vaccines as BCG, DPT, polio, need special mention.

Secular increasing trend of expectation of life at birth may be taken as an indicator of mortality transition. This has been presented in Table 12.7.

This table indicates an increasing trend of expectation of life at birth. This higher expectation of life at birth can be attributed to improvement in public health and disease control measures. Indian population experience expectation of life at birth about 61 years for the period 1991- 96. If the existing trend continues Indian male and female would achieve expectation of life at birth about 64 and 65 years respectively by 2006.

Crude death rate often regarded as an indicator of mortality transition. Three years moving average of crude death rate has been presented in Table 12.2b for the period 1980-1995. The series of crude death rate follows a declining trend which reflects that mortality is in the process of transition.

From Table 12.8 mortality indicators in India from 1980 to 1993 can be viewed at a glance. Infant mortality has been shown in

Table 12.7
Expectation of Life at Birth for India, 1901-2001

Period	*Expectation of Life at Birth* e_0		
	Male	*Female*	*Combined*
1901-10	22.6	23.3	22.9
1911-20	19.4	20.9	20.0
1921-30	26.9	26.6	26.8
1931-40	32.1	31.4	31.8
1941-50	32.4	31.7	32.1
1951-60	41.9	40.6	41.3
1961-70	46.4	44.7	45.6
1970-75	50.5	49.0	49.7
1976-80	52.5	52.1	52.3
1981-85	55.4	55.7	55.4
1986-90	57.7	58.1	57.7
1991-96p	60.6	61.7	61.2
1996-2001	62.4	63.4	NA
2001-06	64.1	65.5	NA
2006-11	65.6	67.2	NA
2011-16	66.9	68.8	NA

P = from 1996 onwards the figures are projected.
NA = Not available

Table 12.8
Mortality Indicators in India 1980-93

Year	*Neonatal Mortality Rate*			*Postnatal Mortality Rate*			*Perinatal Mortality Rate*			*Still Birth*		
	R	U	T	R	U	T	R	U	T	R	U	T
1980	76	39	69	48	26	45	60	36	56	12	8	11
1985	67	38	60	40	26	37	52	30	48	11	9	10
1990	57	31	53	29	20	27	52	34	48	12	11	12
1991	55	32	51	31	21	29	49	33	46	11	10	11
1992	54	33	50	31	20	29	50	34	48	12	10	12
1993	52	28	47	28	16	26	48	31	44	11	9	11

earlier table. Neonatal, Postnatal, Perinatal mortality rate follows a declining trend from 1980 to 1993. Rural areas experience higher Neonatal, Postnatal and Perinatal mortality compared to urban areas of India.

Still birth fluctuates around 12 and 11. Improved medicine, use of vaccine, consciousness about health are the major contributing factor to this declining mortality.

Age Pattern of Mortality

Age pattern of mortality for different time period is an important indicator of mortality transition for any country. An important feature of the age pattern of mortality in countries with high mortality like India is that it follows a roughly U shaped curve, representing the high mortality of infancy and the right hand value, representing high mortality old ages. In Table 12.9 and Figure 12.5 age specific mortality for 1993 have been represented to trace, the age pattern of mortality.

The curve for 1993 is flatter compared to steeper pattern for 1982 (not shown). As mortality is in the process of transition infant death rate for 0-4 age group (more than 30%) in 1982 gradually show a declining tendency (24% in 1993). But the developed countries like Japan follows a J shaped age pattern of mortality curve. The J shaped curve reflects lower left stretch for lower infant mortality (about 10%) in 0-4 age group in 1982. But the left hand value of U shaped mortality curve for India represents high mortality of infancy and right hand value represents high mortality of old ages.

Couple Protection Rate and Expenditure on Health and Family Planning

Couple protection rate CPR (Table 12.10) has increased continuously since 1980 indicating increasing use of family planning methods. This has contributed to declining fertility.

Expenditure on family welfare and health and Government budget has been presented in Table 12.11. Increasing trend in expenditure on health, family welfare and Government budget is observed over the years 1985-86 to 1995-96. But the striking feature is that the share of family welfare expenditure to health

Table 12.9
Estimated Age Specific Death Rates by Sex in India, 1993

Age Group	*Rural*			*Urban*			*Combined*		
	Male	*Female*	*Person*	*Male*	*Female*	*Person*	*Male*	*Female*	*Person*
0-4	25.3	27.9	26.6	13.4	13.3	13.4	22.7	24.8	23.7
5-9	2.6	3.1	2.8	0.4	0.5	0.5	2.0	2.5	2.2
10-14	1.3	1.7	1.5	1.1	1.3	1.2	1.2	1.6	1.4
15-19	1.9	2.6	2.2	1.0	1.2	1.1	1.6	2.2	1.9
20-24	2.4	3.4	2.9	1.4	2.1	1.7	2.1	3.0	2.6
25-29	2.6	3.5	3.0	1.6	2.1	1.8	2.3	3.0	2.7
30-34	3.1	3.2	3.2	2.2	1.5	1.9	2.9	2.7	2.8
35-39	4.4	3.2	3.8	3.0	1.9	2.5	4.0	2.8	3.4
40-44	5.4	4.4	4.9	4.4	2.6	3.6	5.1	3.9	4.5
45-49	8.8	6.1	7.4	6.2	3.0	4.8	8.0	5.3	6.7
50-54	14.2	10.1	12.2	10.7	5.3	8.3	13.2	9.0	11.2
55-59	22.1	16.4	19.3	16.0	8.0	12.1	20.6	14.4	17.6
60-64	33.3	26.4	29.3	23.4	17.7	20.6	30.7	24.2	27.5
65-69	48.9	38.6	43.7	37.3	22.4	29.5	46.2	34.6	40.3
70+	101.1	89.8	95.2	75.7	55.8	65.5	94.5	81.1	87.6
All ages	10.6	10.5	10.6	6.3	5.2	5.8	9.5	9.1	9.3

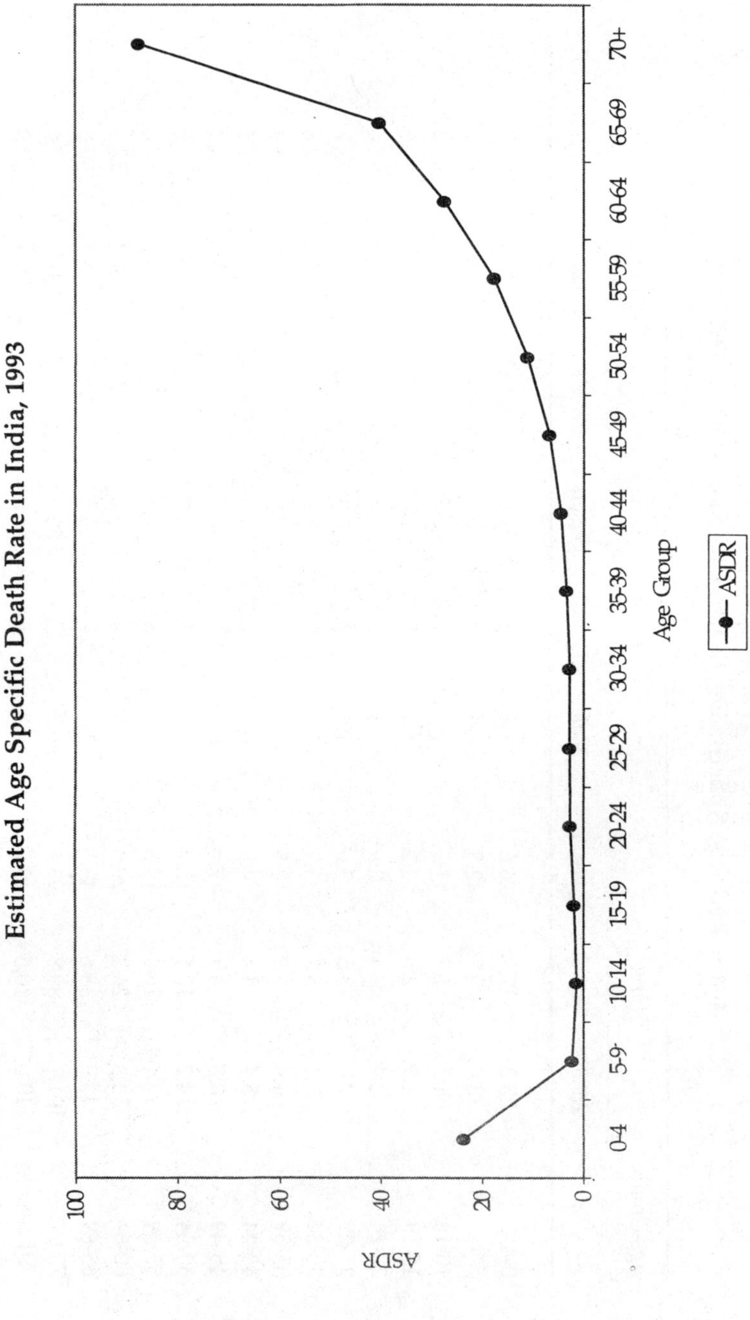
Estimated Age Specific Death Rate in India, 1993
ASDR
100
80
60
40
20
0
0-4
5-9
10-14
15-19
20-24
25-29
30-34
35-39
40-44
45-49
50-54
55-59
60-64
65-69
70+
Age Group
ASDR

Figure 12.5

Table 12.10
Percentage of Effective Couple Protection Rate Due to All Methods in India as on 31 March 1980-96

Year	*Complete Protection Rate*
1980	22.3
1985	32.1
1986	34.9
1987	37.5
1988	39.9
1989	41.9
1990	43.3
1991	44.1
1992	43.6
1993	43.5
1994	45.4
1995	45.8
1996	46.5

expenditure and Government budget follows a gradual decreasing trend. Though Government is paying much attention to family welfare programme, share of family welfare expenditure to Government budget needs to be increased. Share of health expenditure to total Government budget expenditure should be increased.

Overview

In the second half of twentieth century fertility started to decline in the developing countries like, India, China and Sri Lanka. But there is wide disparity in levels, trends and patterns of fertility decline due to great diversity in socio-economic, cultural and political situation prevailing in these countries. Chinese have reached below replacement level fertility by raising age at marriage, reducing fertility of married woman of age 26. Chinese family planning includes the stated official policy on voluntarism, mandatory family planning, national limit on the number of children per couple and one child pledge. Chinese family planning programme

Percentage of Effective Couple Protection Rate Due to All Methods in India as on 31 March, 1985-96

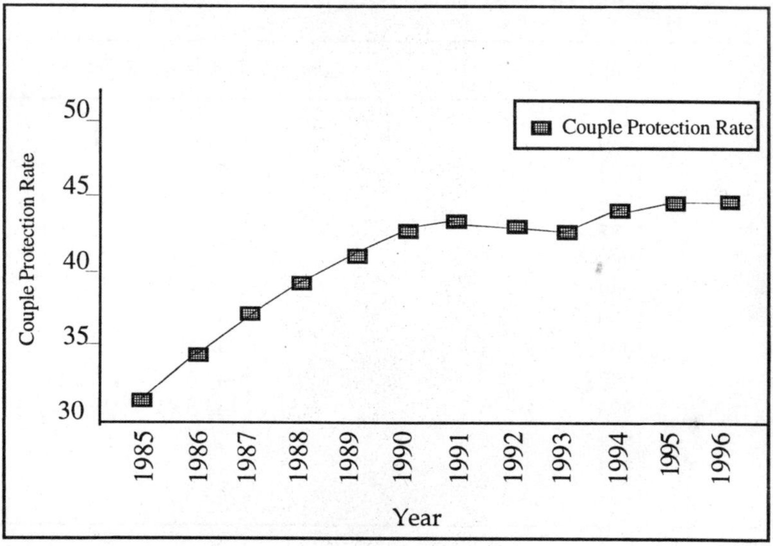

Figure 12.6

is forceful though there is no physical force. The success lies in the fact that Government enjoys goodwill power and confidence of great majority of people.

Fertility transition in Sri Lanka is contradictory to classical theory of demographic transition which stresses importance of economic development, mortality decline and modernisation as major causes of fertility decline. The fertility transition of Sri Lanka can be explained in terms of social development hypothesis which states that fertility decline can take place under condition of poverty if there is social development indicated by literacy status of woman, health equality and social justice. Sri Lanka enjoys better health, longer life, higher education for both boys and girls, welfare institution providing minimum subsistence level food for the masses, better communication and transportation.

India's fertility transition is taking place under

(*a*) regional variation in socio-economic condition,
(*b*) Government sponsored programme,

(*c*) dynamic family planning programme,
(*d*) large democratic Government,
(*e*) force of socio-economic transformation and modernisation.

There can be little doubt that the major contribution to the decline was from the family planning programme. India's TFR 3.5 in 1993 suggest that India still needs a long way to reach below replacement level fertility. However keeping in view the present level of achievement, it is expected that Net Reproduction Rate, NRR=1, *i.e.*, replacement level fertility would be achieved in the period of 2011-16 A.D.

Table 12.11
Family Welfare Health and Total Government Budget by Year (Centre, States and UTs)

(Rs. in Crores)

Year	*Family welfare expenditure*	*Health expenditure**	*Total Govt. expenddituree*	*2 as % of 4*	*2 as % of 3*	*3 as % of 4*
(1)	(2)	(3)	(4)	(5)	(6)	(7)
1985-86	536.54	4006.47	76015.35	0.71	13.39	5.27
1986-87	570.23	4638.23	91180.88	0.63	12.29	5.09
1987-88	642.14	5386.15	101554.37	0.63	11.92	5.30
1988-89	712.92	6987.39	115828.96	0.62	10.02	6.03
1989-90	819.74	6591.43	137662.65	0.60	12.44	4.79
1990-91	932.57	7496.38	155141.47	0.60	12.44	4.83
1991-92	1065.60	8402.10	176995.94	0.60	12.68	4.75
1992-93	1055.02	9320.03	198489.59	0.53	11.32	4.70
1993-94	1342.86	10879.28	225842.16	0.59	12.34	4.82
1994-95RE	1445.33	10536.73	262602.10	0.55	11.53	4.77
1995-96BE	1635.05	13773.67	286715.55	0.57	11.87	4.80

* = Includes medical, public health, family welfare, sanitation and water supply.
RE = Revised Estimates
BE = Budget Estimates
Source : Department of Economic Affairs/Ministry of Finance.

Though India experiences declining trend in mortality over the past years, the mortality rate is still high compared to the other developing countries of the world. The average expectation of life is still very low compared to other developing countries of the world. Hence it is true that present mortality conditions are better compared to past, but they are far from satisfactory. Much more remains to be done. Caldwell (1986) examined Third World mortality experience to identify the ways through which poor countries can achieve low mortality without waiting for economic growth. He has given examples of Sri Lanka, Costa Rica, Kerala (an Indian State) which have achieved a considerable low level of mortality on account of improved status of women and their education, radical political tradition and use of improved medical facilities. In general low mortality can be achieved under following conditions

(a) health service to all,
(b) universal immunisation,
(c) female autonomy,
(d) improvement in reproductive health.

India is in the process of demographic transition. Demographic transition and economic development are intertwined. The trend of demographic indicators of economic developments highlights that demographic transition and economic development are complimentary to each other. But India has to move a long way to reach post-transitional level of demographic process.

ANNEXURE

Definitions

Term	Definition
Crude Birth Rate	Number of Births per 1,000 population in a given year.
Crude Death Rate	Number of Deaths per 1,000 population in a given year.
General Fertility Rate (GFR)	Number of live births per 1,000 women in reproductive age-group (15-49 years) in a given year.
General Marital Fertility Rate (GMFR)	Number of live births per 1,000 married women in the reproductive age-group (15-49 years) in a given year.
Total Fertility Rate (TFR)	Average number of children that would be born to a woman if she experiences the current fertility pattern throughout her reproductive span (15-49 years).
Total Marital Fertility Rate (TMFR)	Average number of children that would be born to a married woman if she experiences the current fertility pattern throughout her reproductive span (15-49 years).
Gross Reproduction Rate (GRR)	Average number of daughters that would be born to a woman if she experiences the current fertility pattern throughout her reproductive span (15-49 years).
Net Reproduction Rate (NRR)	Average number of daughters that would be born to a woman if she experiences the current fertility and mortality patterns throughout her reproductive span (15-49 years).
Age Specific Fertility Rate	Number of live births in a year to 1,000 women in any specified age group.

Age Specific Marital Fertility Rate	Number of live births in a year to 1,000 married women in any specified age group.
Age Specific Death Rate	Number of deaths per 1,000 population in a specified age group in a given year.
Infant Mortality Rate (IMR)	Number of infants dying under one year of age in a year per 1,000 live births of the same year.
Neonatal Mortality Rate	Number of infants dying within the first month of life (under 28 days) in a year per 1,000 live births of the same year.
Postnatal Mortality Rate	Number of infant deaths at 28 days to one year of age per 1,000 live births in a given year.
Perinatal Mortality Rate	Number of still births plus deaths within first week of delivery per 1,000 births in a year.
Expectation of Life at Birth e_0	Average number of years' a new born child is expected to live under current mortality conditions.
Child-women Ratio [C (0-4)/W (15-49)]	Ratio of child aged 0-4 to woman aged 15-49, expressed per 1,000.
[C (5-9)/W (20-54)]	Ratio of child aged 5-9 to woman aged 20-54, expressed per 1,000.

References

1. Bongaarts John and Potter R.G., 1983, *Fertility, Biology and Behaviour*, Academic Press, New York.
2. Bohua, Li, "Levels, Trends and Determination of Fertility," *Asia-Pacific Population Journal*, Vol. 5, No. 1990, pp. 3-16.
3. Bhende, A.A., and Kanitkar, Tara, 1991, *Principles of Population Studies*.
4. Chaudhury, Mahinder, "Demographic Transition Theory and Developing Countries — A Case Study of India," *Demography India*, Vol. 11, No. 1, 1982, pp. 73-113.
5. Cheng, C.Z., "The Fertility Decline in China: The Contribution of Changes in Marital Status and Marital Fertility," *Asia-Pacific Population Journal*, Vol. 8, No. 2, 1993, pp. 52-72.
6. Caldwell, J.C., 1976, "Toward A Restatement of Demographic Transition Theory," *Population and Development Review*, Vol. 2, Nos. 3 and 4, pp. 344-50.
7. Caldwell, John, 1981, *The Theory of Fertility Decline*, (London: Academic Press).
8. Easterlin, R.A., 1969, "Towards a Socio-Economic Theory of Fertility," in Behraman, S.J., Corsa, C., and Freedman, R. (eds.), *Fertility and Family Planning: A World View*, University of Michigan Press.
9. National Family Health Survey 1992-93, *India*: Summary Report, IIPS, Bombay.
10. National Family Health Survey (1995), *India*, IIPS, Bombay.
11. Sharma, A.K., and Misra, B.D., 1978, "Fertility Differentials in India — An Analysis of Census Fertility Data," *The Journal of Family Welfare*, Vol. 25, No. 2.
12. United Nations, 1973, *The Determinants and Consequences of Population Trends*, Vol. 1, (New York), Chapter IV.
13. United Nations, 1973, *The Determinants and Consequences of Population Trends*, Vol. 2.
14. United Nations, 1967, Methods of Estimating Basic Demographic Measures from the Incomplete Data, Manual IV, Population Studies No. 42, ST/50 Series A-42, New York.
15. WFS, World Fertility Survey: Major Findings and Implications, 1984.
16. William Brass, 1968, Methods of Analysis and Estimation. In Brass W., and Coale A.J. (eds.), *Biological Aspects of Demography*, Taylor and Francis Ltd., London.

CHAPTER 13

A Biography of Professor Amartya Sen: A Pioneer in Welfare Economics

Biswanath Ray

Mrs. Amita Sen, an aficionado of Rabindranath Tagore gave birth to a son on 3 November 1933 in a hut at Gurupally, Santiniketan around 3-45 P.M. This child used to be called affectionately as 'Bablu' by the nearest and dearest ones but Rabindranath named him 'Amartya.' His father Ashutosh Sen was a lecturer in chemistry at the University of Dhaka at the time of his birth. His grandfather was Sharada Prasad Sen and maternal grandfather was Kshiti Mohan Sen, a close associate of Rabindranath. His father was a member of the Public Service Commission during the tenure of Dr. Bidhan Chandra Roy as Chief Minister of West Bengal. His ancestral home was at Manikgunj, Dhaka. Bablu's sister Manju was born in 1938 and Rabindranath too named her as 'Superna.' Both Bablu and Manju used to spend their childhood days with maternal grandparents Kshiti Mohan Sen and Kiran Bala because of transferable nature of service of his father elsewhere. Dressed in green clothes, his mother used to act in the dance drama of Tagore and was called as 'Green Beauty (Fairy)' by Abanindranath Tagore. This shows the intimate relationship of this family with Tagore's.

Bablu was admitted to a convent school at Mandalay, Burma in 1938 as his parents shifted there for an assignment for three years. After the completion of this assignment, Ashutosh Sen returned to Manikgunj and Bablu studied at St. Gregory School for a while. The student life of Bablu began at Path Bhawan in the year 1942 in Class IV. His student life at Santiniketan spreads over Shishu Bhawan, Path Bhawan and Viswa Bharati. During student days,

Bablu loved to keep his daytime busy with chats, debates, social work, etc. and used to spend studying upto late night. In other words, he was a 'night bird.' He is till now maintaining this habit. He was an extraordinary student and used to be top in all his examinations in school, however he never kept himself busy only with studies. Apart from studies, his interest spread over various hobbies such as literature, cartoons, drawing, photography, recitation, magic, quiz, acting, kite flying, soccer playing and bicycle riding. It is to be noted that Rabindranath once embraced Amartya for his record in sack race, at an annual sports at Santiniketan. He developed the habit of writing in his childhood and used to concentrate himself either on writing stories, articles or on commenting as a critique of the drama. Many of his writings were also published at his young ages. His article "In search of a Man" (Manusher Sandhane) was appreciated by his teachers. He published the magazine 'Sphulinga' in collaboration with poet Alok Ranjan Dasgupta. Eminent writers and poets such as Premendra Mitra, Hirendranath Datta, Pramatha Choudhuri, Kshiti Mohan Sen and so on used to cover this magazine with their writings. Artist Nanda Lal Basu printed the cover of 'Sphulinga.' He had also an intimate relationship with 'Sahityika.' He was keen on literary meetings, picnics, travelling and similar matter. He also loved to spend his spare time in reading detective stories written by Sharadindu Bandopadhyay and English poems.

Bablu spent his childhood and youth in the company of a few eminent and scholarly people of Bengal at that time who are famous in their own right. Definitely his association and interactions with these eminent people greatly influenced his later life. 'Pratichi' is his parental house at Sripalli. His neighbours include eminent men of various spheres such as Kshiti Mohan Sen (maternal grandfather), Prabhat Kumar Mukhopadhyay, Nanda Lal Basu, Hari Charan Bandopadhyay, Nityananda Binod Goswami, Jagadananda Roy, Satya Charan Mukhopadhyay, Kumud Roy, Nepal Chandra Roy and others. Apart from them, he came in contact with a few great teachers like Nityananda Goswami, Tanayendra Ghosh and others at Path Bhawan. He was also very affectionate and very close to Sąnti Deb Ghosh, Kanika Bandhopadhyay, Krishna Kripalani and his mother (Asram Kanya) Amita Sen.

He grew up in an environment of high thinking and with close interactions with those great people apart from Tagore. This enriched his thinking and tastes. Thus a touch of humanity is observed in his writings. His observations and experience with Great Famine of Bengal during 1942 (Bengali year 1350) greatly disturbed his mind and conscience. He started in believing that the scarcity of food is not the only reason behind famines. Probably, the seeds of developing economics especially for human development were sown at that young age which made him a Nobel Laureate in later life.

After passing Matriculation examination, Amartya was admitted to I.Sc. Class at Shiksha Bhawan in Santiniketan. He stood first in his I.Sc. examination in 1950 and was admitted into The Presidency College, Calcutta. He was lucky to have a few fellow students who are successful in later life either as an economist or a bureaucrat. Prominent among his colleagues at the Presidency College were: Sukhamoy Chakraborty, Jyoti Sengupta, Tarun Datta, Mihir Rakshit, Ashok Ranjan Guha, Pranab Bardhan and many more. After passing his B.A. examination with first class, Amartya left India to study at the University of Cambridge, England. He obtained TRIPOS from this University and was awarded "Adam Smith Prize" as the best student of the year. He received his M.A. as well as Ph.D. from the Trinity College in 1959.

Amartya married a famous litterateur Nabanita Deb Sen in 1960 and had two daughters: Antara and Nandana by this marriage. Unfortunately his marriage to Nabanita did not last long. After that, Amartya married Eva, a professor of economics and had one son Kabir and one daughter Indrani by this marriage. The second marriage ended because of Eva's death; and Amartya then married Ema Rothschild.

He was in the Faculty of various universities around the world. He served in the Faculty of Economics in many universities such as Jadavpur University, 1956-58, as a Fellow at Trinity College, London, 1957-63; Professor of Economics at Delhi School of Economics, 1963-71; Professor of Economics at the London School of Economics, 1971-77; Professor of Economics at the University of Oxford, 1977-80; White Professor at Large, 1978-84; Lamant Professor of Economics and Philosophy at the Harvard University, 1987-97; Master at Trinity College and Lamant Emeritus Professor at the University of Cambridge, 1998-99. He served most of the top Universities around the world, which probably enriched him in his research through interactions with various scholars and students. Scholars and students around the world were also keen to have some direct interactions with Professor Sen in order to get better equipped themselves for research. For these reasons, Prof. Sen was invited as a Visiting Professor by many universities and organisations around the world. He held the position of visiting assistant professor at the Massachusetts Institute of Technology (MIT), 1960-61 and visiting associate professor at the Stanford University, 1961. He served as a visiting professor in the University of California, 1964-65; and University of Harvard, 1968-69. Thus his professional career spread over several universities and institutions of international reputation. All these illustrate the recognition of his scholarly activities in fundamental research around the world.

During 1960s, Amartya Sen published several valuable articles. He did research in the area of poverty, famine, hunger, social inequality and gender discrimination. He extended his research in the branches of economics that are mainly dominated by either Arrow or Samuelson or Mid. A major part of his research also included the economy of the Indian subcontinent of Bangladesh, India and Pakistan. Poverty is dominant in this region. Quality of life had been improved in many parts of the world, which are unprecedented in history. However, he was puzzled regarding the failure of the Indian subcontinent to achieve such development. In his opinion floods, epidemics, and natural calamities were not the main reasons for this underdevelopment but illiteracy, malnutrition, failure in immunisation, and gender discrimination *i.e.*, mismanagement of the Governmental System. (Editorial, *Desh* 14 November 1999). Most of the research of Professor Sen was around the welfare of the poor. He constructed an index to judge the improvement in poverty. Human Development Index of the United Nations was also the idea of Professor Sen. Amartya published his Ph.D. thesis as his first book on economics: *Choice of Techniques* in 1960. This book is dedicated to his parents. In 1970, his book: *Collective Choice and Social Welfare* was published which dealt with the incompleteness of Arrow's model on personal choice to social choice and established a new law in this respect. This new law of choice is known as Sen model. He published *On Economic Inequality* in 1973 and *Welfare and Rights* in 1978. In his book *On Economic Inequality*, he stressed that the scarcity of food is not the only reason for famine in many countries around the world. This is his principal contribution to Welfare Economics.

A discussion on how to eradicate famine, reduce the effect of famine and so on is there in his book on *Hunger and Public Action* jointly with Jean Derez. Most of the research of Prof. Sen was on development economics and the welfare of the poorest section of the people. In his opinion, per capita income is not an adequate measure of development of any country in this world. Education health, nutrition, infant mortality, etc. are also important factors for human development. His research in this respect along with Mohaboob-Ul-Haque is adopted by UNESCO in their *Annual World Development Report* as an index to measure the development of all the countries in the world. This index is known as Human Development Index as stated by UNESCO in the *Annual World Development Report*. Among his many books a few need to be remembered as pioneering works: *Employment, Technology and Development; Poverty and Famines; Choice Welfare and Management; Resources, Values and Development; Inequality Re-examined; Jeevan Jatra O Arthaniti; Indian Economic Development and Social Opportunity* and so on. Besides these, he has innumerable research articles. Because of his innovativeness and high quality research, Professor Sen was appointed advisor to many international organisations and professional bodies from time to time. For example, Chairman: Advanced Skill and Technology, United Nations; Member: Special Committee on the Evaluation of Development of Asia and East Asia; Honorary Director: Agricultural Economic Research Centre, University of Delhi; Reviewer: Review of Economic Studies; Member: Theory and Divisional Committee, University of Oxford; Member, Editorial Board: Economic and Social History Review, Journal of Peasant Studies; Member; Editorial Board: Pakistan Development Review; Executive Member: Econometric Society; President: American Economic Society; and Member: Council as well as Executive Working Committee: Royal Economic Society.

Institutions and universities of international reputation around the World bestowed upon Professor Sen honorary Degrees and Awards in recognition of his fundamental research in economics. A few of those awards are Mahalanobis Award 1976; D. Lit: University of Saskawchuan 1979; Deshikottam: Viswa Bharati 1980; D. Lit: Viswa Bharati 1983; D. Lit: University of Essex

1984; D. Lit: University of Kath 1984; Frank Sadman Distinguished award in Political Economy 1986; D. Lit: University of George Town 1987; Doctor of Law: University of Tulane 1990; D. Lit: University of Jadavpur 1990; D. Lit: University of Kalyani 1990; International Award of Senator Geovanni Agnelli 1990; Alseson Finstein Award on World Hunger 1990; D. Lit: University of Guildhall 1991; Indira Gandhi Gold Medal: Asiatic Society 1994; Edinborough Medal: 1997; D. Lit: University of Guild 1999; Bharat Ratna: Government of India 1999. For his fundamental research on Welfare Economics, Swedish Academy awarded the prestigious Nobel Prize in Economics to Professor Sen on 14 October 1998. The prize money of this greatest award is about four crores fourteen lakhs rupees.

He is also a connoisseur of Rabindra literature. His economics is directed towards humanity and is intertwined with Philosophy. He is not only an economist of world eminence but also a great social scientist. He still maintains his Indian citizenship despite his living abroad for nearly three decades. His works stimulate many branches of the World Economy. Amartya, as a man professes several qualities such as patriotism, kindness, patience, perseverance, courtesy, love for humanity, and friendliness. All these qualities collectively turn Amartya as one of the greatest man of the modern world.

References

1. Basu, Mitava (1999), *Amartya Sener Chhele Bela*, (Calcutta, Taraknath Book Syndicate, 1999).
2. Publishers, Anand (1999), *Anand Mela*, (Calcutta, Anand Publishers, 1999), 16 December 1999.
3. Publishers, Anand (1999), *Desh*, (Calcutta, Anand Publishers, 1999), 14 November 1999.
4. Sen, Prithviraj (1999), *Novel Jaye Amartya Sen O Janakalyan Arthaniti*, (Calcutta, Shyama Prasad Sarkar, 5 Nabin Chandra Pal Lane, 1999).
5. Roy, Moinak (1999), *Amartya Sen O Unnayan Arthanitir Punarjanmya*, (Calcutta, Radical Impression, 1999).

Index